RECONSTRUCTION AT SEWANEE

The Founding of the University of the South
and its First Administration
1857-1872

By

ARTHUR BEN CHITTY

A facsimile edition, with a preface
by the author

PROCTOR'S HALL PRESS • *Sewanee*

*A Facsimile Reproduction
of the 1954 Edition
with a New Preface by the Author*

*New Material Copyright © 1993
by Arthur B. Chitty, Jr.
All rights reserved*

Printed in the United States of America

*Published by Proctor's Hall Press
Proctor's Hall Road
P.O. Box 856
Sewanee, Tennessee 37375-0856*

International Standard Book Number: 0-9627687-6-6

Library of Congress Catalog Card Number: 54-9459

PREFACE

This facsimile edition of *Reconstruction at Sewanee* reproduces the text of 1954. To my astonishment, there have been no factual errors reported in forty years. There are two additions, both given in this Preface.

The first is a modification of Note One, page 74—the origin of the name "Sewanee"— new information that surfaced after the 1954 edition was published. The clue which seems to outweigh the speculations of Note One come from a 397-page collaborative effort titled *Walum Olum,* in which nearly two dozen scholars in the disciplines of linguistics, history, archeology, ethnology, and anthropology examined a curious "document," i.e., a collection of painted sticks. This "history book" was produced by an Asian tribe migrating across the Bering Straits about two thousand years ago. The elders cherished their past but could not write. Instead, they passed their tribal story to their children by word of mouth, using the sticks as mnemonic aids. While members of the tribe were still able to recite their story, Dr. Constantine S. Rafinesque, a professor at Transylvania College in the 1830s, took down with phonetic spelling the account of their migration. He later translated it into the Algonquin dialect used by Indians moving from Indiana to Delaware about A.D. 1600. For our purposes, only one word is important—Saawaneew. It referred to a large segment of the tribe which went south. "Sewanee" apparently applied to the southern cousins who came to Middle Tennessee—the Cumberland River and Plateau area.

Was the name "The University of the South" chosen because it was located at a place known to the Indians as "South" or "Southern Region"? Probably not. There seems ample evidence that the founders simply wanted to identify the new institution with the self-conscious section about to become, briefly, a nation. The Indian connection is pure coincidence. (The Sewanee Mining Company and the University's post office, however, are both directly from Indian words.)

The second addition includes a few words about the Civil War hiatus in the University's affairs, which took place between October 1860—the laying of the cornerstone— and March 1866, when Quintard and Fairbanks returned. The July 4, 1863, skirmish at University Place was not included in the 1954 edition because it had no significant effect on the academic or physical developments. That editorial decision deserves reconsideration. The academic dreams of Polk and his colleagues were drastically reduced by the effects of the Civil War. Similarly the destruction of the temporary log and frame structures had no important meaning for the re-founders who got the institution open between March 1866 and September 18, 1868, when the first nine students began their studies.

This segment of the Preface is simply a bow to such Civil War buffs as myself who want to know how the military actions of the Army of the Cumberland (Northern) and the Army of Tennessee affected University Place. When Jefferson Davis appointed his relative-by-marriage Braxton Bragg the commanding general of the Army of Tennessee, he sealed the fate of the Confederacy in what was then called "the West." Although Bragg was a man of high character and culture, he was ultra-conservative in military discisions. Whereas when Robert E. Lee had a 51 percent chance of success, he would fight, Bragg apparently wanted the odds ten-to-one in his favor before committing his troops. After the ill-fated foray into Kentucky and the fall of Nashville, military actions in Bragg's area took place on or near the Nashville and Chattanooga Railroad (later the N.C. & St. L. and the L.&N., now CSX). This is the road which after 1850 went under Sewanee's mountain and through the Cowan tunnel. After 1856, the Tracy City spur came through University Place to dead-end at the coal fields.

On a freezing New Year's Day in 1863, Braxton Bragg, at Stone's River near Murfreesboro (between Sewanee and Nashville), suffered the most ignominious of all defeats. He was outflanked by George Henry Thomas and William Starke Rosecrans. All through the spring, with only sporadic action, Bragg pulled his troops southeastward toward Sewanee Mountain. Here his generals expected him to make a stand with his artillery a thousand feet up the slope, commanding the enemy's advance. Instead, Bragg retreated across the undeveloped campus in June. Actually, Bragg took the train through the tunnel and three of his generals saw the future university's site with which their names afterward would be connected. Leonidas Polk, the principal founder (who died a year later, before the Battle of Atlanta), William J. Hardee, for whom the football field would be named, and B. Frank Cheatham, whose daughter and grandchildren (the Hodgsons) would become prominent in its history.

There were a few shots fired before and after July 4, and the polished marble cornerstone was blown up as a prank. The colonel, an Episcopalian, vowed to court-martial the perpetrators if he caught them. A Confederate rear-guard covered the retreat of Hood's Texans.

Robert W. Daniel summarized the story in the 1947 *Sewanee Alumni News:* "That Sewanee was the setting for a Confederate victory in a cavalry engagement on July 4, 1863, has now been established by the discovery of a contemporary account of the skirmish, written three days afterwards by a Confederate chaplain who took part, and printed in the Houston, Texas, *Telegraph* on August 19, 1863.... The tragically fraternal character of the War is emphasized by the fact that the Northern troops who charged the Texans at Sewanee were all Kentuckians: 'the 1st, 5th, and 9th Kentucky regiments,' Chaplain Bunting wrote, 'the fifth being in the center—with whom we had the severe fight.' They were opposed by the 8th Texas Cavalry, known as Terry's Texas Rangers, whom R. S. Bunting served as chaplain. The engagement was one of the rear-guard actions during the campaign. . . . During the retreat of the Army of Tennessee into northern Georgia, some of the infantry crossed the the University Domain by way of the Brakefield Road. The march was covered by the Texans, posted at the edge of the Mountain; and it was here that they withstood the assault of the Kentuckians, though outnumbered three to one. At first thrown into confusion by the heaviness of the odds, the Texas regiment stopped the enemy by a volley of buckshot and pistol-fire at five paces. Then, as the contemporary account tells it, 'D, K and G companies charged the enemy's cavalry and repulsed them handsomely.' About thirty of them were killed, including a colonel and twelve other officers. The Texans suffered nine casualties, only one of whom was killed. 'Such was our loss,' Chaplain Bunting writes complacently, 'on the 4th of July near Sewanee's University of the South, on Cumberland Mountain.' If the regiments were anywhere near full strength, close to two thousand men must have been engaged in this skirmish."

The most annoying gunfire to disturb the top of the plateau lying between University Place and Beersheba Springs thirty-five miles away came from Bushwhackers—lawless brigands including deserters from both sides who roamed about stealing livestock, food, and whatever property they could carry away. They were responsible for burning the few pre-War cottages, except Fairbanks' Rainsford Place, which federal troops destroyed in 1863.

For those wishing to read more about "the War at Sewanee" there are three monographs, written by Robert W. Daniel, George L. Reynolds, and Edgar Legare Pennington, and a book by Howard M. Hannah. All are available in the Torian Archives along with several letters written by Union soldiers describing the cool springs and lovely summer they spent on the Mountain before advancing on to Chattanooga for the battles of Lookout Mountain, Chickamauga, and Missionary Ridge, where altogether there are more soldiers buried than anywhere else except Gettysburg.

One might say Sewanee just "sat it out" during the War, but at its end there remained intact the largest piece of real estate ever owned by an educational institution up to that time, and there became available as teachers a remarkable group of men, including three Confederate generals.

ARTHUR BEN CHITTY

University of the South
Sewanee, Tennessee
September 1993

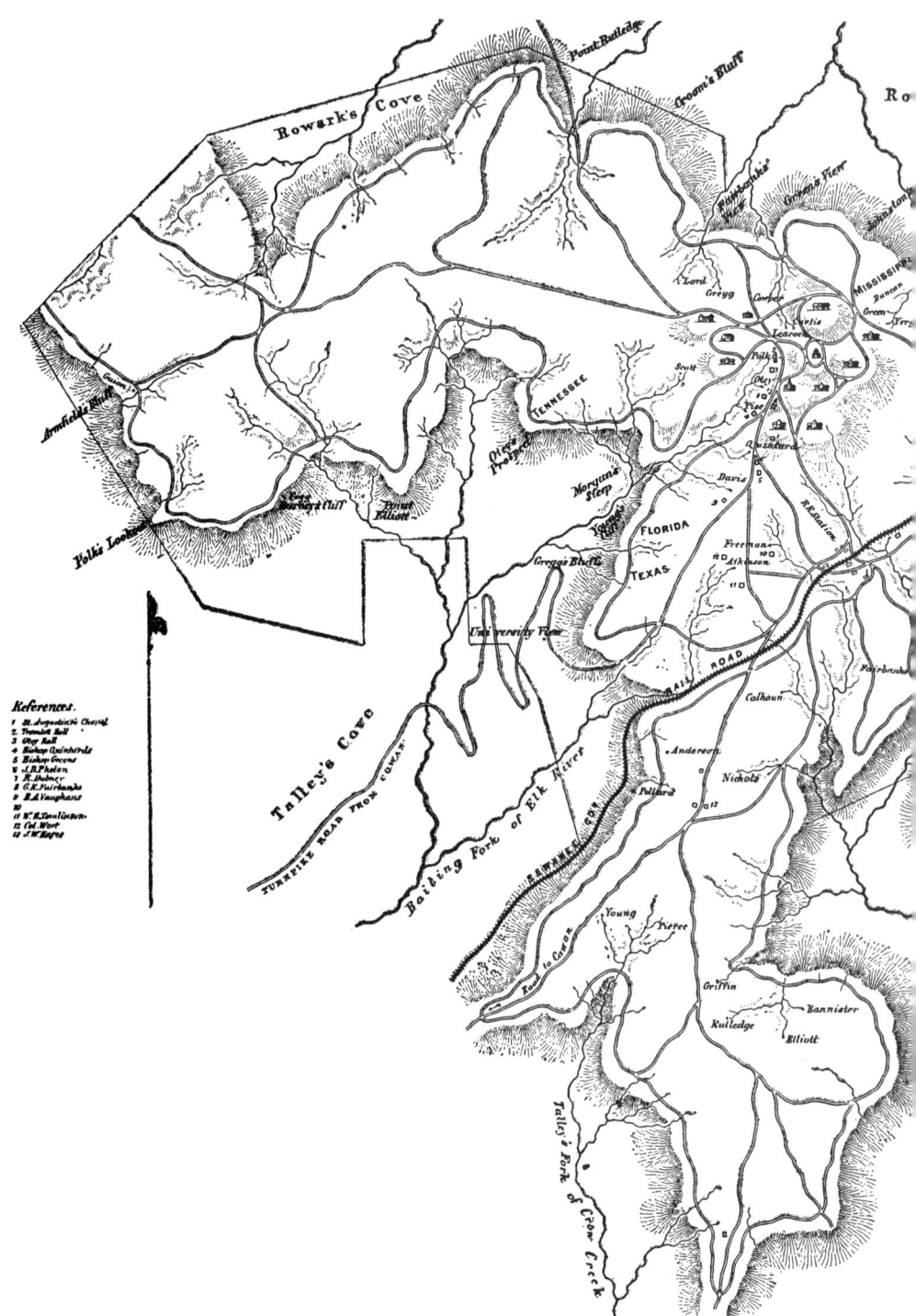

ABOUT 1870
PLAN OF THE LANDS
OF THE
UNIVERSITY OF THE SOUTH,
ON THE
SEWANEE PLATEAU
of the
CUMBERLAND MOUNTAINS
2000 feet above the level of the Sea
University Place, Franklin Co. Tenn.

Scale 4000 Feet to the Inch.

Note. The group of Buildings represented on the upper portion of the Map indicate proposed location of University Buildings not yet errected. The names Otey, Polk &c. are attached to Springs thus named. Avenues are indicated which are not yet opened. So' 1-13 indicate existing Buildings.

RECONSTRUCTION AT SEWANEE

First Printing
1000 Copies
This book is Number

Copyright 1954 by Arthur B. Chitty, Jr.

TYPOGRAPHY AND BINDING BY
BENSON PRINTING COMPANY
NASHVILLE, TENNESSEE

RECONSTRUCTION AT SEWANEE

The Founding of the University of the South
and its First Administration
1857-1872

By
ARTHUR BENJAMIN CHITTY, JR.

Published in anticipation of the Centennial
of the University in 1957.

The University Press
Sewanee, Tennessee
1954

This book I inscribe to my wife
Mary Elizabeth Nickinson Chitty

INTRODUCTION

There were few lights to illumine the tragic times of southern Reconstruction but that emanating from a Cumberland mountaintop was one of them. Sewanee was one of the few successful creative efforts of the disconsolate time initiated by southern people. The career of the Episcopal Church's sole effort at university-building has been largely ignored by general historians. Beyond its own circle of enthusiasts, its significance has been missed.

It is now almost a half century since George Rainsford Fairbanks, "the last of the founders," published the first and only *History of the University of the South*. This present book, compiled in preparation for the Centennial of the University in 1957, is not as ambitious as his in scope but it examines more closely than did his the founding, refounding, and the administration of the first vice-chancellor.

Reconstruction at Sewanee is an expansion of a master's thesis done at Tulane University in 1952 under the direction of Dr. Wendell H. Stephenson. It deals with the founding of the University of the South in 1857, sponsored by ten dioceses of the Episcopal Church in the deep South, and with its opening to students in 1868. Contrast is noted between its development as an idea in the high noon of southern prosperity and of the implementation of that idea in the postwar South. Reconstruction postponed financial security but simultaneously promoted the assembling of a faculty ordinarily unobtainable by educational enterprises.

Strict Reconstructionists will wonder why this story was stopped in 1872 rather than the more proper 1878. The reasons are two. The important relationships of the University with the context of the time had been established by 1872. Second, the story has a natural dramatic cohesion if stopped at the end of Bishop Quintard's administration. In 1878 the institution was undergoing an organizational crisis which, distressing as it was at the time, did not change the pattern established by the first faculty and administration. The functions of faculty, vice-chancellor, and trustees in 1954 resemble those of 1872 more than those of 1878.

The organization of this work is basically chronological, with pause for development of atmosphere in Chapter IV and ingathering of implications in Chapter V. On occasion, at the expense of rapid movement, space has been accorded to quotations which have more human than historic interest.

The conclusions are reached that the founders' plans, involving the acceptance of excellence as a criterion, were sound for this regional institution and that the refounders formulated in four years (1868-1872) a pattern combining the cultural and ethical implications of the Oxonian, southern, West Point, classical and Episcopal traditions.

ARTHUR BEN CHITTY

University of the South
Sewanee, Tennessee
April 1, 1954

TABLE OF CONTENTS

INTRODUCTION 5

PICTORIAL SECTION 9

CHAPTER ONE—VISIONS AND VIEWERS (1857-1861)

    Religious Influence Predominant — Learning Gave Prestige — Episcopal University Proposed — Otey, the Educator — Polk, Man of Action — Elliott, the Classicist — The Founding — Ideal Location sought — Site and Name selected — Charter Granted — Money Sought — Forerunner of the Endowment Idea — The Domain — Plan for a "Heavenly City" — A Physical Beginning — Constitution and Statutes — Broad Scope of Curriculum — Gathering Clouds — The Power and the Glory
. . . . 41

CHAPTER TWO—IDEAL REVISITED (1861-1868)

    The Supporting Church — Tennessee Initiates Revival — Reunion of the Church — Quintard, the Refounder — Mendicant Unashamed — Fairbanks, Good Right Arm — To Recall a Dream — Sewanee College at Winchester — Trustees Approve Revival — Green, the Fourth Chancellor — Diocesan Divinity School — Joint Sponsorship Sought Again — Eyes Turn to England — Sewanee as Anglican Missionary Enterprise — British Friends Respond 83

CHAPTER THREE—OF WILL AND WAY (1868-1872)

    Josiah Gorgas — A Time Disconsolate — School Begins — Second Term Optimism — Instruction and Discipline — Same Goal but Slower Page — Hollow Fiscal Structure — Faculty Enlarged — Academic Evaluation — Report to a Constituency — The First Bequest — From School to College — Theological Training — The Coming of DuBose — Others of That Company 115

CHAPTER FOUR—PLOUGH AND SCYTHE (1866-1872)
    The Village — Benefactor Unsung — Homogeneity — Academic Diversion — The Halls — Student Life — Athletics — Extra Curricular — Two of the Boys — Intimation of Importance 150

CHAPTER FIVE—FIRST FRUITS (1872)
    Fanfare with Trumpets Muted — Realist in their Midst — Conclusion: Founders' Plans Survive — The Regional Idea — The Five-Fold Tradition (The Oxonian, The Military, The Classical, The Southern, The Episcopal) — A Tale of Two Times 169

ACKNOWLEDGEMENTS 185

PERMISSIONS 188

BIBLIOGRAPHY 189

INDEX 197

PICTORIAL

To produce a picture section for a book ending in 1872 is not easy. Photography was in its infancy. The first good action shots were made during the Civil War. Leonidas Polk, even with his genius for planning, forgot to "cover" the laying of the cornerstone. There was no photographer on hand, not even a stray *Harper's* artist.

The archives of the University of the South yield only six efforts to show what the eye saw at Sewanee before the War. Five of these are the watercolors of Bishop Hopkins of Vermont, preserved by chance from twenty-eight he painted. They show the sylvan beauties of the domain. "Natural Bridge" reproduced here is typical.

The sixth prewar sketch is a simple pen-and-ink reproduction of one of the first three homes at Sewanee, the residence of George R. Fairbanks, which in 1860 stood on the north escarpment, west of Green's View, near the present Peter J. Garland home. This is all we have of prewar Sewanee. Perhaps future discoveries in attics will prove that an unsuspected photographer was present at the laying of the cornerstone.

There were, of course, portraits and daguerreotypes of the principal people. They are faithfully presented here with preference given to those which have not appeared before in print.

JAMES HERVEY OTEY

The Right Reverend James Hervey Otey, first Bishop of Tennessee, first Episcopal priest west of the Great Smokies, was first Chancellor of the University of the South. He deserved the honor. He had labored faithfully for over twenty years to bring to life a comprehensive institution of higher learning. Otey was a nationalist, an ardent foe of secession. He was determined to maintain the catholicity of this educational enterprise. He began the long-continuing ascendency of Tennessee among the owning dioceses.

LEONIDAS POLK

The Right Reverend Leonidas Polk, first Bishop of Arkansas and (later) of Louisiana, was the second Chancellor and was principally responsible for the University's location, its endowment, and its constitution. He was briefly, by virtue of his seniority, titular head of the nascent institution after the death of Otey in 1863, although during that year he never presided over a meeting of the Board. He conceived a real university in the modern sense with graduate work and fellowships. This lieutenant general, this pioneer bishop, may well be remembered in distant days as a genius in American education.

STEPHEN ELLIOTT

The Right Reverend Stephen Elliott, first Bishop of Georgia and second Presiding Bishop of the Confederacy, was the third Chancellor. It was at his call that the meeting of 1866 was held which led to the revival of the University. He was a close friend of Otey but was especially admired by Polk for his breadth of learning and his love of the classical. One of the significant acts of his later life was to charge a young Confederate Chaplain named Quintard to preserve at all costs the University of the South.

CHARLES TODD QUINTARD

The Right Reverend Charles Todd Quintard, second Bishop of Tennessee, was first Vice-Chancellor of the University. The original planning was a composite work. Great as was Polk's contribution, especially as to breadth of scope, he was flanked by others of almost equal greatness. But Quintard, after the deaths of the first three, was the *sine qua non*. Without him, it is hard to believe that the University could have revived. His courage, his ingenuity, his unquenchable enthusiasm made him the outstanding southern bishop of his day.

GEORGE RAINSFORD FAIRBANKS

Major George Rainsford Fairbanks was a versatile man. He was also a dogged, determined, relentless, humble follower of idealists—which is not quite the same as, though it may be even rarer than, an idealist. Before the War, he was the first to build a home at Sewanee with Polk and Elliott—an act of great confidence. After the holocaust he was the first to build beside Quintard—an act of unwarranted optimism. When a man of cultivation, of scholarship, an author and barrister, moves his family to a wilderness, he has faith. That man was Fairbanks.

WILLIAM MERCER GREEN

The Right Reverend William Mercer Green, first Bishop of Mississippi and fourth Chancellor, was the principal link between the Sewanee that was planned and the Sewanee that was. Bishop Green moved to Sewanee, lived at Sewanee, brought to its shaky beginnings his prestige, his quiet assurance. Most of his contemporaries agree on one descriptive adjective—saintly.

ALEXANDER GREGG

The Right Reverend Alexander Gregg, first Bishop of Texas and fifth Chancellor, maintained summer residence at Sewanee for a quarter century. He buttressed the institution by encouraging precisely the sort of backing which almost a hundred years later promised to make Sewanee financially secure. He was the first to take the support of their University to the parishes.

JOSIAH GORGAS

Brigadier General Josiah Gorgas, Lee's chief of ordnance, the "second genius of the Confederacy" according to Freeman, attended Sewanee's first chapel service, returned to teach in the second term. He was the first headmaster of the "junior department" and the second Vice-Chancellor, succeeding Quintard in 1872. He brought quiet competence, courtly dignity, and a great lady to the secluded domain.

WILLIAM PORCHER DUBOSE

The Reverend William Porcher DuBose came to Sewanee as Chaplain in a narrow escape from the bishopric of South Carolina. He became Sewanee's greatest teacher, greatest personality, greatest theologian. His students became disciples and his influence on the Episcopal Church may be unparalleled in America. He bridged the gulf between theoretical religion and reality in a way which made sense both to theologians and to people.

JABEZ WHEELER HAYES

Jabez Wheeler Hayes made his fortune in Newark as a jewelry manufacturer. Sewanee in his mellow maturity combined his two chief hobbies, horticulture and Christian education. He came to the University of the South to plant fruit trees and to assist a cause he thought important, the training of youth in Christian virtue.

FRANCIS W. TREMLETT

The Reverend Francis W. Tremlett of London was the fitting recipient of Sewanee's first honorary degree. From the time he first heard of the missionary enterprise, this Confederate-at-heart kept its interests before his friends, who were, happily, some of the most distinguished Lords and Ladies of Victoria's England.

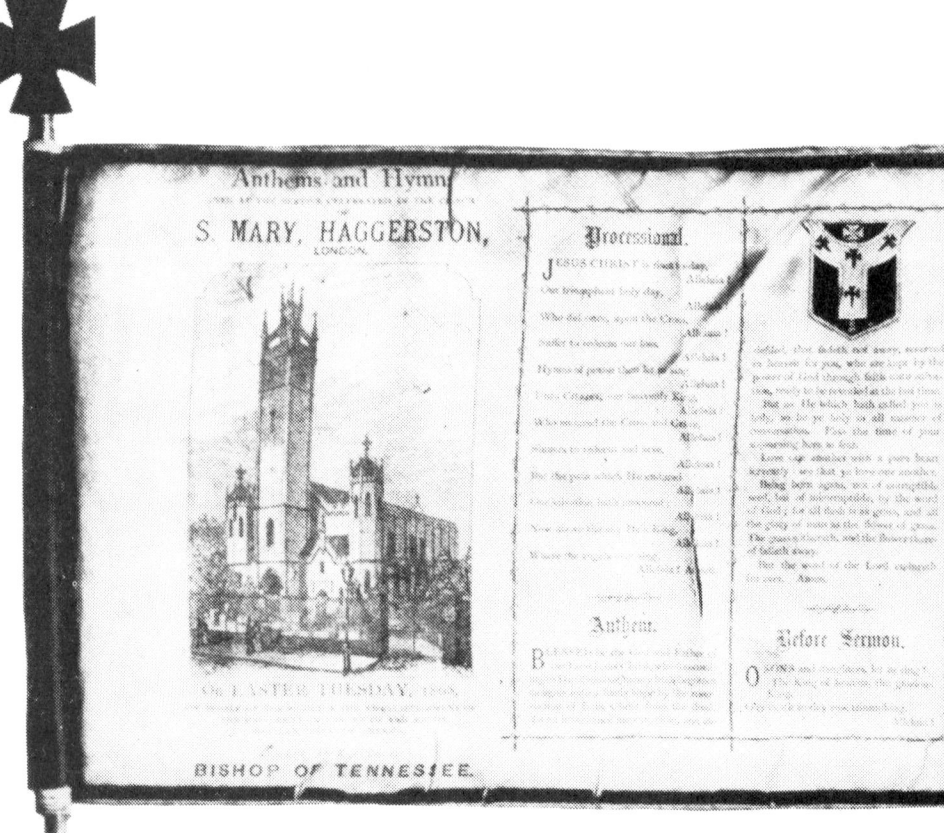

Bishop Quintard preached more than a sermon a day for six months in England while raising the vital £2,500 which was to open the University of the South. This program chronicles his appearance at St. Mary's, Haggerston, London.

Bishop Quintard brought back enough money to the impoverished plateau to build frame buildings and hire teachers. The first dormitory, appropriately enough, was named for the first "Commissary of the University of the South," the Reverend Doctor Tremlett. Tremlett Hall stood on the site of the present home of Mrs. Henry M. Gass.

The Right Reverend Nicholas Hamner Cobbs, first Bishop of Alabama, prominent among Sewanee's first trustees.

The Right Reverend Henry Champlin Lay, first Secretary of the Board, later Bishop of Arkansas and of Easton.

The Reverend David Pise, second Secretary of the Board, clerical trustee from the Diocese of Tennessee.

Colonel T. Frank Sevier, first Proctor, first commandant, disciplinarian, Instructor of Commerce and Trade.

Brigadier General and the Reverend Francis Asbury S h o u p, mathematician, metaphysician, brilliant teacher.

John Barnwell Elliott, M.D., son of Bishop Stephen Elliott, first Health Officer and Professor of Chemistry.

Robert Dabney, first Professor of English Literature, Virginian, scholar, "most popular of the early teachers."

Caskie Harrison, first Professor of Ancient Languages, stern young perfectionist, defender of the classical.

ST. AUGUSTINE'S CHAPEL

Although it doubled for classroom building and auditorium in the first years, St. Augustine's Chapel, named for the famous Anglican mission college at Canterbury, achieved a curious dignity. Its clapboard walls witnessed in solemn processions the leading figures of the southern Episcopal Church.

LIBRARY

The first library was material for jest. The 2,000 volumes which had been given by Oxford and Cambridge Universities crowded its shelves. It later became the chapter house of Sewanee's first fraternity, Alpha Tau Omega, which still occupies the same site.

BRIERFIELD

Josiah Gorgas built a house which he named nostalgically for the iron works he had left to rust in Brierfield, Alabama. Under the talented hand of his wife Amelia, Brierfield became one of Sewanee's great homes. It has maintained its tradition of hospitality under its present owner, Mrs. Telfair Hodgson.

When the Diocese of Tennessee authorized the opening of a theological school at Sewanee after the War (it was uncertain whether other dioceses would again join in support of the educational venture), the first building constructed by its action was Otey Hall. It served as academic building, dormitory, and finally as residence before burning down in 1881.

Even among the pleasant homes of Sewanee, one stood out above all others. It was Fulford Hall, the home of Bishop Quintard and later of his son-in-law Vice-Chancellor Wiggins, and the Vice-Chancellor's home today. Here distinguished visitors were welcomed. Here the Bishop gathered his sentimental treasures from British and American admirers. It was only of logs but its owner knew queens.

The name Kendal given the Bishop Green place at Sewanee went back to some ancestral home in England. Miss Lily Green, who survived her octogenarian father by almost a half-century, made it famous among Sewanee students and visitors.

The Rectory, built by Chaplain DuBose in 1871, became a mecca for Sewanee's early students, especially those who had been personally recruited in South Carolina by the popular young clergyman. Ice cream, games, and fireside conversations were among the attractions.

Rebel's Rest, built for the Fairbanks family in 1866, was completed just after Bishop Quintard's Fulford Hall next door. When Fulford burned in the 1890's, it became the oldest residence at Sewanee. Here was held the first meeting of the Board of Trustees after the War and here met for the first time the E. Q. B., fortnightly faculty club now nearing its first century of uninterrupted existence.

WILLIAM CRAWFORD GORGAS

Sewanee was to turn out no more remarkable product in its first hundred years than Major General William Crawford Gorgas, conqueror of yellow fever at Panama, surgeon general of World War I, Knight of the British Order of St. Michael and St. George. Willie went barefoot as a grammar school boy in 1869 and took honors in the second graduating class of the college in 1875.

This almost-candid shot of students in front of St. Augustine's Chapel is the nearest approach to a modern unposed photo to be taken of early Sewanee. It is one of several stereopticon slides preserved in the archives. Sewanee had three-dimensions even in 1873!

Debating was relished by students and faculty. Interminable orations were devoured by eager listeners and societies were formed to encourage the forensic arts. The Pi Lambda (for Polk Leonidas) and the Omega (Otey) societies merged to form Pi Omega in 1872 and this group competed with the older Sigma Epsilon (Stephen Elliott) for three-quarters of a century before they both became casualties of World War II. Key to the names of students in the Sigma Epsilon photo below will be furnished any visitor to the University archives.

One of twenty-eight watercolors painted by Bishop John Henry Hopkins during his visit in the winter of 1859-60 is this fairly accurate impression of Natural Bridge, located at the east edge of the Domain. On the opposite page is a sketch of the frame residence built by George R. Fairbanks on the north escarpment on the site of the present Garland home. There are no known photographs of prewar Sewanee.

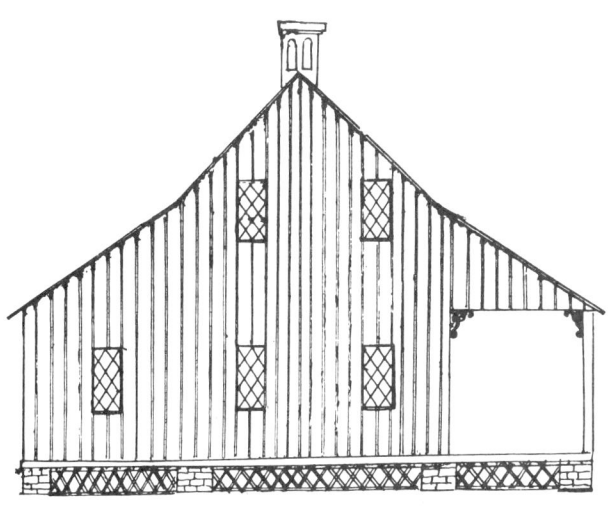

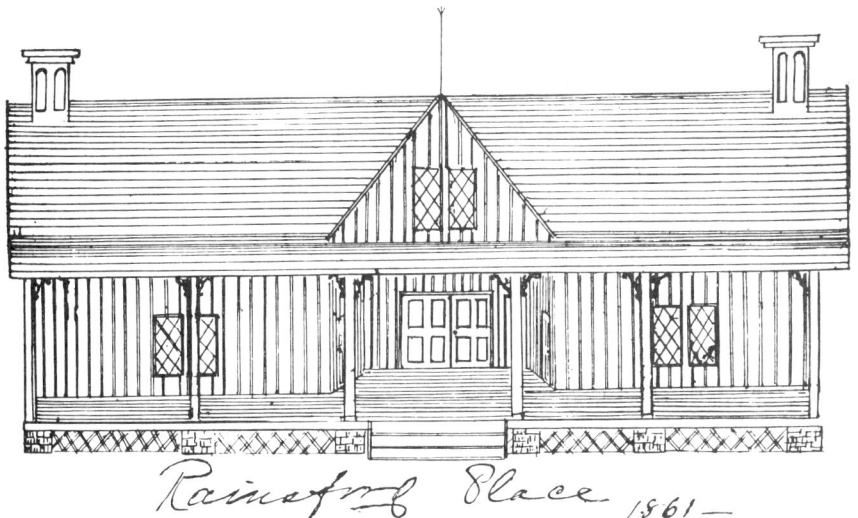

Rainsford Place - 1861 -

Education is an ornament in prosperity and a refuge in adversity.

ARISTOTLE

CHAPTER ONE

VISIONS AND VIEWERS
1857-1861

THE OUTLOOK facing the University of the South at its opening in the Reconstruction year of 1868 was in bleak contrast to the vision of Bishop Leonidas Polk and his collaborators who proposed the Episcopal institution in the late 1850's. Here, on an isolated Tennessee mountain at a place known to the Indians as Sewanee,[1] the first nine students met four teachers. The simple clapboard and log buildings and the few thousand dollars that had been laboriously collected represented a pathetic deterioration of the plan of the rich 1850's for a university born fullgrown, with the largest endowment and landed domain in the country.

In the four years before the war for southern independence, ten Episcopal dioceses united to found an institution of higher learning on a scale not previously envisioned in the South. The regional experiment had received unprecedented support when it became a casualty of the Civil War.

The decade in which the University was projected brought unprecedented prosperity to most of the nation. In the North there was marked increase in wealth. The reaper and the Bessemer process were in use, a new revolver by Colt was on the market, and Goodyear was announcing new developments in rubber. Steam railways were only twenty years old. Texas and most of the far West had recently been acquired. But there were storm warnings for the South. Steel rails and cross-ties, flow of reciprocal trade, and streams of immigrants were forging the North and Northwest into a single economic and social pattern. The southern plantation, long under fire on moral and political grounds, was attacked on economic grounds as a wasteful system. A single county in Massachusetts boasted real estate values exceeding those of South Carolina. The white population of Massachusetts and Illinois equalled that of all the cotton states together.[2]

The ominous twist which history was to give some of these facts was not apparent to many Southerners in the fifties. They marshaled statistics of their own. During the ten-year span good prices and bumper crops were pushing the cotton growers' income from $100 million to $250 million. Two thirds of the 1860 cotton crop was exported to form a major portion of the world's supply.[3] In England millions depended on cotton manufactures and derivative industries. The same was true in New England. Southern economists believed that cotton was the key to worldwide prosperity. Yet this vaunted crop was worth only half as much as the unglamorous hay harvest of the North.[4]

Railroad construction, although lagging in comparison with that of the North, nevertheless increased from 2,068 to 10,386 miles in this magic decade. The lumber industry doubled and flour production increased. A line of ships gave the South direct and regular commercial contact with Europe.[5] The prevailing spirit was bullish. The South had developed a sectional consciousness which soon would tragically ignite as southern nationalism.

Education in the South was conducted in a religious atmosphere. There were several state universities, but the spirit of the large Protestant denominations prevailed in most of them. Of the five southern states in the Union before 1800, North Carolina and Georgia had mentioned education in their constitutions,[6] and in the half century which followed the opening of the University of North Carolina in 1795,[7] state institutions were established in Georgia, South Carolina, Virginia, Alabama, Tennessee, Mississippi, and Louisiana. But, as one historian ironically puts it, the states exercised great self-control in supporting their universities.[8]

RELIGIOUS INFLUENCE PREDOMINANT

Presbyterians, Methodists, and Baptists were in control of more than half of the colleges of the section.[9] The Presbyterians, inspired by their success at Princeton, opened Hampden-Sydney in 1776, Washington College in 1782, and subsequently founded Davidson, Oglethorpe,

Erskine, and Centre. The Methodists set up Randolph-Macon in 1832, and then established Emory, Emory and Henry, Wofford, and Trinity.[10] The Baptists founded Mercer in 1833, and Wake Forest, Richmond, Baylor, and Furman. Spring Hill at Mobile was established by the Roman Catholics who, despite early advantages in Louisiana and Florida, remained one of the minor denominations of the planter civilization.[11]

The Episcopal Church had met little success in operating colleges and seminaries in the South. William and Mary in Virginia, though Anglican in origin, was now nonsectarian.[12] Madison College and Ravenscroft College in Tennessee were failures. Kentucky's theological seminary which flourished at Lexington for several years following 1834 [13] closed some time before 1845.[14] Its failure followed dissension in 1837 between members of its faculty and the bishop of the diocese. Kentucky also operated Shelby College for a number of years.[15] In Mississippi St. Andrew's College was opened in Jackson in 1852 and Rose Gates College at Okolona in 1859. Neither survived the Civil War. Two "Episcopal ventures in education" in Texas, St. Paul's College, Anderson (1852-1856), and Wharton College at Austin (1858-1865) were short-lived.[16] St. Paul's College at New Orleans appeared in church almanacs from 1855 to 1858 but then disappeared.

Four factors appeared necessary for the successful establishment of a denominational college: conviction of the importance of education, denominational organization, sufficient membership, and wealth.[17] Episcopal lag could be laid principally to late organization. All of the bishops concerned in the founding of the University of the South except those of the Carolinas and Arkansas were first bishops of their dioceses.[18]

The Episcopal Church, however, enjoyed a peculiar status in the South. Historian William E. Dodd stated the matter pleasantly enough:

> Although there may be other roads to the Celestial City, no gentleman would choose any but the Episcopalian way. It may be doubted whether there were twenty thousand Episcopalians in all the region from Charleston to Galveston at the outbreak of the Civil War, yet members of "the church" were almost invariably found in the seats of the mighty.[19]

As this analysis suggests, the ratio of Episcopalians to total population was low. In 1860 the highest Episcopal ratio was one for every 38 persons in Connecticut, whereas in the cotton states the range varied from one in each 114 in South Carolina to one in each 1,209 in Texas.[20]

LEARNING GAVE PRESTIGE

Higher education in the South looked good when compared statistically with the rest of the nation. There were 260 colleges and universities, 1,500 teachers, and 25,000 students in 1860, more than half the institutions in the land and almost half of the teachers and students.[21] Twice as many young men per thousand of white population in the South were attending college as in other sections. The income of higher educational institutions of the area rose to $708,000 in 1860, an increase of 100 per cent since 1850. Most of the college enrollments were around 100, with a few as high as 400. Between 1850 and 1860 nearly every college in the South doubled in attendance.[22] The college degree carried social prestige and, surprisingly enough by standards of a half century later, its possession was a solid political asset.

Some of the ablest teachers of the time taught in the lower South. Ethnologist Josiah C. Nott at the University of Alabama had a national reputation. Frederick Augustus Porter Barnard, later president of Columbia, was professor of natural history at Alabama in the beginning of the South's great decade. In 1854 he went to the University of Mississippi where in 1856 he became chancellor. Francis Lieber offered superior instruction in political science at South Carolina until he was lured to Columbia College in 1856. Joseph LeConte in Charleston was abreast of Charles Darwin in developing the theory of the origin of species. Louis Agassiz was strongly tempted to resist the blandishments of Harvard to continue teaching biology in Charleston. J. D. B. DeBow was pioneering in commerce courses in New Orleans. And yet all was not well. The University of Virginia was charged in the late 1850's with stifling academic freedom. In 1856 a professor at the University of North Carolina was dismissed for expressing antislavery views.[23] The trustees of the University of Georgia tried to throttle the spirit of scientific revolt.[24] Despite the flowering of its higher education the South was still in a state of comparative cultural poverty and, as its institutions progressed, they usually found with dismay that the Yankees had done twice as much in half the time. In its museums, in its fine music and drama, and especially in its public education, the South could point only to a few bright spots.

EPISCOPAL UNIVERSITY PROPOSED

This was the atmosphere into which, on July 1, 1856, the Right Reverend Leonidas Polk of Louisiana projected his 4,000-word letter on education to brother bishops of the other nine dioceses of the lower South and Southwest.[25] The Bishop of Louisiana declared that the Episcopal Church should consider itself responsible for the spiritual well-being of all 5,800,000 souls in the dioceses concerned. "Our mission is to all," he said, "as well to those who differ from us as those who agree with us." Despite its promises for the future, he wrote, higher education in the South, as sponsored by other religious denominations and state governments, compared unfavorably with institutions of highest grade abroad or in the northern states. The Episcopal Church faced a diminishing of its power for good if it failed to sponsor higher education. Individual dioceses were too weak to build institutions "so enlarged and so liberal as to leave nothing to be desired" but together with joint control a university of breadth and comprehensiveness could be established. A theological seminary must be a part of the plan because of the need for a native ministry and there must be a fine grammar school since the preparatory level of education had also been neglected by the Episcopal Church in the South.[26] Polk's letter was so specific as to suggest locating the institution in the lower Allegheny range, where newly completed railroads converged with easy access to all parts of the South. Further, the mountain air and pure water would insure against epidemics fostered by miasmas of the coastal plains.

Polk's plan was adopted by the nine bishops of the South meeting at the general convention of the Episcopal Church in October, 1856. So mature was Polk's outline, so complete and carefully documented, that, rewritten by Bishop James Hervey Otey of Tennessee[27] without essential change, it was used by the southern prelates in their manifesto on a church university issued from Philadelphia on October 23.[28]

This address, distributed throughout the South, contained nine proposals for organization. The university would be Protestant Episcopal, its board of trustees would include the bishop, one clergyman, and two laymen elected by each owning diocese. At least $500,000 would be raised before the university could be put in operation. There would be a university treasurer in each diocese who would annually send to the corporation treasurer the interest on endowment held by that diocese. The amounts subscribed would revert to the dioceses in event of dissolution. Each bishop would place before his next annual council a plan for inaugurating the project, the senior bishop by consecration would be chancellor, and the university would be located near Chattanooga.

It is a tragic fact that of the nine bishops who signed this document, only one, William Mercer Green of Mississippi, took an active part in the postwar struggles of the university. Otey, Polk, and Stephen Elliott, the three principal instigators, did not live to see the first student admitted.[29] These three were professional men before they entered the ministry—Otey a teacher, Polk a soldier, and Elliott a lawyer. In that order they became the first bishops of Tennessee, Arkansas (later of Louisiana), and Georgia. In that order they entered the history of Sewanee and emerged as its leaders.

OTEY, THE EDUCATOR

Otey was born in 1800 in Bedford County, Virginia. He graduated from the University of North Carolina in 1820, the first student there to win the degree bachelor of *belles lettres*.[30] He married Elizabeth Pannill of Petersburg in 1821. The same year he opened a school in Maury County, Tennessee. Next year he became headmaster of Warrenton Academy in North Carolina and while in that post was baptized and confirmed in the Episcopal Church. In 1827 he was ordained priest and two years later became the first minister of his faith to be heard west of the Alleghenies.[31] In 1833 he was elected bishop of Tennessee. For three years after 1841 he had missionary jurisdiction over Florida, Mississippi, Arkansas, and the Indian Territory. In 1857 he met with the first board of trustees of the University of the South on Lookout Mountain, where he made the principal address. Elected first chancellor, he took part in the laying of the cornerstone in 1860 at University Place and died in 1863 in Memphis.

Bishop Otey was pre-eminently an educator.[32] His diocese was an educational diocese and many of his clergy were or became teachers. In 1856 he ordained to the priesthood the man who was to succeed him, Professor Charles Todd Quintard of the Memphis medical college faculty. Quintard, as second bishop of Tennessee, continued the educational tradition of the diocese until his death in 1898. Otey was a man of wide reading, and intellectual versatility.[33] In politics he was a Whig, and his address at Lookout Mountain showed no sympathy for sectional rivalry.[34]

The Reverend Moultrie Guerry names 1832 as the year in which the idea of the University of the South had its origin.[35] In that year, the thirty-two year old Otey, who had been only eight years a member of the Episcopal Church, sponsored a resolution at the third annual convention of the Tennessee diocese to establish a classical and theological seminary within the state.[36] No action was reported in 1833. The following year Otey, by then bishop, regretted that the time was inauspicious for pushing educational plans. Nevertheless the matter was referred to the diocesan standing committee which included the new rector of St. Peter's Church, Columbia, young Leonidas Polk, and Francis B. Fogg of Nashville, who was influential twenty-four years later in obtaining the charter of the University of the South.

From 1834 onward, Polk and Otey were close friends and zealous co-workers for church-sponsored education. In 1835 plans were discussed for an interdiocesan institution to be operated jointly by the dioceses of Tennessee, Mississippi, and Louisiana. It would include a liberal arts college, a theological seminary, and a teachers' college. The Panic of 1837 halted solicitation for funds for this institution but hope still justified securing a charter for a less ambitious enterprise to be located in Madison County, Tennessee. Madison College was never opened. In 1838 Polk, nominated by Otey, was elected missionary bishop of Arkansas and given jurisdiction over the southwestern United States and the Republic of Texas. Before Polk left Tennessee, he assisted Otey in opening the Columbia Female Institute, which finally closed after World War I.

At Columbia, in 1844, Otey opened Mercer Hall which closed after four years. He then started Ravenscroft College near Columbia, which also failed for lack of funds. His health broke in 1850 and he took a trip to Europe, an event having some significance years later for the University of the South. This six-foot-three Virginia frontiersman, who looked "very like a Cherokee Indian,"[37] was received with wondering enthusiasm in England and his quiet eloquence attracted the Archbishop of Canterbury.[38] When Otey's successor, Quintard, went to England in 1867 to solicit a critical £2,500 for opening the University, he found that the reputation of "My Lord Bishop of Tennessee" had preceded him.

POLK, MAN OF ACTION

Polk came from a family of soldiers.[39] Robert Pollock, a Scot, served under Cromwell. He came to Maryland in 1689. He shortened the name which was to be borne by many descendants, among them President James K. Polk. Robert's grandson, Thomas, was identified in North Carolina with the Mecklenburg Declaration of 1775. Serving with Washington at Valley Forge, he later became a brigadier general. Thomas' son William was in the Revolutionary army at eighteen with the rank of major. William's second wife was Sarah Hawkins, mother of Leonidas. In 1823 William Polk obtained a United States Military Academy appointment for his son who had entered the University of North Carolina at fifteen.

At West Point Polk came under the influence of Chaplain Charles P. McIlvaine, later bishop of Ohio for forty-one years, who baptized and confirmed the young cadet under dramatic circumstances in the Academy chapel. After graduating eighth in his class he entered the Episcopal seminary at Alexandria, Virginia.[40] He was ordained deacon in 1830 and was married the same year to the wealthy Frances Devereux. In 1833 he was ordained priest and that year traveled in Europe. On his return he settled on a Maury County, Tennessee, farm provided by his father. The Devereux family supplied the slaves. While living there he worked closely with Otey in educational endeavors in the diocese.

As missionary bishop of Arkansas, he witnessed pioneer conditions on the southwestern frontier before he was elected first bishop of Louisiana in 1841.[41] In the next fifteen years he lost his personal fortune and that of his wife in a series of plantation disasters but he established the Episcopal Church firmly in Louisiana.[42] Polk lived to see his idea of a university enthusiastically accepted, the funds raised, the cornerstone laid. After southern secession he thrice declined but finally accepted a commission as major general from Jefferson Davis, served with the Army of Tennessee, retreated across the Sewanee domain in July, 1863,[43] and was killed the following year at Pine Mount near Kennesaw, north of Atlanta.

Polk never considered himself a well-educated man.[44] Sometimes his clergy would criticize his conducting of a service or his reading of the rubrics.[45] He was particularly attracted to Stephen Elliott, whose scholarly and cultural attainments exceeded his own.

ELLIOTT, THE CLASSICIST

Elliott was born in Beaufort, South Carolina, in 1806, the same year as Polk, and was reared in an atmosphere of sensitive refinement. His father, Stephen Elliott, was a famous naturalist, president of the first state bank of South Carolina, founder and editor of the *Southern Review*, and highly regarded in political life.[46] His mother, Esther Habersham, came from an equally respected family. At six young Stephen read Greek. At sixteen he entered Harvard as a sophomore, transferred to South Carolina College the next year in order to be educated in his native state,[47] and graduated with third honors. He practiced law for six years in Beaufort and Charleston. He married Mary Barnwell and after her death he married Charlotte Bull Barnwell of Beaufort. He was converted to the Episcopal faith in 1832,[48] ordained priest in 1836, and, while chaplain of South Carolina College at Columbia, was elected first bishop of Georgia in 1840, when the entire state contained only seven Episcopal clergymen and three hundred communicants.[49]

Bishop Elliott indicated his interest in education by becoming head of the Montpelier Female Institute in 1845. He personally assumed its debts, and its closing in 1853 left him virtually penniless. Elliott came to know Polk well; in Elliott, Polk saw the cultural ideal for the University. Elliott at first reacted timidly to the magnitude of Polk's plan of 1856, but the Louisianian's aggressive optimism [50] persuaded him of the desirability of a new university. He accompanied Polk on the whirlwind fund-raising campaign of 1859 [51] which brought home $400,000 from Louisiana alone. Elliott lived through the war and succeeded William Meade of Virginia as presiding bishop of the Protestant Episcopal Church in the Confederate States of America. He maintained a close attachment to Bishop John Henry Hopkins [52] of Vermont, presiding bishop at the critical Philadelphia triennial which brought the northern and southern factions of the church together in 1865. After the death of Polk, Elliott became senior bishop of the owning dioceses of the University and as chancellor called the 1866 meeting of the University's trustees. Two months after this meeting Elliott died in Savannah.

After Polk's letter to the bishops and their joint *Address to Members and Friends,* eight steps led to the laying of the cornerstone. Officers of the University were elected at the first meeting of the trustees, July 4-6, 1857, and principles upon which the institution would be established were declared.[53] A name and a site for the University were selected at Montgomery on November 27-28.[54] The charter drafted at that session was granted by the Tennessee legislature on January 6, 1858.[55] Arrangements to take title to the lands were made at Beersheba Springs, near Sewanee, at the meeting held July 3-6, 1858.[56] The commissioners for endowment reported to the trustees at Beersheba August 10-12, 1859, that sufficient funds had been pledged—about $478,000.[57] The constitution, studied extensively in New Orleans February 8-13, 1860,[58] was adopted at the first session of the board held at the site of the University, October 9-12, at which time the cornerstone was laid.[59]

THE FOUNDING

At Lookout Mountain on Saturday, July 4, 1857, and continuing on Sunday and Monday, the new institution, still nameless and still without a location, began its existence. In an effort to influence the selection of Chattanooga as the site of the university, the city of Chattanooga entertained the members of the board at Col. James A. Whiteside's Lookout Mountain Hotel.[60] Seven bishops, seven clergymen, and six laymen attended as official representatives of nine dioceses.[61] Secretary Henry C. Lay, future bishop of Arkansas, recorded the first meeting of the Sewanee board:

A wild and picturesque spot had been chosen for the exercises, and a rude stand provided upon the elevation afforded by a rock. Beneath the stand the bishops sat in a group; the band was stationed in the rear; and on one side, under the shade of a large tree, was placed the choir, extemporized for the occasion, with a suitable musical instrument, while the rest of the company were scattered irregularly upon the cliffs, the fences, or beneath the trees. Thus, the services proceeded with undisturbed quietness and decorum.[62]

Of the unofficial accounts of the day, that recorded by Albert Miller Lea of Knoxville supplies some of the most colorful details. He tells of ascending by a five-mile trail from Chattanooga to the Mountain House hotel. It was a bright day and many sightseers added a "promiscuous concourse" of four or five hundred persons to the "small but very choice body of delegates." Bishop Polk asked Major Lea to serve as marshal for the procession at eleven o'clock Saturday morning. Mrs. Stephen Elliott played the melodian. The congregation sang the hundredth Psalm, Bishop Green read the twenty-second chapter of Joshua, all sang the St. Ambrose *Te Deum,* Bishop Nicholas Hamner Cobbs prayed, and the company chanted *Gloria in Excelsis.* All joined in "The Star Spangled Banner,"[63] played by the brass band from Chattanooga.

Bishop Otey gave the principal address on national unity. "We affirm that our aim is eminently national and patriotic . . . not of political schism. . . . We contemplate no strife, save a generous rivalry with our brethren, as to who shall furnish to this great republic the truest men, the truest Christians, and the truest patriots."[64] As he spoke the United States flag, which had been carried in procession by a young boy and a veteran of the Revolution, wrapped itself around him and "arrested his discourse" until Lea drew it away.[65] After the address, Otey, the senior bishop in point of consecration, was elected president of the board by the trustees. Of thirty accredited to this public meeting, twenty were present. On Sunday the clergy preached in the churches of Chattanooga. On Monday Bishop Elliott presented a preamble and ten resolutions concerning the institution, following in spirit the bishops' joint address of 1856.

Bishop Green proposed the name "The University of the South," but the motion was tabled. Committees suggested by Polk were appointed for location, charter, ways and means, organization, and construction.

Although a clause or two in the resolutions indicated unPolklike compromises, the whole sweep of the action was imaginative and the perspective long. Certainly Otey's address revealed statesmanship of high order and the staging of the event showed in Polk a sense both for the dramatic and for the fitness of things. The Lookout Mountain meeting received some attention from the general press and wide coverage in Episcopal publications. The effectiveness of the publicity soon was shown by the number and quality of offers made to induce the University to locate in sundry communities.

IDEAL LOCATION SOUGHT

Bishop Polk took charge of the investigation of potential sites. His committee on location was ready to report to the trustees in November, 1857. Meeting in Montgomery at the same time as the annual gathering of the southern dioceses, now known as the Provincial Synod, seven bishops, seven presbyters, and six laymen of the Sewanee board represented nine dioceses—all except Arkansas.[66] The committee on location had been thorough in its investigation. It sought the services of Colonel Walter Gwynn, engineer for the Blue Ridge Rail Road and geologist of Anderson, South Carolina.[67] Polk wrote prominent persons in the localities concerned, telling them of the nature of the examination to be conducted and securing from them agreement to pay the expenses of the investigating party.[68] Beginning on September 14, 1857, Gwynn set out with three engineers including Charles R. Barney of Baltimore, a friend of Polk's at West Point.[69] Gwynn was armed with a formidable list of eighteen "Enquiries," devised by Polk, which included such items as elevation; extent of flat surface; agricultural possibilities; nature of soil; type of timber; prices (for delivery at the site) of dressed lumber, stone, sand, lime, brick, and coal; average seasonal readings of barometer, thermometer, and hygrometer; access to nearest town and rail connections of that town with each of the ten states concerned; presence of rivers, streams, or lakes; description of springs near by; and a general sketch showing features of each locality.[70] The results achieved by Gwynn and his group reflect great credit on his energy and on Polk's wisdom in the selection.[71]

Colonel Gwynn's survey covered his personal examination of the sites at Huntsville, McMinnville, Cleveland, Sewanee, and Atlanta. In addition to these, communications in writing contained proposals of varying degrees of attractiveness from Greeneville, Athens, Tullahoma, Franklin, and White's Creek Springs, Tennessee; Gordon Springs, Dalton, and Griffin, Georgia; Jacksonville, Alabama; and Corinth, Mississippi.[72]

A résumé of inducements reveals that Huntsville offered a subscription of $100,000 if either of two sites should be selected for the University. Russell's Hill, 818 feet above the sea, consisted of a 2,000-acre tract of fine soil capped by a 116-foot hill with a 10-acre surface for building. Monte Sano, three miles from Huntsville, boasted 1,000 acres of building surface atop a 900-foot mountain, 1,500 feet above sea level.[73]

Citizens of McMinnville offered $40,000 and 2,000 acres of land on a Cumberland mountaintop 1,854 feet above sea level. Ben Lomond had heavy timber, cheap coal, gray sandstone suitable for heavy construction. Six miles of beautiful views encircled the summit while a flat surface of 508 acres on the generally undulating top was considered good for building purposes.[74] Chattanoogans would give $50,000 and a site on Lookout Mountain. Mayor W. D. Fulton set forth the information sought and virtually invited the trustees to name their terms.[75]

Cleveland proposed a gift of 1,200 acres, free use of a marble quarry, and ample clay for brick. There also Thomas Calloway offered a $50,000 interest in 18,000 acres of land. A. Fitzgerald proposed that the University take its choice of his interest in either of two properties, both considered valuable copper mines, and these two gentlemen together offered $20,000 in stock of the Southern Copper Mining Company.[76] Richard Johnson, chairman for the Atlanta group, reported that at a public meeting on November 18, a resolution had been passed asking the mayor and council to donate 1,000 acres of land, including a lake and a large spring.[77]

Sewanee was the most isolated of the locations. There was no cash consideration but Samuel F. Tracy of the Sewanee Mining Company would donate 5,000 acres of land, a million feet of pine timber on adjacent lands, free transportation of 20,000 tons of freight on the company railroad which ran through the tract, and 2,000 tons of coal. Further, an additional 5,000 acres adjoining the Sewanee Mining Company tract were offered by Dr. Wallace Estill of Franklin County[78] and other citizens.[79]

This property was located twelve miles from the county seat, Winchester, and five miles from the village of Cowan, where the railroad spur from the Tracy City coal mines came down the 1,000-foot mountain to connect with the main line of the Nashville and Chattanooga Railroad.[80] There was a barely passable wagon trail up the mountain whose summit was 1,938 feet above sea level. A few years before, the area had been wild country. Timber was large and abundant. Coal was present a few feet below the surface at several points. There was plentiful sandstone of various colors and much limestone, sand, and clay. Numerous large springs flowing 500 to 1,000 gallons per hour would not be likely to run dry. Unknown then to the board was the fact that a few hundred square miles of the lower Cumberland plateau constitute the only interior portion of the nation in which the annual rainfall is over sixty inches.[81]

Site and Name Selected

In the balloting for a site, the trustees voted "by orders," the bishops voting as one order and clerical and lay trustees as the other order. A two-thirds majority was needed to carry each of the two groups. The vote was also by dioceses, which meant that five bishops and the clergy-laity groups from five dioceses would have to agree on a site. On the first ballot Sewanee received only one vote from the seven bishops [82] and two from clergy and laity. The natural advantages of Sewanee did not win over the more tempting material inducements of the other localities until the seventeenth ballot, when the bishops gave the necessary five votes, and in the other order Sewanee had four, Huntsville two, Atlanta one. The deadlock was broken with a resolution that Sewanee be accepted if satisfactory title and a suitable charter could be obtained.[83]

Athens was chosen in 1801 as the site of the University of Georgia for reasons much like the choice of Sewanee: beauty of site, location on a hill, a spring of water, no evils of town life. The University of North Carolina was built at Chapel Hill in a similar manner, and Jefferson had the same sentiments about the location of the University of Virginia.[84]

The board approved a draft of a charter drawn up by Francis Fogg and proceeded to the selection of a name. Major Fairbanks moved that the previous suggestion of Bishop Green, "The University of the South," be adopted. The Reverend J. Wood Dunn of Texas proposed "The Church University," and Bishop Thomas Atkinson "The University of Sewanee." The first motion prevailed.

Bishop Cobbs announced the first large gift to the enterprise, an endowed professorship of scientific and practical agriculture,[85] to be given by his fellow Alabamian Isaac Croom. Colonel Croom was president of the State Agricultural Society and the Alabama Historical Society, and a former member of the legislature.[86] He was never called upon to make good his pledge, for he died during the war. Croom's Bluff on the north escarpment of the Sewanee domain commemorates his offer.[87] Bishops Polk and Elliott were elected commissioners to canvass the dioceses for other subscriptions.

CHARTER GRANTED

The charter was granted by the State of Tennessee on January 6, 1858.[88] It was accepted by the trustees at their next meeting in July at Beersheba Springs, a mountain resort about thirty miles from Sewanee toward McMinnville. There was some fumbling connected with the charter. Either the trustees did not know what they wanted or they did not know how much the state was willing to grant. The original charter was routine except for its clause exempting a thousand acres of the University tract from taxes.[89] In 1860 an amendment was secured giving the right to establish police and municipal regulations. Authority was later given to enforce municipal regulations pertaining to restriction of business and inspection of food. In 1874 the chancery court of Franklin County gave authority to "levy and collect taxes for municipal purposes," a provision which was used only briefly.[90]

Had a clear idea been formed of what was wanted, it seems likely the legislature would have granted it in the first place. The original charter should have specified what finally in practice was secured, tax exemption for the whole domain. It also should have reserved for the University community all powers ordinarily granted incorporated municipalities.[91] For practical purposes, however, the University was able to maintain the domain inviolate against the "evil-minded persons" whose intrusion was feared by the makers of the charter.

The site was reconsidered at the 1858 meeting of the board. Although the Alabama faction headed by Bishop Cobbs was inclined to favor the plain rather than the mountain, the site was confirmed unanimously. The reasons for selection of Sewanee were then published [92] in order to advertise the project and quiet further objections. The seclusion of the site had been a deliberate choice since "it would be preferable to create a society around the University which should receive its tone from . . . and be in a measure dependent upon the University." The peroration called for "men of the South to rally round us" with "your wealth, your counsel, your active cooperation."

The mailing piece mentioned a factor destined to influence the University for the first forty years of its existence. The school would run through the summer months and send the students home at Christmas for a winter vacation.

> During these hot months . . . plantations are deserted. . . . It is inconvenient for . . . [the parents] to have their sons returned. . . . They do not wish to introduce them . . . to the dissipated society of watering places. . . . For the South, the proper vacation of a University is the winter . . . when he [the student] can engage in the sports which make him a true Southern man, hunting, shooting, riding; when he can mingle freely with the slaves who are in the future to be placed under his management.[93]

It was not foreseen in those days of uninhibited planning that the winter vacation would make possible the economical construction of light frame buildings with no basements or expensive heating plants. In the lean postwar days scarce dollars were thus stretched. Until after the turn of the century, Sewanee halls were uninhabitable and homes almost so in winter. Not until 1908 was it thought necessary to abandon cold weather holidays for the sake of conforming to customs of other institutions.

Colonel Barney was at work at Sewanee in the summer of 1858. On August 10 the University entertained its neighbors in Franklin County with a barbecue at which Polk, Green, Barney, Colonel Armfield, Squire Hawkins, and Dr. Abernathy were among those present. On August 15

VISIONS AND VIEWERS   57

at Barney's cabin Bishop Green held a religious service. About 130 persons sat on hastily constructed seats and heard the bishop read Morning Prayer, followed by an earnest and informal discussion of the peculiarities of the Episcopal religion—the distinctive dress, written prayers, baptism of infants, regeneration, conversion, apostolic succession. A witness said, "Men's eyes in this region look into you as if they were sighting you along the barrel of a rifle."[94]

MONEY SOUGHT

The University's first printed solicitation for funds,[95] published February 24, 1859, elaborated the financial plan, a plan which would be abandoned after the war. Money received for the University would be invested, the principal remaining in the various dioceses. The interest alone would be used, first for buildings, then for supplemental operating income. It is difficult now to evaluate the wisdom of Polk's financial plan. The idea of having regular annual income from each diocese was good. Possibly a bishop would be more willing to raise money if it remained in his own diocese. The ten diocesan treasurers might have become ten fund-raisers constantly increasing the University's endowment. The administrative responsibility for investing funds would remain in the dioceses, at least until some one made a direct gift which presumably would not be declined because it did not come through a diocese. There might have been a greater concern for an institution to which the diocese sent large checks each year. Furthermore, dioceses might have been encouraged to raise endowments for themselves, something only a few then attempted, none successfully. There were drawbacks, however, to Polk's plan. Inevitably there would have been disproportionate contributions and dioceses best able to give would feel justified in holding back. Less interested dioceses would have set the rate of giving. New dioceses among the owning group or the withdrawal of sponsorship would have brought difficulty. Dispersion of invested endowment throughout the owning dioceses had both virtues and defects.

The fund-raising plan was aimed at large gifts. No passing the plate in churches was contemplated by Polk.[96] The benefactor-elect was asked to guarantee the annual interest on the gift he planned to make and to remit the principal at his convenience. The benefactor of a $25,000 scholarship might agree to send $2,000 per year from the time of the commitment and then provide for the $25,000 principal in his will. Psychologically, the idea had the advantage of coaxing a large initial pledge, encouraging continuous support, and holding open the possibility for a substantial bequest. Fund-raisers a century later had developed no better approach.

For two months in the spring of 1859 Polk and Elliott made personal calls in Louisiana, concentrating on the wealthy planters of the coast and of the Mississippi and Red rivers.[97] When the trustees met on August 10 for a three-day session, again at Beersheba Springs, the bishops reported "in cash, bonds, and notes, payable in available periods . . . $363,580. Besides this . . . to be fulfilled within a short period, about $115,000."[98] Although the cash portion of this total was very small, there were no oral promises involved. All pledges were in the form of notes considered negotiable.

Again the astuteness of Polk can be discerned in this focusing of effort on one state. The amount needed could have been secured in less time with less trouble by "skimming the surface in the associated Dioceses," but Polk wanted a thorough canvassing of all ten participating groups and he set the example in his own diocese. Elliott, inspired by his intensive work with Polk, felt certain he could raise $3,000,000 in Georgia alone. Cobbs hoped for $250,000 from Alabama.[99] The appeal of the Sewanee plan and the effectiveness of Polk and Elliott may be measured by a comparison with the vastly more numerous Baptists who began in 1857 to build a theological school at Greenville, South Carolina. Their raising $100,000 in that year and another $100,000 in the succeeding two years was considered "remarkable."[100]

FORERUNNER OF THE ENDOWMENT IDEA

In a modern age of huge educational endowments, it is easy to forget what was then the value of a million dollars. Put aside the optimistic estimate of Elliott and take the more conservative expectation of Polk that $3,000,000 could be raised in *all ten* dioceses.[101] The annual income from this amount at the 7 per cent contemporary interest would be about $200,000 per year. In the 1870's a large stone building was constructed at Sewanee for $30,000, a stone library building for $10,000. At this rate within a few years a substantial campus could be built by using interest alone. The annual income would then be reserved largely for instructional costs. This idea was not new but at the time it had never been carried into effect on the scale contemplated by the southern bishops. South Carolina College in the 1850's was receiving only $6,000 per year from the state to supplement student fees. The University of Georgia was receiving a like amount plus the income from a land grant of 80,000 acres. The University of Virginia was receiving $15,000 per year from the state.[102] Polk was thinking of an institution which would have more than ten times the annual subsidy of the best southern university.

The fund folder revealed that there would be instruction at the graduate level, with emphasis on original research and creative effort by faculty, students, and fellows.[103]

> This highest scholarship, which is necessary as a standard . . . it is our desire to furnish. . . . The existing institutions [of the South] will continue to supply . . . the scholarship they are now giving. . . . When their students shall have graduated, if we can offer them a maturer cultivation, they will spend additional years at the University.[104]

Perhaps this institution would be the one for which historian Jared Sparks had hoped. In a letter to George Bancroft thirty years before, the then editor of the *North American Review* said:

> It is a great mistake to call any of our institutions . . . universities. They are neither such nor ever can be, without radical change. . . . I do not believe that a university can be engrafted on any of our old colleges. There are so many shackles on Harvard. . . . Let us have an establishment where we can teach young men something about the operation of their own minds, the doings of the world, the business of life. Europe is full of such institutions; it is time for one at least in America.[105]

THE DOMAIN

In the spring of 1859 Colonel Barney surveyed the entire domain[106] and drew a contour map, scaled 400 feet to the inch, showing ten-foot changes of elevation in the central area. He was ready with his findings when Otey called to order on August 10 at Beersheba the fourth meeting of the board of trustees.[107]

At least six men participated in securing the 9,525 acres of land reported to the assembled trustees. Fogg, with his great influence on Nashville's capitol hill,[108] worked with John Armfield and John Bass to register the deeds. In Franklin County Dr. Wallace Estill, Arthur Middleton Rutledge, and Arthur St. Clair Colyar begged or bought a dozen tracts, raising the money among themselves and from citizens of the county. Colyar procured titles to the following parcels:[109]

Sewanee Mining Company	5,000 acres
Heirs of Wallace Estill, Jr.	2,500 acres
W. B. Shapard	610 acres
A. M. Rutledge	410 acres
Abraham Bowers	250 acres
Moreland Tract from J. B. Hawkins and infant heirs	200 acres
Miles Vassar Tract from Henry Garner	130 acres
Decherd Tract	120 acres
Lawson Rowe	100 acres
D. Barnes	100 acres
Houghton and Hines	80 acres
Allen Gipson	72 acres

There were conflicting lines between some tracts, and the total acreage credited here is larger than the size indicated by survey of the outside boundaries. The conveyance from the Sewanee Mining Company included a clause which was to have ominous portent later. It stated that if the school were not in operation within ten years, the lands would revert to the company.

The fourth meeting also handled other routine matters. Fogg was elected first registrar and all documents were placed in his charge. Bishop Elliott reported that quantities of the printed solicitation, with accompanying maps, were on hand in Savannah. Barney was paid $1,811.96 for his services, authorized to draw $500 more for additional plats of surveys, and appointed engineer and surveyor for the ensuing year at a salary of $2,000. Two cabins were reported built with $200 furnished by Armfield. Commissioners Polk and Elliott were authorized to appropriate $5,000 each for expenses. Bishop Cobbs moved two important resolutions which were passed: that an executive committee be appointed with authority to proceed with laying the cornerstone as soon as notified of the completion of the drive for $500,000, and that the committee provide for landscaping the campus.

PLAN FOR A "HEAVENLY CITY"

The landscape gardener was the versatile Bishop John Henry Hopkins of Vermont, an engineer, painter, musician, lawyer, and preacher. He was building Vermont Episcopal Institute and would use his Sewanee salary to finish its chapel. He took six months' leave from his diocese and on December 5 arrived at University Place.[110] Through the bare trees good views could be had of the whole area. He wrote his wife: "I occupy the best of a set of log houses, in which is the office of Col. Barney (the skillful engineer and general manager of the University estate). It is a good large room, with a fine open fire. The logs are hewn smooth, outside and in, and my bed and table are both very comfortable."[111] Polk and Elliott came to spend Christmas day with Hopkins in the wilderness. They planned to lay the cornerstone of the principal building on July 4.[112]

The New Englander was impressed with the surroundings. Besides drafting maps of roads and sites for buildings, he sketched over two dozen water colors of scenes on the domain.[113] The extreme healthfulness of the region, Bishop Hopkins thought, marked it beyond any spot within his knowledge as the place for such an institution. "If Lake Champlain could be thrown in," he said, "it would be absolute perfection."[114]

The constitution and statutes were the principal order of business at the next meeting of the trustees, held in New Orleans February 8-13, 1860, at the aldermen's chambers.[115] The sixteen trustees present accepted a provisional draft of the constitution, which was ordered printed for further consideration and held over for final passage at the next meeting. Secretary Lay had become bishop of Arkansas and on Polk's motion the Reverend David Pise of Tennessee succeeded him.

Theoretically each of the ten dioceses united in the organization of the University provided four trustees, the bishop, a presbyter,[116] and two laymen, a potential attendance of forty. Actually the largest attendance at the first six meetings of the board, including the laying of the cornerstone, was twenty-two.[117] As events developed, the two new bishops succeeding Bishop George W. Freeman of Arkansas, who held provisional jurisdiction in Texas, were Henry C. Lay for Arkansas and Alexander Gregg for Texas, both of whom had been regularly attending trustees' meetings as clerical members from Alabama and South Carolina respectively.[118]

All members of the board—divided equally between clergy and laity—had to be communicants of the Episcopal Church. Attendance at the meetings by bishops was good, by presbyters fair, and by laymen poor.[119] Twice—at Montgomery and New Orleans—meetings coincided with annual interdiocesan conferences, involving in most cases no extra time or expense for the delegates, but four times the trustees met exclusively as a university board. The board was divided into a group which seemed vitally interested and a group which was not.

The best aspect of the attendance record was the geographical representation. Six dioceses had at least one man at every meeting and two others went unrepresented at only one meeting. Texas and Arkansas, neither fully organized as dioceses, were represented respectively at three meetings and at one. Tennessee most often had full delegations, followed by Alabama, Florida, and Louisiana.

A PHYSICAL BEGINNING

The new educational idea was paraded in full dress before the public at the laying of the cornerstone. On October 9, the day before that prescribed for the great occasion, trustees to the record number of twenty-two began arriving at University Place [120] by coach and by rail. They found the residences of Polk and Elliott near the proposed central building and that of Fairbanks a half mile out on the north bluff. There were several cabins occupied by Barney, his crew, and their gear. Near Polk Spring [121] a row of one-story buildings connected by an encircling piazza, canvas covered, housed long rows of cots for the overnight guests. The benches from a shed which seated 3,000 people could be removed and tables brought in to accommodate 500 for meals. A caterer from Nashville contracted to supply and serve food. That evening under the stars the Reverend Doctors Charles T. Quintard of Nashville and J. Freeman Young of New York, later bishops respectively of Tennessee and Florida, rehearsed the impromptu choir for its part in the performance the next day.[122]

Among the complex preparations which preceded such a convocation as this, the hauling of the cornerstone was not the least. The six-ton piece of marble[123] was pulled roughhewn up the mountain from the quarry near Elk River by Barney's chainman, I. T. Miller, driving eight yoke of oxen.[124] Six weeks were required to polish it. Since plans for the central building had not been decided upon, the cornerstone was laid on a false foundation of massive sandstone blocks at the apex of a gentle slope, the highest point on the domain.

"Almost like magic the mountain plateau teemed with life, the shriek of arriving railway trains, the rumbling of omnibuses and carriages brought up for the occasion, the throng of people from the surrounding country.... A band ... from Nashville poured forth its martial strains, and booths and peddler wagons indicated a gala day."[125] Estimates of the size of the crowd ranged from 4,000[126] to 10,000.[127] Most eyewitnesses agreed on 5,000. Many were mountain people from the surrounding coves and valleys, who swarmed by foot, wagon, and mule-back, bringing their children and their provisions. Others were miners of Tracy City, transported on company trains which whistled in every hour.

With Colonel Rutledge as marshal, the procession moved off at eleven o'clock through the forest four abreast. The choir and band were followed by specially invited laymen, the trustees, the architects, clergy, and bishops. As the procession reached the palisaded enclosure, the visitors opened ranks, and the bishops and clergy, clad in black robes and white surplices, the choir and band, the architects and trustees came through and stood around the stone. The ladies were invited within the enclosure. The band struck up "Hail Columbia."

The eight bishops in the procession were Atkinson of North Carolina, Francis Huger Rutledge of Florida, Green of Mississippi, Cobbs of Alabama, Elliott of Georgia, Polk of Louisiana, Otey of Tennessee, and Benjamin Bosworth Smith of Kentucky.[128] The hundredth Psalm was sung, Bishop Rutledge read the scripture, Bishop Atkinson delivered the exhortation. Bishop Cobbs read the collects, and the choir sang the *Jubilate Deo*.

Bishop Elliott then deposited in the cornerstone a Bible, a prayer book, copies of the constitution and the church canons, a bound volume of University documents, copies of the journals of the participating dioceses, assorted Episcopal publications, a church almanac for 1860, and, sad to say, several silver coins. Rumors of this treasure prompted Federal soldiers three years later to blow up the cornerstone.[129]

The slab was sealed and Bishop Polk, striking it three times, pronounced the dedication of the University to "the cultivation of true religion, learning, and virtue, that thereby God may be glorified and the happiness of man may be advanced." The *Benedicite* was sung by the choir with instrumental accompaniment, led by Young and Quintard.

The listeners then repaired a hundred and fifty yards west to the assembly shelter. Bishop Otey presented the orator, John S. Preston of South Carolina. This wealthy planter became famous as a speaker when he welcomed home the Palmetto Regiment from the Mexican War. He made his most dramatic oration on the floor of his state's secession convention not long after his appearance at Sewanee and then became a brigadier general of the Confederacy.[130] Preston's address has been quoted by so many Sewanee speakers that it would be well to give his central theme:

> All power is with the people. . . . All are to govern. All therefore must be taught to govern. Education must be given to all. Unless we are taught to use them in the right way our civil and religious liberties are worthless and dangerous boons. . . . Admit this and there cannot be a holier or higher purpose than to furnish instruction to our people.[131]

Closing prayers were said by Bishop Green, the *Gloria in Excelsis* was sung, a benediction given, and the ceremonies were recessed for the midday banquet. The band played intermittently during the meal and between the speeches which followed.

The first speech was by a former pupil of Otey's, Commander Matthew Fontaine Maury.[132] The next speaker was Chancellor Frederick A. P. Barnard of the University of Mississippi. He called attention to the fact that the University of the South would be unique in American education in having been created "not through the slow growth of years, but immediately and at once."

Congressman John M. Bright of Tennessee made an address. The last speaker was the able, peppery, and diminutive Bishop Benjamin B. Smith of Kentucky. He was invited in a subtle effort to secure the active participation of his diocese. Of those present that day, he alone is known to have viewed the enterprise, especially the location, with a jaundiced eye, though he made no allusion to this in his talk.[133] Perhaps he remembered his own failure with the Lexington seminary. A memorandum scribbled by Bishop Smith at the time and pasted in one of Bishop Quintard's scrapbooks grumbles:

> Sewanee . . . totally unpractical . . . manners and dress of professors and their families will become careless, rude, provincial: and those of the students boorish. . . . If an ecclesiastical epidemic should break out, it will rage horribly—Puseyism—Revivalism and what not, will find a congenial atmosphere here, for their wildest devastations!!! Class intercourse between clerical professors exceptionally narrowing—between their ladies even worse. I have no motive but the love of good letters—sound morals—and pure and undefiled religion, for wishing the Sewanee enterprise abandoned, and a St. Paul or St. Stephens—or St. James—or Racine substituted in its stead, either at Huntsville or Winchester.[134]

Happily the Bishop did not broadcast his dark forebodings at the ceremony and apparently nothing disturbed the "most beautiful, bright, and cheerful day."[135] One journalist concluded ecstatically that this "undertaking is the most important ever inaugurated in the South, and from it . . . incalculable advantages may be derived by Southern people."[136]

The less formal aspects of the occasion have been described by one of the barefooted mountain children playing in the background.

> It was in 1860, I believe, that my grandfather, J. F. Anderson who lived about 12 miles from what is now Sewanee, gathered up all of his numerous family to attend the laying of the Corner Stone of what was intended to be the first building of the University of the South. . . . The trip was made by wagon and horseback through the mountains, and we camped out one night on the way. I was then about 10 years old, and remember being scared by the screaming of a wildcat during the night. . . . I will never forget the exciting events of that day. There were certainly enough startling events to excite an ignorant country boy. . . . The

first thing I noticed was the great throng of country people, more than I had ever seen or have seen since. . . . They had come as we had come on foot, horseback and in wagon, drawn by all sorts of teams, from afar and near, and they had come prepared to enjoy the day, bringing provisions for man and beast; also intoxicating liquor. . . . I saw fighting, horse-trading, gambling, all conducted openly and vociferously and without the least regard for the ceremonies that were being conducted around the corner stone, not over two hundred yards away, where was assembled also a large throng of better dressed and more orderly people around the church dignitaries dressed in their caps and gowns. . . . I could not get close enough to hear anything, and I doubt if much was heard by anyone more than a few yards away.[137]

CONSTITUTION AND STATUTES

On Wednesday, October 10, after the triumphant ceremony, the trustees convened with Polk acting as president. The principal item of business was the adoption of the constitution and statutes.[138] Earlier at New Orleans, Polk outlined to the trustees his efforts "to obtain . . . the programmes and examine the working machinery of the most eminent institutions of learning in our own country and in Europe."[139] He acknowledged aid from the President of the United States [140] and embassies in England, France, and the German states. Besides foreign publications there were outlines of organizational systems of American schools and memoranda of numerous individuals, supplemented by personal inspection of committee members.[141] Looking back, Mrs. Polk remembered:

> I now, for the first time [winter of 1849-1850], heard my husband speak of his wish to establish a university which should enlist the sympathy of all the States. . . . In the spring of 1852 he began to collect information relative to the educational systems of England, France, and Prussia, and to consult with some of his friends.[142]

There need be no hesitation in giving to Polk a large share of credit for the organizational scheme. Bishop Green made a clear statement in his Chancellor's Address of 1869 [143] that he considered Polk primarily responsible, with assistance from Otey and Elliott. Of Polk, Hopkins says:

Visions and Viewers

He brought with him at that time [December, 1859] a large box entirely filled with . . . correspondence with . . . the Old World, as well as laboriously and thoroughly digested projects for a southern university which, when completed, was to be the noblest and best-endowed in Christendom. . . . I was amazed and delighted at the combination of original genius, lofty enterprise, and Christian hope with the utmost degree of practical wisdom, cautious investigation, exquisite tact, and indefatigable energy, which far surpassed all that I could conceive in the bounds of human efficiency.[144]

The nineteen articles of the constitution and the twenty-three statutes exceed five thousand words.[145] They were so detailed as to make it obvious that the authors planned frequent revision, especially of the statutes. For instance, salaries of several officers were specified. The ideas expressed in the previously published addresses were incorporated, namely, perpetual ownership by the Protestant Episcopal Church and government by a board composed of the bishop, a clergyman and two laymen from each of ten listed dioceses, the clergymen and laymen elected and accountable to their respective diocesan conventions. A quorum of trustees was fifteen if there were present at least one bishop, one clergyman, and one layman. The board, not self-perpetuating but perpetual by the succession of bishops and elected representatives, would be virtually impossible to stack, buy, or put pressure on. The base of power would be spread over a wide geographical area. The board could accept at its pleasure applications from other dioceses to join in the support and government of the University.[146]

Few men were better qualified than Fairbanks to make an interpretation of the nature of the University's board of trustees. It was, Fairbanks thought, a body corporate, not a convention of delegates. Each trustee had the same power as any other trustee.[147] Votes were of equal weight, whether episcopal, clerical, or lay. Trustees were to act individually and separately, not in conjunction with co-trustees elected from the same diocese. No trustee was amenable to or under the control of any other. A majority of votes cast determined the question. Vote by orders was optional, this bicameral feature requiring a majority among bishops as one order and a majority among clerical and lay trustees voting together as the other order. The vote by orders presumably would counterbalance the idealistic and spiritual thinking of the bishops against the hard practicality of the realistic laymen and would prevent domination by either group.

The government envisioned by the founders was oligarchical in form, with virtually all power residing in the nonresident board of trustees or in an executive committee designated by them. The trustees "shall have the entire management and supervision of the affairs, concerns, and property of the University." Ample financial means were taken for granted. The trustees reserved to themselves not only large stated powers but all unstated powers.[148] Unless it was assumed that the board would delegate powers very freely, it must be admitted that the centralizing of administrative power as well as policy control in the hands of trustees who only met once a year was unwise. The trustees, not the administrative head, theoretically appointed and removed professors, assistant professors, lecturers, and fellows.

The statutes directly contradicted the constitution by allowing the vice-chancellor "control over all . . . departments." A handsome salary of $6,000 was designated for him. His recommendations to the annual session of the trustees were limited to those which were approved by a committee of senior professors called by the Oxonian title of hebdomadal board. The statutes are not explicit but presumably the vice-chancellor would not teach. He probably was not expected to raise money. When a professor or officer became negligent, the vice-chancellor could "advise and remonstrate"[149] with him, and upon continuance of such negligence, must, after first giving notice of his intention, file with the erring one a copy of the protest which he planned to make to the trustees. A weak "control" to be sure, but indubitably Oxonian.

As demonstrated during the administration of Josiah Gorgas (1872-1878) and his successors in the vice-chancellorship, the constitution and statutes imposed unsatisfactory restrictions on the executive head. This handicap did not become apparent under Bishop Quintard, the first vice-chancellor, when an executive committee of trustees, meeting frequently and awed by his personality, gave the authority of the board to the vice-chancellor as that authority was needed. At the close of Quintard's administration the executive committee was abolished and, although reinstated later, never had adequate authority until the 1930's, when a

VISIONS AND VIEWERS

board of fourteen regents, acting as the trustees' executive committee, was given sufficient authority to allow consummation of necessary transactions in the interim between annual meetings.

The constitution and statutes said nothing about requiring officers, professors, or students to be Episcopalian, though all trustees would be. Nothing was said about doctrine but chapel attendance would be required of students, faculty, and staff.[150]

BROAD SCOPE OF CURRICULUM

The ambitious nature of the project is seen by an enumeration of the "schools" which would be established:[151]

Greek Language and Literature
Latin Language and Literature
Mathematics
Physics
Metaphysics
History and Archaeology
Natural Science, with Cabinets and Gardens
Geology, Mineralogy, and Paleontology
Civil Engineering, Construction, Architecture, and Drawing
Theoretical and Experimental Chemistry
Chemistry Applied to Agriculture and the Arts
Theory and Practice of Agriculture with Farm Attached
Moral Science and Evidences of Christian Religion
English Language and Literature
French Language and Literature
German Language and Literature
Spanish Language and Literature
Italian Language and Literature
Oriental Language and Literature
Philosophy of Language
Philosophy of Education
Rhetoric, Criticism, Elocution, and Composition
American History and Antiquities
Ethnology and Universal Geography
Astronomy (with Observatory) and Physical Geography
Political Science, Political Economy, Statistics, Law of Nations, Spirit of Laws, General Principles of Government and Constitution of the United States

Commerce and Trade, including History and Laws of Banking, Exchange, Insurance, Brokerage, and Bookkeeping
Theology
Law
Medicine
Mines and Mining
Fine Arts, including Sacred Music.

Each "school" would be headed by a professor and would correspond to a modern "department." Diplomas would be granted by each school on completion of specified work. The A.B. degree would be conferred on an individual who held diplomas from the schools of moral science, Greek, Latin, mathematics, physics, and English. Presumably other studies would not add credit for the bachelor of arts degree. The A.M. requirements were metaphysics, chemistry, political science, rhetoric, French (including the ability to speak the language), and another modern language. The vagueness of this section, in view of the ornate curriculum, may have resulted from the realization that the yet unhired faculty would have contributions to make to academic patterns. Appropriate degrees for professional schools were left to the several professors of those schools. The hebdomadal board would award degrees subject to the approval of the trustees who alone would award honorary degrees.

The statutes introduced one concept [152] which marked the life of the University until the turn of the century. The students would live with private families in groups of twelve or less that they might be under the refining influences of home life during college days. Bishop Elliott thought that the domain would attract the best society of the South, that hundreds would own summer homes, and that retired persons would contribute to the atmosphere of gracious living which it was planned to encourage.

With the adoption of the constitution and statutes an executive committee of seven trustees was appointed with "full power and authority ... to attend to all those matters connected with the success of the University, which they may deem necessary."[153] The finance committee reported expenses of $18,153.63 since the last meeting, and estimated that cornerstone ceremonies would cost about $8,000. As assets, the com-

VISIONS AND VIEWERS

mittee listed notes deposited with the University treasurers in the following dioceses:

Louisiana	$264,160.00
Alabama	52,259.99
Tennessee	28,480.00
Mississippi	7,320.00
Texas	1,240.00
North Carolina	1,180.00
Miscellaneous	13,450.00
	$368,089.99

To this they added subscriptions of $25,400 and the promise of $25,000 made by T. D. Warren, not yet reduced to a note, for a total of $418,489.99. The committee evaluated other assets as follows:

The domain at Sewanee	$100,000
Transportation on Sewanee railroad	20,000
20,000 tons coal	7,000
1,000,000 feet of lumber	3,000

These assets, added to the approximately $375,000 net from subscriptions, gave a total of $505,000, enough to qualify for the minimum figure set in the original proposals.

The executive committee was instructed to lay out streets and give two months' notice of readiness to lease lots on the domain. They were authorized to select the winning plan from artists' drawings for the principal building and to pay $400 for it.[154]

GATHERING CLOUDS

During the winter of 1860-1861 University Place was occupied by the families of Bishops Polk and Elliott, Postmaster W. H. Tomlinson and his family, and Colonel Barney and his workmen. The small settlement shared the political tension of the South. When South Carolina seceded in December, the Elliott children raised their version of a Confederate flag in front of their house.[155] Bishop and Mrs. Elliott were "hot for secession." Colonel Barney had painful misgivings.[156] Christmas was celebrated that week with eggnog at the Elliotts' and charades at the Polks'. In February, Franklin County, under the spirited leadership of

Colonel Peter Turney, grew tired of the hesitation of Tennessee and joined the militant southern states by passing its own ordinance of secession at a popular meeting in Winchester and petitioning for annexation to Alabama.[157]

On March 23 Polk and Elliott addressed a circular letter from University Place to the bishops whose dioceses were in the Confederate States. They proposed a convention to be held in Montgomery on July 3, 1861, for the purpose of considering the relationship of the southern dioceses to the Protestant Episcopal Church in the United States.[158] Bishop Elliott presided over the convention which resolved that it was necessary that the dioceses within the seceded states form an independent organization.

On the evening of April 12, when the first shell was fired from Fort Johnson at Fort Sumter, unknown persons at Sewanee set fire to the Elliott and Polk houses. The Elliotts had gone to Georgia two days before, but Mrs. Polk and her children had remained. They barely escaped. Later other attempts were made to burn the University buildings and Colonel Barney's residence. Bishop Polk in New Orleans was outraged. "Such a diabolical spirit and heart I never before heard of." His son and biographer feels that it was then that he entered into the solitary inward struggle which resulted in his taking arms.[159]

He had entered the Confederate army before the next meeting of the board of trustees, October 14-21, 1861, in Columbia, South Carolina. Seventeen trustees [160] met there simultaneously with the council convened to adopt a constitution for the Protestant Episcopal Church in the Confederate States of America.[161] The prevailing atmosphere of the meeting was optimistic as far as the University was concerned. The executive committee was given full discretionary powers with reference to the domain and was specifically authorized to establish a preparatory school at Sewanee as funds contributed for the purpose might become available. Bishop Elliott resigned as endowment commissioner, wanting "to place everything in as snug a condition as possible, and wait events."[162]

After the Columbia meeting Bishop Otey placed the University domain in the care of Fairbanks, a fellow member of the executive committee. Fairbanks remained at Sewanee with his family until the fall of

Nashville and then went to Marietta, Georgia, where he entered the Confederate forces,[163] serving as a major in the commissary department which supplied the hospitals of the Army of Tennessee.

THE POWER AND THE GLORY

The Sewanee idea exceeded in scope anything previously attempted on the North American continent. About it was a Utopian air. Despite Otey's stout nationalism, much of the overwhelming response had been for the glory of the South. The idea was a natural concomitant of the growing southern self-consciousness of the 1850's. In the high noon of southern history, building a great educational and cultural center had a civic as well as religious appeal which Polk was not slow to seize upon.[164] The idea received immediate public acceptance. Pressed forward with diligence, its progress was unchecked. Every expectation was justified, the most optimistic goals appeared attainable. Each of the nine proposals in the joint letter of 1856 had been followed. A remarkable domain had been received. Financial stability seemed secure. In 1856 Polk had written to Elliott:

> There is no reason why . . . we might not in five years have a Church University which would rival the establishment at Harvard or Yale. . . . A movement of some kind is indispensable to rally and unite us, to develop our resources and demonstrate our power. We must rise above diocesan considerations.[165]

In 1860 he was able to report to his diocese: "No similar enterprise in this country has ever met with so much consideration or been the recipient of so large an amount of substantial aid, at so early a period of its career."[166]

Twenty-five years before the laying of the Sewanee cornerstone, a French visitor to America had written a study of the nation pitched in sympathetic tones. But at Washington City, Alexis de Tocqueville had smiled with incredulity.

> The Americans traced out the circuit of an immense city on the site which they intended to make their capitol, but which, up to the present time is hardly more densely peopled than Pontoise, though, according to them, it will one day contain a million inhabitants. They have already rooted up trees for ten miles around, lest they should interfere

with the future citizens of this imaginary metropolis. They have erected a magnificent palace for Congress in the center of the city and have given it the pompous name of the Capitol.[167]

The imagination of Polk and his fellow-dreamers is not unlike that which dictated the selection of the site at Washington. Many years ahead of their time, these men knew a measure of success, for, until matters were taken out of their hands by the irrepressible conflict, success was at their grasp.

Notes for Chapter One

[1] The origin of the name Sewanee is unknown but several theories have been advanced: (1) a variant of "Shawnee" from Creek word *Sawani* meant "echo"; (2) a derivative of the Shawnee word *Shawano* connoted "southern"; (3) *Sewanee* in Shawnee meant "lost" as of a river sinking underground to rise further on (Lost Creek Cove below Point Disappointment is bounded on three sides by the University domain and is fed by Sewanee springs); (4) *Th'wanwee* in Shawnee meant "foggy" or "misty"; (5) both Cumberland River and Cumberland Mountains were called *Shawan, Shawne,* or *Sewanee* by the Indians; (6) *Suwannee,* the river, is thought to be a corruption of the Spanish *San Juan;* and (7) the *Sawanee* Indians, migrating from the Rocky Mountains eastward, gave their tribal name to a village on the east bank of the Mississippi above Memphis and also to the Cumberland plateau and river. Sources (all in Sewanee Archives), in order, are (1) J. W. Parnell to S. D. Hinman, November 14, 1885; (2) *ibid.;* (3) S. D. Hinman to Telfair Hodgson, December 5, 1885; (4) *ibid.;* (5) William Giles Dix, "Address, 1859," Telfair Hodgson (ed.), *University Papers,* Ser. A, No. 1 (Sewanee, 1888), *Reprints of the Documents and Proceedings of the Board of Trustees of the University of the South Prior to 1860,* p. 142, hereafter cited as Hodgson (ed.), *Reprints of Documents Prior to 1860;* (6) John M. Lea to Hodgson, December 6, 1885; and (7) A. S. Colyar to Hodgson, n.d. [*circa* 1885] (Sewanee Archives). The story that *Sewanee* meant "Mother Mountain" seems to be apocryphal. The present authority at the Smithsonian Institution, John P. Harrington, thinks the second theory is correct.

[2] William E. Dodd, *The Cotton Kingdom* (New Haven, 1921), 111 n.

[3] Francis B. Simkins, *The South Old and New* (New York, 1947), 111.

[4] Arthur C. Cole, *The Irrepressible Conflict* (New York, 1934), 59.

[5] Simkins, *South Old and New,* 110.

[6] Edgar W. Knight, *A Documentary History of Education in the South Before 1860,* 5 vols. (Chapel Hill, 1949-), II, 135.

[7] George H. Denny, "Universities and Colleges of the South," Samuel C. Mitchell *et al.* (eds.), *The South in the Building of the Nation,* 12 vols. (Richmond, 1909), X, 243.

[8] Robert S. Cotterill, *The Old South* (Glendale, 1936), 285.

[9] Dodd, *Cotton Kingdom,* 111.

Visions and Viewers

[10] Albea Godbold, *The Church College of the Old South* (Durham, 1944), 7-43.

[11] Charles W. Ramsdell, "The Southern Heritage," William T. Couch (ed.), *Culture in the South* (Chapel Hill, 1934), 3.

[12] Sydney G. Fisher, *Church Colleges* (Philadelphia, 1895), 14, 15. William and Mary ceased to be church-owned in the disestablishment following the American Revolution. It partially burned in 1859.

[13] Henry Caswell, *The Martyr of the Pongas: being a Memoir of the Rev. Hamble James Leacock* (London, 1857), 16-31. Dr. Caswell was a professor in the seminary.

[14] W. Robert Insko, "Benjamin Bosworth Smith, First Bishop of Kentucky, 1832-1884, Ninth Presiding Bishop, 1868-1884," *Historical Magazine of the Protestant Episcopal Church* (New Brunswick, N. J.), XXII (June, 1953), 192-198. The Lexington seminary was revived under its original charter in 1951.

[15] Nash K. Burger, "William Mercer Green, First Bishop of Mississippi, 1850-1887," *Historical Magazine of the Protestant Episcopal Church,* XIX (December, 1950), 345.

[16] Walter Prescott Webb (ed.), *The Handbook of Texas,* 2 vols. (Austin, 1952), II, 531, 890.

[17] Godbold, *Church College of the Old South,* 76.

[18] The Diocese of South Carolina was founded in 1795, North Carolina in 1823. The others consecrated their first bishops as follows: Tennessee, 1834; Georgia and Louisiana, 1841; Alabama, 1844; Mississippi, 1850; Florida, 1851; Texas, 1859. Arkansas consecrated its first bishop in 1838 but remained a missionary district, except for the duration of the war, until 1871. Linden Morehouse (ed.), *The Living Church Annual, 1950,* (New York, 1950), 155, *passim.*

[19] Dodd, *Cotton Kingdom,* 99.

[20] Undated, unidentified clipping in Charles Todd Quintard Diary (Sewanee Archives), February 20, 1878, quoting *The Church News* (St. Louis, n.d.). In 1950 by comparison the nationwide Episcopal ratio was about one in each hundred of population.

[21] Cotterill, *Old South,* 287. At least seventy of these institutions were still in existence in 1909. Denny, "Universities and Colleges of the South," Mitchell *et al.* (eds.), *South in the Building of the Nation,* X, 255-58.

[22] Cole, *Irrepressible Conflict,* 47.

[23] Clement Eaton, *A History of the Old South* (New York, 1949), 393. Benjamin Sherwood Hedrick was professor of chemistry.

[24] Cole, *Irrepressible Conflict,* 46-48.

[25] Leonidas Polk, *A Letter to the Right Reverend Bishops of Tennessee, Georgia, Alabama, Arkansas, Texas, Mississippi, Florida, South Carolina, and North Carolina* (New Orleans, 1856).

[26] There were 3,000 academies in the South. Simkins, *South Old and New,* 89. Contemporary newspapers advertised many of these as being under Episcopal influence.

[27] George R. Fairbanks, *History of the University of the South* (Jacksonville, 1905), 21.

[28] James H. Otey *et al, An Address to the Members and Friends of the Protestant Episcopal Church in the Southern and South-Western States* (Philadelphia, 1856).

[29] Senior bishop of the group, James H. Otey, died in 1863. Lieutenant General Polk was killed by artillery fire at Pine Mountain in 1864. Stephen Elliott of Georgia died in 1866, Nicholas Hamner Cobbs of Alabama in 1861, George W. Freeman of Arkansas in 1858, and William Mercer Green of Mississippi, the sole exception, lived to be chancellor of the institution (1866-1887). Francis Huger Rutledge died in 1866 and Thomas F. Davis of South Carolina went blind during the 1860's, dying in 1871. Thomas Atkinson of North Carolina became ill after the war, attended only one trustees' meeting at Sewanee, contributed little to the development of the University, and died in 1881. Dates are from Morehouse (ed.), *Living Church Annual, 1950*, 395-97.

[30] Moultrie Guerry, *Men Who Made Sewanee* (Sewanee, 1932), 2.

[31] Frank H. Gailor, "Sewanee in the Years Before the Civil War" (Sewanee Archives).

[32] Arthur H. Noll, *History of the Church in the Diocese of Tennessee* (New York, 1900), 118, 119.

[33] His love for string music was the occasion of a story he told on himself. On an episcopal visitation he was playing a violin in his room when a servant looked in and said: "Massa, better put up dat fiddle. Dere's a preacher in de house." Guerry, *Men Who Made Sewanee*, 2.

[34] James H. Otey, "Diary, November 3, 1840," William Mercer Green, *Memoir of Bishop Otey* (New York, 1885), 25. "Went to town. Voted Whig ticket."

[35] Guerry, *Men Who Made Sewanee*, xiii.

[36] Noll, *History of the ... Diocese of Tennessee*, 120, 121.

[37] Sarah Barnwell Elliott, *Sewanee: Past and Present* (Sewanee, 1909), 17.

[38] Green, *Memoir of Bishop Otey*, 50.

[39] Guerry, *Men Who Made Sewanee*, 12-26.

[40] Polk's father, when asked by a friend where his son was stationed, said, "Stationed! Why, by thunder, Sir, he's over there in Alexandria at the Seminary!" *Ibid.*, 16. Legend identifies the friend as Andrew Jackson. W. Dudley Gale to writer.

[41] The bishop of a missionary district, elected by the House of Bishops, can accept election in a diocese. The bishop of a diocese cannot transfer to another diocese. *Constitution and Canons for the Government of the Protestant Episcopal Church in the United States of America* (Chicago, 1943), 99.

[42] William Mecklenburg Polk, *Leonidas Polk, Bishop and General*, 2 vols. (New York, 1893), I, 180.

[43] George L. Reynolds, "Sewanee and the Cumberland Plateau in the Civil War" (Sewanee Archives), 9.

[44] Walter H. Stowe, "Polk's Missionary Episcopate," *Historical Magazine of the Protestant Episcopal Church*, VII (December, 1938), 341-59.

[45] Polk, *Leonidas Polk*, I, 184.

[46] *National Cyclopedia of American Biography*, 35 vols. (New York, 1892-1916), IV, 508.

[47] Hubert B. Owens, *Georgia's Planting Prelate* (Athens, 1945), 8.

[48] Elliott had been playing whist one evening when a member of the party read in a spirit of ridicule the announcement that a Presbyterian revivalist, Daniel Baker, wa

preaching in an Episcopal church. All went in merriment and eight of the eleven, including Elliott, were converted. Guerry, *Men Who Made Sewanee,* 26, 27. The Episcopal Diocese of Dallas in 1952 operated Daniel Baker College in Texas, a former Presbyterian institution, retaining the name of a minister of another faith.

[49] *National Cyclopedia of American Biography,* V, 425.

[50] Polk, *Leonidas Polk,* I, 207, 208, 213, 214.

[51] Guerry, *Men Who Made Sewanee,* 30.

[52] [John Henry Hopkins, Jr.], *Life of the Late Right Rev. John Henry Hopkins, First Bishop of Vermont and Seventh Presiding Bishop* (New York, 1873), 313.

[53] Hodgson (ed.), *Reprints of Documents Prior to 1860,* pp. 21-50.

[54] *Ibid.,* 51-79.

[55] *Ibid.,* 94-97.

[56] *Ibid.,* 80-125.

[57] *Ibid.,* 125-62.

[58] *Ibid.,* 163-92.

[59] *Ibid.,* 193-227.

[60] The entertainment of the visitors cost the city $434. Gilbert E. Govan and James W. Livingood, *The Chattanooga Country, 1540-1951* (New York, 1952), 156.

[61] Present were Bishops Otey, Polk, Elliott, Cobbs, Green, Rutledge, and Davis; Reverend David Pise, Francis B. Fogg, and John Armfield of Tennessee; Reverend William T. Leacock and George S. Guion of Louisiana; Reverend Henry C. Lay, Charles T. Pollard, and L. H. Anderson of Alabama; Reverend William W. Lord of Mississippi; Reverend Alexander Gregg of South Carolina; Reverend Moses Ashley Curtis and T. D. Warren of North Carolina; and Reverend J. Wood Dunn of Texas.

[62] Henry C. Lay, "Proceedings of a Convention of the Trustees of a Proposed University for the Southern States, under the Auspices of the Protestant Episcopal Church, Together with a Narrative, and the Address of the Rt. Rev. Jas. H. Otey, D.D., Bishop of Tennessee," Hodgson (ed.), *Reprints of Documents Prior to 1860,* pp. 21-50.

[63] Albert M. Lea to Charles T. Quintard, "All-Saints' Day," 1879, inserted in Quintard Diary. Lea was sometime professor of mathematics in East Tennessee University (now University of Tennessee). Charles M. Seymour, *A History of One Hundred Years of St. John's Episcopal Church in Knoxville, Tennessee, 1846-1946* (Knoxville, 1947), 4.

[64] Hodgson (ed.), *Reprints of Documents Prior to 1860,* pp. 48 *et passim.*

[65] Lea to Quintard, "All-Saints' Day," 1879. The much-traveled flag now hangs in All Saints' Chapel at Sewanee.

[66] *Ibid.,* 51, 52.

[67] *Ibid.,* 59, 99.

[68] *Ibid.,* 61.

[69] The other two engineers were James L. Randolph and Theodore S. Garnett of Virginia. "Colonel Barney," Lily Baker, Charlotte Gailor, Rose Duncan Lovell, and Sarah Hodgson Torian (eds.), *Sewanee* (n.p., 1932), 13.

[70] Hodgson (ed.), *Reprints of Documents Prior to 1860,* pp. 69, 70.

[71] Gwynn's report is dated November 17, 1857. *Ibid.*, 66-68.

[72] *Ibid.*, 65.

[73] *Ibid.*, 62, 70, 71.

[74] *Ibid.*, 63, 74-76.

[75] *Ibid.*, 63, 78, 79.

[76] *Ibid.*, 76, 77.

[77] *Ibid.*, 64-66, 77, 78.

[78] Estill had received his land by grant from the state about twenty years before. James Otto Hill, "Sewanee, A Unique Community," unpublished master's thesis, Middle Tennessee State College, 1952 (Sewanee Archives).

[79] Especially Arthur St. Clair Colyar and Arthur Middleton Rutledge. Fairbanks, *History of the University of the South,* 34.

[80] Colonel V. K. Stephenson, president of the line, directed Polk's attention to Sewanee and accompanied him on a horseback tour of the mountaintop. *University Record* (Sewanee), I (August, 1873), 31. The line is now known as the Nashville, Chattanooga, and St. Louis.

[81] Walter P. Webb, *The Great Plains* (New York, 1931), 18.

[82] Probably Polk, the only member of the board who had visited the site. Fairbanks, *History of the University of the South,* 30.

[83] Hodgson (ed.), *Reprints of Documents Prior to 1860,* p. 55.

[84] E. Merton Coulter, *College Life in the Old South* (New York, 1928), 10, 11.

[85] Hodgson (ed.), *Reprints of Documents Prior to 1860,* p. 53. The amount was $25,000. Fairbanks, *History of the University of the South,* 31.

[86] William Garrett, *Reminiscences of Public Men in Alabama for Thirty Years* (Atlanta, 1872), 397, 398.

[87] Edward McCrady, Jr., "Map of the University of the South and Environs" (n.p., *circa* 1940).

[88] Francis B. Fogg and Russell Houston of Nashville secured the charter. Hodgson (ed.), *Reprints of Documents Prior to 1860,* p. 57.

[89] *Ibid.*, 94-97.

[90] Fairbanks, *History of the University of the South,* 155.

[91] Failure to secure such powers has resulted in the University's inability to receive percentage rebates on state sales taxes collected at Sewanee.

[92] Stephen Elliott *et al.,* "Address of the Board of Trustees of the University of the South to the Southern Dioceses . . .," Hodgson (ed.), *Reprints of Documents Prior to 1860,* pp. 98-107.

[93] *Ibid.*, 100, 101.

[94] Winchester *Home-Journal,* August 28, 1858, September 23, 1858.

[95] Leonidas Polk and Stephen Elliott, "Address of the Commissioners for Raising the Endowment of the University . . .," Hodgson (ed.) *Reprints of Documents Prior to 1860,* pp. 108-25.

[96] Fairbanks, *History of the University of the South,* 60, 61.

[97] *Proceedings of the Board of Trustees of the University of the South at their Session Held at University Place, Sewanee, Tenn., July 11th-14th [16th], 1870* (Macon, 1870), 28-30. Hereafter cited as *Proceedings, 1870*. Titles vary.

[98] Hodgson (ed.), *Reprints of Documents Prior to 1860,* pp. 134, 135.

[99] Greenough White, *A Saint of the Southern Church* (New York, 1897), 151.

[100] Dodd, *Cotton Kingdom,* 110.

[101] Polk, *Leonidas Polk,* I, 203.

[102] Cotterill, *Old South,* 286.

[103] Masters of arts would be eligible for fellowships from trustees. Tenure would be five years, stipends $500 per year and quarters. Statutes, Art. IX, Sec. 5, Hodgson (ed.), *Reprints of Documents Prior to 1860,* p. 222.

[104] Hodgson (ed.), *Reprints of Documents Prior to 1860,* pp. 119, 120.

[105] John S. Bassett, *The Middle Group of American Historians* (New York, 1917), 124.

[106] Domain, as used here and elsewhere, applies to the whole tract of the University's lands, approximately 10,000 acres.

[107] Hodgson (ed.), *Reprints of Documents Prior to 1860,* pp. 125-38.

[108] Undated clipping from Nashville *American,* inserted in Quintard Diary, April 13, 1880. Fogg died April 12, 1880.

[109] Hodgson (ed.), *Reprints of Documents Prior to 1860,* pp. 130-32. The date of the conveyance from the Sewanee Mining Company was September 23, 1858. The first nine students were matriculated almost ten years later on September 18, 1868. The Estill family and Rutledge were residents of Franklin County. W. B. Shapard was a Nashville bank president who owned a summer home on the plateau. W. C. Dowdell to the writer, March 30, 1953. Hawkins, Garner, Barnes, Houghton, Hines, and Gipson are familiar names in Franklin County a hundred years later. Decherd is the name of a nearby community. Lawson Rowe had a cabin near the spring now known as Tremlett.

[110] Hopkins remained three months instead of six, and at his suggestion was paid only half of the $1,500 fee agreed upon, plus his traveling expenses, a sum sufficient to finish his chapel.

[111] [Hopkins], *Life of the Late Right Rev. John Henry Hopkins,* 313.

[112] Winchester *Home-Journal,* January 5, 1860.

[113] Six of these survive and hang in the University library.

[114] In 1951 "Lake Champlain" *was* thrown in. The United States government, to secure water for cooling the Arnold wind tunnel turbines at Tullahoma, laid out an artificial lake in the valley five miles from the west line of the domain.

[115] Hodgson (ed.), *Reprints of Documents Prior to 1860,* pp. 163-93.

[116] Note on terminology: "clergyman," "minister," "presbyter," "priest," and "clerk in holy orders" are roughly synonymous in Episcopal usage. "Rector" is one of these in charge of a parish. All must serve a trial period, usually one year, as "deacon" before being ordained "priest." As titles, "Venerable," "Reverend," "Very Reverend," and "Right Reverend" are properly used only with full name, or with initials and last name, never with last name alone. "Father," "Doctor," "Canon," and "Mister" may be used with last name or full name. A diocesan is a bishop in charge of a diocese.

[117] Summary of attendance of trustees: Lookout Mountain, 1857, twenty; Montgomery, 1857, twenty; Beersheba Springs, 1858, eighteen; same place, 1859, twenty; New Orleans, 1860, sixteen; Sewanee, 1860, twenty-two. There was no bishop of Texas until the election of Gregg in 1859. Bishop Freeman of Arkansas attended no meetings before his death in 1858, and Arkansas, technically a missionary district and not a diocese, did not name clerical or lay trustees before the war.

[118] Lay withdrew from the board in 1869 when he was elected bishop of Easton in Maryland. Easton became an owning diocese of the University in 1946.

[119] Otey, Polk, Elliott, and Green attended all six meetings. Bishops Rutledge of Florida, Cobbs of Alabama, and Lay of Arkansas missed only one each and Gregg two, although as clerical representative he had attended four straight. Atkinson of North Carolina missed three. Davis of South Carolina attended one and Freeman none. Of the ministers, Pise attended six meetings, Lay, Leacock, and Curtis missed one each. Of the remaining ten, the average attendance was less than two. Only one of this group later showed effective interest, J. Jackson Scott of Florida. Of the laymen, Fogg attended all meetings, Fairbanks missed the first but attended every other until his death in 1906. Of twenty-seven lay trustees eligible at different times, twelve never attended a meeting, this group including such prominent citizens as Eugene Hinton and Thomas B. Magruder of Mississippi, Governor Elisha Marshall Pease of Texas, and Thomas Ruffin of North Carolina.

[120] The inchoate community became a post office, "University Place," on October 22, 1859, and was named "Sewanee" on March 24, 1870. V. C. Burke (First Assistant Postmaster General) to Sarah H. Torian, September 6, 1949 (Sewanee Archives). The Sewanee Mining Company at Tracy City applied for the name after the Civil War but there was then a Sewanee in West Tennessee. When this station closed, the alert Fairbanks secured for the University the name by which it became popularly known. "Letter of Colonel A. S. Colyar," *Semi-Centennial of the University of the South, 1857-1907* (Sewanee, 1907), 31. The University *Proceedings* used "University Place" through 1867, then "University Place, Sewanee, Tennessee" through 1871, changing to "Sewanee" in 1872.

[121] Early surveys used this large spring as "zero bench mark." In the 1830's and 1840's the cabin at "Rowe's Spring" (also miscalled Rose Spring) had been a rest stop on the Nashville to Atlanta stage route. Harry Easter, "Prehistoric Sewanee," Baker *et al.* (eds.), *Sewanee*, 3. Rainy Spring was one prewar name. *Winchester Home-Journal*, September 29, 1859. In 1859 it was named for Bishop Polk when the views and springs were named by Bishop Green and Fairbanks. Fairbanks, *History of the University of the South*, 39, 40. After Tremlett Hall was located above it, the spring became popularly known as Tremlett Spring.

[122] Hester Elliott Shoup, "The Laying of the Cornerstone," Baker *et al.* (eds.), *Sewanee*, 14-16.

[123] *Journal of the Proceedings of the 34th Annual Convention of the Protestant Episcopal Church in the Diocese of Tennessee* (Memphis, 1866), 51. Hereafter cited as Tennessee Diocesan *Journal*. Titles vary.

[124] Habersham Elliott, son of Bishop Elliott, rode into Sewanee perched on top. I. T. Miller, "Hauling the Cornerstone," Baker *et al.* (eds.), *Sewanee*, 16. Miller erroneously says it was John B. Elliott. Charlotte Gailor, "Skit Presented by Woman's Club at Sewanee Public School October 9, 1950," Scene I, p. 13 (Sewanee Archives).

[125] J. Freeman Young, *The Church Journal,* quoted in Fairbanks, *History of the University of the South,* 42, 43. This account was written by one eyewitness and edited by another.

[126] New Orleans *Daily Picayune,* October 17, 1860.

[127] Shoup, "The Laying of the Cornerstone," Baker *et al.* (eds.), *Sewanee,* 14.

[128] Absent were Lay of Arkansas, Gregg of Texas, and Davis of South Carolina. Davis opened a diocesan theological school in Camden in 1859. Although interrupted by the war, it survived through the lifetime of Bishop Davis. The school moved to Spartanburg about 1870 and closed before 1880. Theodore DuBose Bratton, *An Apostle of Reality, The Life and Thought of the Reverend William Porcher DuBose* (New York, 1936), 45.

[129] Reynolds, "Sewanee and the Cumberland Plateau in the Civil War" (Sewanee Archives).

[130] Lucien Lamar Knight (ed.), *Library of Southern Literature,* 16 vols. (New Orleans, 1907), XV, 353.

[131] Hodgson (ed.), *Reprints of Documents Prior to 1860,* p. 59. The reader is left to assume that "people" meant "white people." No mention is made of the exclusion of any race here or in the constitution and statutes.

[132] Matthew Fontaine Maury was Otey's candidate for vice-chancellor. Charles T. Quintard to George R. Fairbanks, December 26, 1867 (Sewanee Archives).

[133] Hodgson (ed.), *Reprints of Documents Prior to 1860,* pp. 77, 78.

[134] Baker *et al.* (eds.), *Sewanee,* 11, 12. Edward Bouverie Pusey (1800-1882) advocated return to pre-Reformation forms and a consciousness of primitive antiquity. Certainly Green and Quintard, and possibly Polk, Otey, and Elliott, were in a general way sympathetic to the Anglo-Catholic viewpoint. "Revivalism" would be one of several opposing points of view. The three institutions preferred over Sewanee by Bishop Smith have either closed or been lost to the Episcopal church.

[135] Fairbanks, *History of the University of the South,* 58.

[136] Nashville *Republican Banner,* October 13, 1860.

[137] John W. Gonce to Charles W. Underwood, January 1, 1923 (Sewanee Archives).

[138] Hodgson (ed.), *Reprints of Documents Prior to 1860,* p. 200. An interpretation of the founders' plans was delivered by Fairbanks as a report to the trustees in August, 1886, and is printed in the *Proceedings, 1886,* pp. 61-70.

[139] Hodgson (ed.), *Reprints of Documents Prior to 1860,* p. 166. Oxford, Cambridge, Queen's University, Ireland, King's College, London, and the University of London are named in the news stories. Winchester *Home-Journal,* January 19, 1860.

[140] Millard Fillmore, Franklin Pierce, and James Buchanan were presidents in the period 1850-1861. The Bishop's distant cousin James K. Polk had gone out of office in 1849.

[141] David G. Haskins, *A Brief Account of the University of the South* (New York, 1877), 39.

[142] Polk, *Leonidas Polk,* I, 182. In 1875, when Bishop Quintard was in England on his second trip soliciting funds for the reviving institution, he noted in his diary a call on the Reverend G. E. Jelf: "Mr. Jelf's father was for many years ye head of King's College London, & had a long correspondence with Bp. Polk as to ye organization of ye University of ye South." Quintard Diary, December 11, 1875.

[143] *Proceedings, 1869,* p. 42.

[144] John Henry Hopkins to Mrs. Leonidas Polk, February 14, 1867, Moultrie Guerry, "Beginnings of the University of the South," *Historical Magazine of the Protestant Episcopal Church,* VII (December, 1938), 380.

[145] Hodgson (ed.), *Reprints of Documents Prior to 1860,* pp. 208-27.

[146] In ninety years the board expanded from 40 to 100. Twenty-two dioceses in 1952 furnished 88 members. A constitutional amendment added six trustees nominated by the alumni, and coadjutor bishops have been added. Retired bishops retain their seats on the board as honorary members.

[147] Fairbanks, *History of the University of the South,* 282.

[148] Hodgson (ed.), *Reprints of Documents Prior to 1860,* p. 209.

[149] Statutes, Art. II, Secs. 4, 5, Hodgson (ed.), *Reprints of Documents Prior to 1860,* p. 181.

[150] *Ibid.,* 223.

[151] *Ibid.,* 219, 220.

[152] *Ibid.,* 226.

[153] *Ibid.,* 201.

[154] One plan gave dimensions of the main building, located at the end of a 200-foot-wide avenue, as 272 feet long, 135 feet deep, with an auditorium for 2,500 in the center, a library in one wing, art gallery in the other, "not unlike the general plan of the Capitol at Washington." Fairbanks, "Plans of the Founders," *Proceedings, 1886,* p. 66.

[155] Mrs. W. S. Lovell, "The First Confederate Flag," Baker *et al.* (eds.), *Sewanee,* 23.

[156] Charles R. Barney to George R. Fairbanks, January 2, 1861 (Sewanee Archives).

[157] "Franklin County Secedes," Baker *et al.* (eds.), *Sewanee,* 22-23.

[158] Fairbanks, *History of the University of the South,* 64, 65.

[159] William M. Polk, "Letters to Mrs. Polk," Baker *et al.* (eds.), *Sewanee,* 20.

[160] *Proceedings, 1861,* p. 3.

[161] Fairbanks, *History of the University of the South,* 68 n.

[162] *Proceedings, 1861,* p. 8.

[163] Fairbanks, *History of the University of the South,* 68, 69.

[164] Cole, *Irrepressible Conflict,* 47.

[165] Polk to Elliott, July 23, 1856, Polk, *Leonidas Polk,* I, 209.

[166] *Journal of the Twenty-Second Annual Convention of the Protestant Episcopal Church in the Diocese of Louisiana* (New Orleans, 1860), 16. Hereafter cited as Louisiana Diocesan *Journal.* Titles vary.

[167] Alexis de Tocqueville, *Democracy in America* (Paris, 1836), 277.

CHAPTER TWO

IDEAL REVISITED
1861-1868

THE TEN-YEAR period of grace allowed by the Sewanee Mining Company land grant was prophetically accurate. Conditions in the South were such that no progress in building a university could be made until hostilities ceased. Then three and a half years were scarcely enough in which to collect funds and make arrangements for a school which, when it opened, could be titled a university only by courtesy.

The military actions of the Civil War had little direct influence on the physical properties of the University. Three accounts have been written of the minor engagements which took place on the domain.[1] The few frame buildings were burned, most of them by neighboring Union sympathizers, some by Federal troops.[2] There was something dramatic about Polk's retreating over Sewanee mountain in July, 1863, just eleven months before he was killed. He must have been oppressed by the desolation there and by the knowledge of the far greater loss the University had suffered in the reversals of the southern planters who had seemed prepared in 1859 to support it so generously. There was a sadness about the destruction of the cornerstone and the scattering of papers, records, and letters by Federal soldiers.

After the summer of 1863 the quiet of the forest remained relatively unbroken until the war was over. Underbrush covered the charred timbers. An occasional passerby stopped to refresh himself at the cool springs which slaked the thirst of some hundred thousand men during the seesawing military movements.

As the various Confederate commanders surrendered during April, 1865, beginning with Lee at Appomattox and ending with Edmund Kirby-Smith[3] in Texas, there were many more elemental problems in the South than resurrecting universities. Countless plantations were out of production. Land values declined as much as 90 per cent. Food was short, money almost nonexistent. Cotton had been confiscated.[4] Sherman's path of destruction was the longest and widest but there were other areas of devastation. And where lands had not been laid waste, there was a labor problem. Hundreds of thousands of former slaves were on the road, moving toward no particular destination, just traveling. In some cities matters were even worse. Atlanta lay in ashes. An ammunition explosion had shattered twelve blocks of Mobile.[5] Strife-torn New Orleans was in the third of a fifteen-year period of occupation and reconstruction in which one bitter mistake was piled on another. The railroads of the South were three-fourths inactive.[6] True, the Nashville and Chattanooga was still in operation. For reasons which were no better understood than other aspects of his military strategy, General Braxton Bragg did not blow up the long tunnel under Sewanee mountain when he retreated across the plateau on his way to bloody Missionary Ridge.[7] Access to Sewanee from the outside world still existed by way of the coal spur from Cowan.

THE SUPPORTING CHURCH

Devastation to church buildings throughout the South was widespread. Diocesan journals of the sixties detail the evidence and the record of Tennessee is typical. Its churches were used as hospitals, ordnance depots, stables, and barracks. St. Paul's, Chattanooga, later collected $3,640 from the Federal government for damages but few others were so fortunate. Immanuel Church, La Grange, a brick building, was used for ammunition storage. Its blinds were broken, chancel furniture destroyed, pews used for coffins, stoves stolen, and the bare walls defaced. St. Paul's, Franklin, was so disfigured that it lost its character as a church and was used after the war as a carpenter shop. Ravenscroft Chapel near Randolph was in ruins.[8]

In Louisiana, Sewanee's trustee, the Reverend William T. Leacock, told the twenty-fifth convention of the diocese: "Our church edifices have almost all been injured and some totally destroyed. Our people have been so deeply impoverished that they can neither repair their

IDEAL REVISITED

edifices nor support their ministers."⁹ In 1866 there were only two self-supporting parishes in the diocese of Florida. In South Carolina there was no self-sustaining parish outside the city of Charleston. The clergy of South Carolina earned their living by "fishing, farming, and mechanic arts."¹⁰ Surely there was reasonable excuse for putting idealistic educational plans in the background. If an attempt to create a community on a wild mountaintop in 1857 had been a challenging task, what would it be now with the South almost a wasteland?

TENNESSEE INITIATES REVIVAL

For five months after the war ended there was no sign that the University of the South would revive. Of the ten dioceses which had equal responsibility for the institution, Tennessee was the only one which took positive action at its first postwar convention. In September the clergy and the lay leaders of that diocese assembled at Nashville to name a bishop to succeed Otey, who had died two years before. The election of the Reverend Charles Todd Quintard, chaplain of the Army of Tennessee, marked the point at which the University of the South returned from the realm of dead hopes. The convention resolved:

> That a standing committee to consist of five members, of whom the bishop of the diocese shall be the permanent chairman, be appointed . . . to consult with the executive committee of the University of the South,¹¹ and . . . [establish] a theological training school on the domain. . . .
> That said committee shall have full power to act for the diocese of Tennessee . . . and be authorized to . . . present this subject to other dioceses . . . and to solicit funds for the immediate erection of buildings . . . and salaries of at least two professors.¹²

Although this resolution was proposed by Quintard, whose remarkable talents and unquenchable enthusiasm later made the University a going concern, the importance of two trustees should not be overlooked. They were the Reverend David Pise, secretary of the board, and George R. Fairbanks, both members of the executive committee appointed at the 1861 meeting in Columbia. Earlier in September they had met Quintard on the train and the three had discussed the possibility of reviving the University.

In the history of Sewanee, the reunion of the Episcopal Church in 1865 is a matter of some importance. Other denominations which split in the sectional dispute continued separation after the war. Had the Episcopal Church remained divided, the support of northern bishops would not have been obtained by Quintard on his trip to England to secure funds to open the University. Without northern aid at critical times, small as it was, the University might well have failed. Indeed, Sewanee became a focal point in the southern church for an attitude of moderation. Its first three vice-chancellors had ties with the North, Quintard and Josiah Gorgas by birth and Telfair Hodgson [13] by rectorship of a parish in New Jersey. Quintard's diary convincingly records his desire to wipe out the war's bitterness.

Although Elliott, presiding bishop of the southern church, did not take initiative toward reunion, an obstacle had been removed by the death of Polk, whose "defection" to enter the Confederate army had received almost unanimous disapprobation in the North. On the other hand a vexing problem had been raised by the consecration in 1862 of Bishop Richard Hooker Wilmer of Alabama without the approval of the northern dioceses. Southerners wanted his consecration recognized. The status of Arkansas, raised from a missionary district to a diocese by the southern church, was another issue. Most serious bar to reunion was the strong anti-southern feeling of the Radicals in the northern church.[14]

REUNION OF THE CHURCH

No other northern bishop felt toward the South as did John Henry Hopkins of Vermont who by seniority of consecration became presiding bishop for the critical triennial of 1865. On his landscaping visit the idea of the University had impressed him. He thought Polk particularly able. Hopkins' friendship with Elliott was close. His son had been a tutor in the Elliott home and the two families had preserved that bond.[15] Bishop Hopkins felt he had a personal stake in the southern educational enterprise and felt grateful for the modest monetary contribution it had made to his Vermont chapel. On July 12, 1865, he addressed a letter to the southern bishops: "I trust I shall enjoy the precious gratification of seeing you . . . at the regular triennial meeting." He asked the northern bishops to join him in signing this letter, but when only three replied, none willing, he sent it over his own signature.[16] Hopkins' statesmanship, influenced by southern attachments and revealed in astute conciliatory maneuvers, stamped him with greatness and gave the unopened University a unique, if coincidental, importance in Episcopal history.

Bishops Atkinson and Lay, relatives by marriage, and Bishop-elect Quintard presented themselves at the convention and were warmly received.[17] The drama of the occasion was highlighted when the secretary began the unaltered roll call with "Alabama." Bishop Wilmer was not present but his consecration was accepted. Bishop Lay was willing to have Arkansas revert to a missionary jurisdiction. Bishop Elliott passed by the opportunity of leading the southern church back into the fold not because of personal antipathy to the idea but because of the feeling that his position demanded a judicious detachment.[18] Quintard was consecrated bishop in Philadelphia on October 11 with Bishop Hopkins as consecrator. Five northern bishops and Bishop Francis Fulford of Montreal took part in the consecration of the former Confederate chaplain. So it was

> The consecration of Bishop Quintard for the vacant Southern diocese of Tennessee [that] crowned the work of reunion, so far as it could be consummated at that session, and the wise and loving moderation with which all the delicate points involved were handled insured the voluntary surrender of the Southern organization within a few months.[19]

Significantly, on the very day of his consecration Quintard wrote his friend Reverend John Austin Merrick to meet him at Sewanee to discuss plans for revival.[20]

QUINTARD, THE REFOUNDER

Bishop Quintard, who was to exert an unparalleled influence on the University of the South for the first thirty years of its active existence, was a Connecticut Yankee, born in Stamford on December 22, 1824.[21] His father was Isaac Quintard, of a Huguenot family traced by the genealogist Reverend Charles W. Baird to the early days of the reformed faith in France.[22] Leaving France after the revocation of the Edict of Nantes, the family settled for a while in Bristol and there became identified with the Church of England. In America, the Quintards went to Rhode Island, then New York, and finally Connecticut.

Isaac Quintard was a man of wealth and education. He sent his son to the fashionable Trinity School, New York. Charles Todd left Trinity because of ill health and was tutored by the Reverend James W. Bradin. He attended Columbia College and later received his M.D. from the Medical Department of the University of the City of New York.[23] For a year he interned at Bellevue, then called the Alms House and Prison Hospital. He went to Macon, Georgia, to join in medical practice a relative, Dr. William Nephew King. He moved briefly to Athens and again, because of his health, moved, this time to Roswell. There he married Eliza Catherine Hand on October 19, 1848. He wrote for medical journals and was corresponding secretary of the Georgia Medical Society.[24]

Three years later the Quintards moved to Memphis, where the doctor became a member of the faculty of the local medical school and editor of the *Medical Recorder*. In 1853 he was awarded the honorary degree, master of arts, by Columbia. Years later the health officer of the city of Nashville wrote him, "repeated references to your Medicine addresses and papers published when you were professor at Memphis . . . have given me the highest opinion of your merits as a pioneer in State Medicine."[25]

Vivacious, demonstrative, ardent, the young Episcopalian soon attracted the attention of Bishop Otey. By 1854 Quintard was studying for the ministry under Otey's personal direction. Two parting gifts presented to him by friends of the Memphis medical faculty hint of his personality. One of them was an ornate Bible and the other a gold-headed walking cane with a keen fourteen-inch blade inside.[26] The Reverend Doctor Quintard moved to the Church of the Advent in Nashville in the latter part of 1856. Within three years he became so prominent among the young men of the city that the newly formed Rock City Guard elected him chaplain and the first public parade of the group was to attend Sunday service in the Church of the Advent. On the outbreak of the war he was asked by petition to be chaplain of the First Tennessee Regiment. He first served in the Army of Northern

Virginia, and later retreated with Polk's Corps of Bragg's Army of Tennessee into Georgia.

According to his biographer, he was "probably the most widely known and best beloved" of all the chaplains of the Confederacy.[27] He won the friendship of many soldiers, including an impressive number of high-ranking officers and principal citizens of the Confederacy, not a few of whom he baptized. His war memoirs, written in 1896, are especially valuable since they mention subsequent careers of men he had met in the field. A prolific diarist, he kept almost daily records from 1861 until 1898 and adorned approximately fifty of these volumes with letters, invitations, photographs, and newspaper clippings.[28]

Bishop Quintard was an eloquent preacher. Year after year he was asked to repeat "The Samson Sermon." All of this fire in the pulpit did not, however, prevent an occasional grammar school cadet from nodding in the early service with which Sewanee started each day on its knees. When a tousled head would slump forward, the bishop would point to the young sinner and say, "Wake that boy up. I am talking to him!"[29]

Bishop Quintard's two brothers, George and Edward,[30] underwrote some of his philanthropies. George Quintard gave $50,000 for Quintard Memorial Hall, the present barracks of Sewanee Military Academy. Mrs. George Quintard is said to have joked, "It's fine to have a bishop in the family but it's an expensive luxury."[31]

MENDICANT UNASHAMED

Throughout his ministry Quintard raised money for one cause after another. In Columbus, Georgia, a month before the end of the war, he found that the Reverend William N. Hawks was dying of cancer. Quintard took time from his clerical and medical duties to raise "three or four thousand dollars" to pay off the debts of this Sewanee trustee. On one occasion he remarked that the fitting epitaph for his own tombstone would be "And the Beggar Died."[32] In June, 1866, he went to New York to preach the Commencement sermon at General Theological Seminary. Bishop Hopkins was there and also the influential Bishop Horatio Potter. As though it were an accident, Bishop Quintard wrote that the offertory "was very kindly given me for our own Training School at Sewanee."[33] It was more than coincidence that, everywhere in America and England Quintard went, offerings were earmarked for the University of the South.

When once he directed his enthusiasm toward the University, he never wavered as its most effective advocate. It would be unfair to say that Sewanee came before his diocese, for his episcopacy was remarkably productive and his diocese, at his death, one of the strongest in the South. He was a strong man, usually acting upon mature judgment but not necessarily on form. His diaries reveal that he seized upon every opportunity of potential benefit to the University. His activity was prodigious. He wrote in his diary "one piece of advice ... every now and then to be completely idle. ... I wonder when I shall find time 'to do nothing at all.' "[34] His successor, Bishop Thomas Frank Gailor, said of Quintard and Sewanee: "He pervaded it. Its Sewanee Spirit was his spirit. Its atmosphere was in a large measure his creation. No stranger came here that he did not welcome. There was no sorrow to which he did not minister ... no suffering that he did not try to cheer."[35]

Quintard was not uniformly loved, as implied by Bishop Gailor, nor even universally admired. Twice he considered selling his house at Sewanee, discouraged by the feeling among several critics that "Tennessee had too much influence at Sewanee." He did not, like Polk, enjoy the unreserved approbation of his peers. Resentment was evident at times.[36] His loyalty was always to ideas and ideals, rather than to men. With many, as with Fairbanks, this never caused conflict. With others it did. At the time of General Gorgas' resignation as vice-chancellor in 1878, he was bitterly opposed to Quintard and recorded in his diary, "All [37] believe him unworthy of trust, who have had dealings with him. He is a bad man in my estimation unworthy of the robes he wears, & does his holy calling great wrong in exercising it."[38] After Gorgas' stroke at Tuscaloosa in 1879, Mrs. Gorgas wrote her son William, "He never speaks harshly now, of anyone, even making excuses for Bishop Quintard's inconsistencies."[39]

Quintard lived at Sewanee from 1866 until his death in 1898. He held only one University office, besides the trusteeship conferred by his episcopal status. He was the first vice-chancellor, accepting the post in

1867 when it seemed no one else would take the responsibility. He offered to resign in 1870, and did resign in favor of Gorgas in 1872. His influence was purely that of his personality, his persuasiveness, and the fact that, alone of all persons connected with the University, he was able year after year to raise substantial amounts of money. He was a worthy successor to Polk and probably the most influential Episcopalian in the South during Reconstruction.

FAIRBANKS, THE GOOD RIGHT ARM

George Rainsford Fairbanks, confidant of and collaborator with Quintard and the last surviving founder,[40] has no serious contender for the title of first layman in early Sewanee. He was so closely identified with the University for forty-nine years that an evaluation of the institution requires a brief study of his life. He was born in Watertown, New York, in 1820.[41] He attended Petit Seminaire, Montreal, received a master's degree from Union College, Schenectady, and was admitted to the New York bar. In 1842 he was appointed clerk of the United States circuit court in St. Augustine, Florida, and by 1860, when he moved to Sewanee, he had served as state senator (1846-1847), presidential elector for Lewis Cass (1848), mayor of St. Augustine (1857), and repeatedly as deputy to the Episcopal general convention. He was present at the second meeting of the board of trustees and he attended nearly every succeeding meeting until his death in 1906. He was the first in 1860 to build a home at Sewanee with the first founders, Polk and Elliott; he was the first in 1866 to build beside the second founder, Bishop Quintard.[42] In the Confederacy he was chief quartermaster for the Tennessee army's hospital department. At Sewanee he was the first commissioner of buildings and lands. He divided his time between Tennessee and Florida, where he was one of the state's largest landholders[43] and where he became president of the Florida Fruit Exchange and of the Florida Historical Society, which he helped organize. Called "the foremost historian of Florida,"[44] he edited for a time the *Florida Weekly Mirror* from his winter home (after 1880) in Fernandina. His *History of Florida*, first published in 1871, was adopted in its rewritten third edition by the state school system in 1904. His *History and An-*

tiquities of St. Augustine is linked with the development of that city as a tourist attraction.

Fairbanks is the only man who has written a book-length history of the University of the South. Almost eighty when he began it, he displayed maturity of judgment in the astute interpretations of the ideals of the founders, the concept of the domain, the potentialities of the University as a unifying factor in the southern Episcopal Church. It stands among the best sources of material on the University.

Like Quintard, Fairbanks encountered opposition. The diocese of Tennessee failed to re-elect him deputy to the 1877 general convention.[45] He was removed as commissioner of buildings and lands by the trustees in 1878. William P. DuBose says: "He was not always understood or appreciated . . . his silent endurance and survival of all the trials that beset himself or assailed his trust . . . won him the . . . place he has . . . —the patriarch of Sewanee."[46]

Fairbanks was the *de facto* architect of early Sewanee. He anticipated the modern utilitarians. Though all of his buildings were constructed in the days of the most devious carpenter-gothic, he fastened no gingerbread on University buildings. He built plain, unadorned halls from timber locally cut and locally milled.

Like Quintard, Fairbanks continued his services to the University after he ceased to be a member of the paid staff. He was elected lay trustee from the diocese of Florida and he was actively associated with the successive administrations. He was discussing the University's business with Quintard's son-in-law, Vice-Chancellor Benjamin Lawton Wiggins, over a table littered with maps of the domain, when he had his final heart attack.[47]

In his conduct of the University's affairs and in his *History of the University of the South* Fairbanks was the interpreter of the domain. He seized the founders' concept of a great landed site and held fast to the idea, using every opportunity to teach the second generation what the founders had envisioned. Seclusion, that perfection might be attempted under the most favorable circumstances; insulation, that interference might be repelled or controlled; altitude, that the beacon on a hill might be seen afar—these were the intangibles between lines describing boundaries, trees, springs, coal, and stone.

If the bishops and their fellow dreamers who selected the site of the University in 1857 had known the problems their isolation and altitude would bring—the building and maintenance of roads for automotive traffic, the blasting of pipe lines through solid rock, the repair of miles of power and telephone lines broken in mountain ice storms—some among them still would have wanted the domain at Sewanee. It became a physical expression of what they were trying to do spiritually. Fairbanks intuitively knew this and his life's work was to defend it.

These two men, Fairbanks and Quintard, both from the North and both of the Confederacy, a layman and a bishop, the one patient, methodical, practical, and the other dynamic, inspiring, sophisticated, each with complete confidence in the other—these two formed the team which set the University on its way.

TO RECALL A DREAM

Following the action of Tennessee's convention Quintard, Fairbanks, and Pise directed a letter dated January 13, 1866, to the surviving members of the executive committee of the University, Whittle and Griffin, with a copy to Chancellor Elliott. Retention of the land depended on activation of the educational establishment. They optimistically presumed that endowment held by diocesan treasurers was available and they enumerated the actions taken by the diocese of Tennessee. The letter suggested that the executive committee build, with what funds could be secured for the purpose, simple frame structures "for the accommodation of a boys' classical school," which would be a self-supporting nucleus of a future university and involve no financial liabilities. Bishop Quintard, said the letter, already had collected funds for the establishing of a theological training school. An agent should be appointed to solicit $6,000, a sum necessary to begin the project. Suitable instructors were thought to be available and students ready to enter.[48] Favorable replies were quickly received from all addressees.

The next month construction began with Fairbanks in charge. He consulted frequently with Bishop Quintard, who wrote innumerable memoranda and sent small contributions from every part of the diocese as he went on his visitations.⁴⁹ William P. Ensign secured the lumber and employed the workmen.⁵⁰ A single-room log cabin, fourteen by eighteen feet, was built for the carpenters. The first University building, Otey Hall, had seven rooms and a kitchen in its story and a half. It was ready by May and stood near the front of the present Walsh Hall.⁵¹

Dr. Merrick accepted the appointment of "president of the Sewanee Mission and Theological School" and came to Tennessee the end of March.⁵² On March 22, Quintard, Fairbanks, and the Reverend Thomas A. Morris accompanied him on horseback to University Place.⁵³ With a few workers, some of whom had witnessed the elaborate cornerstone exercises, they gathered around a rude cross twelve feet high. Bishop Quintard announced that the University of the South was re-established. They joined in the Apostles' Creed and sang the *Gloria in Excelsis*.⁵⁴ The planting of the cross was an act of faith which Quintard and Fairbanks promptly supported even more tangibly: both began the construction of dwellings and on June 5, when only two rooms of the log cabin called Fulford Hall were complete, the Quintards moved in.⁵⁵ The Fairbanks family occupied Otey Hall for the summer and in September moved into their log home, Rebel's Rest, next to the Quintards.⁵⁶ Merrick held regular services at Sewanee in 1866 but it is not known if he had any students in the theological training school. He left Sewanee before 1867.

SEWANEE COLLEGE AT WINCHESTER

Meantime, a corollary activity had been started in Winchester, the neighboring county seat. In March the trustees of Carrick Academy there offered Bishop Quintard a building and four acres of land on a ninety-nine year lease if he would operate a male academy. Thinking of it as a feeder for the University and as a collecting point for faculty, he invited the Reverend Franklin L. Knight of New Jersey to take charge as rector.⁵⁷ Quintard addressed the opening exercises on June 8.⁵⁸ The name was changed to Sewanee Collegiate Institute and on September 3 was dedicated under its new title and the resolution of its trustees recorded at the county court. "This school is now a thorough Church institution," wrote Quintard on that day. He named to its board of trustees Fairbanks, Pise, the Reverend George White, and Colonel Peter Turney,[59] war hero and future governor of Tennessee.

Records of student life in this short-lived institute in the valley are rare but an interesting letter of a former student (the same person who had attended the laying of the cornerstone) is extant:

> I was the first person to enter the freshman class of the University . . . [Bishop Quintard had] acquired the use of a school building at Winchester and then started the university course as well as a primary department. That was in 1866. . . . The school was in charge of Dr. Knight as principal and Dr. [H. P.] Hay as teacher of Latin and Greek. There was another teacher or two whom I do not remember. . . . No one ever recited with me in Latin and Greek. I was reading Livy and Xenophon . . . also trigonometry, mental philosophy, and classical literature. I got receipts printed under the style of the "University of the South" when I paid tuition.[60]

The Sewanee Collegiate Institute is described in the letter of another student to a Sewanee vice-chancellor.

> I arrived in Winchester [in] September, 1866, and found there a school of 130 students . . . and four instructors, Dr. Frank Knight, Dr. Henry Palethrope Hay and the Rev. William H. Guilford, M.A., and Mr. Bowers. Major Fairbanks came down occasionaly [sic] to lecture upon History. . . . There were several others seeking orders, H. O. Judd, Henry Dunlap, H. H. Sneed [writer of this letter], Benjamin Bradford and Mr. Drummond. [In] 1867, when Dr. Knight moved with the Theological department to Sewanee . . . I was made professor of mathematics. . . . Dr. Hay and Dr. Knight had some disagreement. . . . I belonged to the Divinity School at Sewanee, and pursued my studies . . . assisted by Bishop Green. . . .[61]

The name of the institute was changed in 1868 to Sewanee College. Sneed and his wife continued to teach there until 1869. In the fall of that year the Reverend Breck Ramsey became head of the school, remaining until it closed on March 31, 1871. The lease was cancelled and the property returned to the town of Winchester. It became a normal school for teachers under local sponsorship. The citizens of Winchester were glad to be rid of the alien Episcopalians. Sneed describes a court scene in which a suit of ejectment was tried. The attorney for the Episcopal Church won the case simply by alluding to the communicant status of Jefferson Davis and Robert E. Lee. For the Southrons of Franklin County, that was enough.

The brief career of the Sewanee school in the valley has interest principally for the antiquarian. Its students apparently considered it a part of the University of the South and the officials of the University, which opened twelve miles away in 1868, did not.

TRUSTEES APPROVE REVIVAL

After some correspondence, Bishop Elliott called a special meeting of the University trustees for October 11, 1866, at Sewanee and invitations were mailed to the board as it had stood in 1861. To the meeting held at Fairbanks' home came four bishops—Elliott, Green, Lay, and Quintard; three clerical trustees; and two laymen,[62] six short of a quorum. The discussion lasted until midnight, and at the end a poll indicated that each man thought the revival of the University was practicable and should be attempted. The executive committee, all of whose members were present except Daniel Griffin of Georgia, asked Quintard to continue to solicit funds, an appointment he accepted "with regret, knowing how much of my time must be taken from ye Diocese."[63]

Three years before, when Polk had passed through Sewanee in July, 1863, he removed from the University vault the deeds and other documents and sent them for safekeeping to railroad president Charles T. Pollard, a Sewanee trustee living in Montgomery. Pollard placed what appeared to be the more valuable papers in the railroad's safe and the others on a shelf. Early in 1865, when the Federal troops threatened Montgomery, Pollard sent the more important University papers with valuables of the company on a special train to Opelika, where it made an untimely junction with a Federal raiding party. Pollard reported with chagrin to his fellow Sewanee trustees the complete destruction of the train and all papers aboard. But, Fairbanks relates,

> During the afternoon of October 12th, while we were in session, a young gentleman came up from the train . . . and brought a letter from Colonel Pollard . . . saying that he had found on a shelf in his office a bundle of papers tied up in a newspaper which he sent along with his messenger . . . he had not examined them. The bundle was laid on the floor.[64]

IDEAL REVISITED 97

Early next morning Fairbanks opened the package, and to his delight there were the deeds to the domain. "It was hailed by us all as an auspicious omen," he wrote.

The next day a group hiked six miles down the Hawkins Cove trail to Cowan. It was the last time the Bishop of Georgia was to see the domain for which he had such great plans. He died nine weeks later. Three chancellors gone and still no university!

GREEN, THE FOURTH CHANCELLOR

The senior bishop in the owning dioceses, the Right Reverend William Mercer Green, Bishop of Mississippi from 1850 until his death in 1887, succeeded Bishop Elliott as chancellor in December, 1866. In January, 1867, he moved out of his diocese and for the rest of his long episcopate maintained residence in Sewanee at "Kendal," returning to Mississippi for regular visitations.[65] His home at Jackson on a site now known as Battle Hill was destroyed during the Vicksburg campaign. Before his election as chancellor he established his devotion to the University by his perfect attendance at trustees' meetings. His service as chancellor was equally faithful.

William Mercer Green was born in Wilmington, North Carolina, May 2, 1798. He was chaplain of the University of North Carolina, his *alma mater,* when he was elected bishop of Mississippi. Green was a great admirer of the first bishop of North Carolina, John Stark Ravenscroft,[66] and from him imbibed a churchmanship high for those days but compatible with the sentiments of Otey, Polk, Elliott, and Quintard. Green was "a mild and saintly man,"[67] not "a hard master given to rebuke. He never quite learned the imperative mood."[68] He was rarely involved in dissension. Though he lacked Quintard's singleness of purpose,[69] he was a steadying influence on the board of trustees and a pacifying influence in the community. His writings included contributions to church periodicals and a biography of Bishop Otey.[70] His residence on the campus, together with that of Quintard and assorted generals, lent distinction to formal occasions, religious or academic.

Like other bishops of his day in the South, Green was a liberal on the race problem. "On several occasions the Church has been open for the freedmen, when their appreciation . . . has been shown by their large attendance. Many worship with the white congregation, and . . . some participate in the Holy Communion."[71]

When he died at the age of eighty-nine,[72] he was the last living signer of the Address of 1856. It was he who proposed the name "University of the South" and he was memorialized at Sewanee by "Green's View," the most popular of the prospects on the north escarpment.

Almost as vital a part of the little community as the chancellor himself was his daughter, Miss Lily Green. She was college mother to scores of students in the early days. She was especially active in the affairs of the village church, later named Otey Memorial, and the people of the village community knew her as their dearest friend.[73]

DIOCESAN DIVINITY SCHOOL

Dr. Knight and his Tennessee divinity students moved to the mountain early in 1867. He became missionary to University Place, and as of March, 1867, reported there were eight families; about twenty-five regular attendants at services, sixteen communicants, twelve children, and a dozen colored persons who came together for instruction after Sunday evening service. He also held services at Lower Coal Banks nearby and was invited to start a mission at Tracy City.[74] In May, 1868, he reported to the diocesan convention that there were nine students in the Sewanee Training and Divinity School, and in 1869 he reported the merger of the diocesan school with the University of the South.[75]

Bishop Green called a meeting of the board of trustees for February 13, 1867, which was held in the home of Charles T. Pollard in Montgomery. Green, Lay, and Quintard welcomed bishops new to the meetings of the board, Richard Hooker Wilmer of Alabama and his cousin Joseph Pere Bell Wilmer of Louisiana. Five familiar names answered to the roll call of clerical members, M. Ashley Curtis of North Carolina, J. Jackson Scott of Florida, William C. Crane of Mississippi, W. T. Leacock of Louisiana, veterans of the prewar board, and William C. Williams of Georgia, secretary, who attended the meeting at Sewanee in 1866. Only three lay trustees were there—Pollard, Fairbanks, and L. N. Whittle of Georgia. The board ratified the actions of its sanguine

IDEAL REVISITED

executive committee and accepted Otey Hall from the diocese of Tennessee. Quintard was elected vice-chancellor and Fairbanks commissioner of buildings and lands at salaries of $2,000 each. Fairbanks was asked to visit Louisiana and accept what could be salvaged from the prewar notes and to act as business manager of the University. Issuance of bonds was discussed and the executive committee was given authority to pay debts from what funds could be found. Diocesan treasurers were asked to send funds to Quintard and Fairbanks, in violation of the prewar constitution. The executive committee was authorized to establish a high school and to proceed with necessary construction. Dr. Curtis was requested to obtain a proffered cabinet of minerals and to see if Bishop Elliott's natural history collection could be had. Kentucky was invited to send delegates to the next meeting. Bishop Wilmer of Louisiana was delegated to "express to Mr. George Peabody, the sense which this body entertains, of the generosity which suggested his munificent donation in furtherance of the educational interests of the Southern States."[76]

JOINT SPONSORSHIP SOUGHT AGAIN

Under date of April 8, 1867, Chancellor Green sent a letter from University Place to each of the other nine dioceses. It may be regarded as the first official notification of the revival of the University of the South as an interdiocesan enterprise. The letter announced that Otey Hall had been transferred to the trustees by the Bishop of Tennessee, that Dr. Knight "was already there in charge of several Divinity Students of his own Diocese," and that his salary would continue to be paid by the diocese of Tennessee. It pointed out that Otey Hall formed an excellent nucleus for "all the Dioceses unprovided with Theological Schools of their own." Another professor could be engaged, whose salary could be paid by joint contribution of the dioceses, which might then send a total of twenty ministerial students, at the rate of $20.00 per month, including washing and lodging.

The letter alluded to "the superior advantages and economy of one central and healthfully located Training and Theological School over a number of small ones." Its tone, though, was singularly uninspired. There were no more visions of grandeur, no reference to the great plans of 1860. It was a timid letter addressed to beaten people. Most dioceses ignored it. Alabama, in convention the following month, deeply regretted its "inability to take any action . . . under the existing circumstances" and resolved that the letter be spread upon the Journal and called to "the attention of Parishes and of individuals desiring to provide for the education of Candidates for Orders."[77]

At Sewanee the tempo of construction increased. For the next three or four years hammer and saw resounded almost continuously as dwellings, stores, stables, and outhouses mushroomed into existence. Leases for the building of private homes in the campus area were originally to have been offered at public bid. The executive committee found this impracticable, set up a lease fee of $40 per year, reduced this in 1867 to $25,[78] and later added a clause allowing faculty and staff members leaseholds at $5 per year. The general plan of the University was to erect

> accommodations for seventy-five to one hundred students this summer . . . in buildings of eight rooms each to avoid too many under one roof and less danger of fire. I wish to put up three of these eight-room buildings . . . to cost $1,200 . . . and one boarding house . . . $1,800.00. . . . The School will be self-supporting when well under way. . . . We now have bedding and room furniture [for] forty pupils.[79]

Even these modest ideas were too optimistic, and money in answer to letters of Quintard, Green, and Fairbanks came slowly.

In the latter part of April, Fairbanks went with Quintard on a fund-raising trip to Louisville where they "received very acceptable aid . . . which enabled us to fit out our present buildings with the furniture requisite, to accommodate a considerable number of students."[80] In June Quintard went to Savannah and Augusta on behalf of the University but the response was slight and illness cut short his trip.[81] He obtained promise of assistance from the Reverend J. H. Cornish of Aiken, South Carolina, who became the first of a long line of unsuccessful financial agents of the University. Returns from these efforts were small and sporadic. The Reverend J. M. McAllister of Augusta wrote: "Since your departure I . . . have received the sum of $50 which you named as the proper proportion from the parish."[82] Quintard and Fairbanks were urgently advised to postpone a visit to Louisiana until a more propitious time, possibly the next fall.[83] There was another discouragement that June. Bishop Charles P. McIlvaine of Ohio, Polk's former West Point chaplain, at the request of trustee M. Ashley Curtis of North Carolina, wrote Governor Rutherford B. Hayes in a fruitless effort to recover the lost maps and Hopkins sketches, thought to have been taken by members of an Ohio regiment.[84]

Construction was well under way on South Wing or Cobbs Hall, a frame building beside Otey Hall, and when the trustees assembled on August 1 their meetings were held in its unpartitioned interior. This third postwar meeting was poorly attended[85] but highly important. The delicate balance between life and death for the University may be judged from the fact that only four dioceses—Mississippi, Tennessee, Georgia, and Florida—were represented. No one came from North or South Carolina, Alabama, Louisiana, Arkansas, or Texas. The presence of the Right Reverend Channing Moore Williams, missionary bishop to China and Japan, and of the Reverend James Craik, five times president of the house of deputies of the general convention, lent distinction, however. Dr. Craik was official observer from Kentucky, but that diocese was not to join the Sewanee orbit as long as Bishop Smith lived.

EYES TURN TO ENGLAND

The most important proposal was introduced by Quintard, that aid be sought from England. The trustees passed a resolution that the chancellor address the archbishops and bishops of England, "setting forth the lamentable condition of the Church in the Southern Dioceses, the history and vast importance of our enterprise," and resolved that the vice-chancellor be authorized to convey in person this request for assistance, with the approval of the presiding bishop, in a direct solicitation for funds in England.[86] Fairbanks, who was handling fiscal affairs of the University, would continue this work and would do what soliciting he could in Quintard's absence.

It was not yet recognized that virtually no funds could be raised in the South. Fairbanks still hoped some of the Louisiana pledges could be collected and thought that "the unnecessary and wanton destruction of the buildings by the troops of the United States, should be a valid claim for reimbursement."[87] Always there was the hope that the next fund-raising scheme would succeed. "The ladies of Savannah organized themselves into an association for ... erecting ... a College Hall in memory of their late beloved Bishop, to be called Elliott Hall."[88] It would have taken only about $3,000 but that was a fabulous sum in the Savannah of 1867.

Fairbanks took pains to dispel an impression that money had been lost by the University. He reported that the total expenditures from 1857 to 1862 were $28,000. To show for this the trustees had at least a 9,000-acre domain even if nothing else were salvageable. He declared that a modest $2,500 would now enable a preparatory school for seventy-five to open.

The trustees gathered on August 2, 1867, to watch the chancellor lay the cornerstone of St. Augustine's Chapel,[89] which was to serve in its ecclesiastical capacity into the next century and for a good part of that time as classroom and assembly hall. St. Augustine's was to find such a place for itself in the hearts of the students, residents, and alumni that, when it was torn down in 1910, its altar, some of its original furnishings and a few deeply initialed pews were transferred to the south transept of the new chapel, All Saints', in order that one physical part of the University should remain almost exactly as it was in the earliest days. At the St. Augustine's ceremony "the doctors of divinity wore their appropriate hoods,"[90] continuing the tone of academic and ecclesiastical formality which began in 1857 at the Lookout Mountain meeting and which has survived.

For the next few months Sewanee news stories carried a London dateline. While buildings continued to go up under the rigid inspection of Fairbanks, Quintard sailed on August 14 for England to attend with other American bishops the Pan-Anglican Conference at Lambeth. In London he met the Reverend Francis W. Tremlett, rector of St. Peter's Church, Belsize Park,[91] an ardent sympathizer with the southern cause [92] and close friend of Commodore Maury. Dr. Tremlett felt that if the help of Archbishop Charles Thomas Longley of Canterbury could be obtained, an appeal to English churchmen would be feasible. On October 15 the archbishop wrote Tremlett sanctioning the effort, making a

IDEAL REVISITED 103

personal donation of £25, and commending "the object to the favorable consideration of the members of our church, in remembrance of the sacrifices which so many of the American bishops have recently made in order to testify their respect and affection for the church of their forefathers."[93]

Before Presiding Bishop Hopkins returned to the States from the Lambeth Conference, he gave a letter of endorsement to Dr. Tremlett as did the bishops of Minnesota, Louisiana, Iowa, New Hampshire, and others. Bishop Hopkins approved the institution "as one which deserves the sympathy and zealous support of every friend to the interests of the Church in England or America. . . . If circumstances . . . rendered such an institution desirable before the war, [the southern states'] condition at the present time makes its establishment far more imperative than ever."[94] The enthusiastic Tremlett formed an imposing committee in behalf of the University.[95] J. A. Shaw-Stewart was named "honorable treasurer" and Tremlett "general honorable secretary." A printed statement, signed by Tremlett, was drawn up inviting subscriptions on four grounds: as an expression of sympathy with a region in great poverty and distress; as support for an enterprise combining higher education and religion; as means of strengthening feeling between the mother country and the United States; and as "a fitting memento of the friendly visit recently paid by the American prelates."[96]

SEWANEE AS ANGLICAN MISSIONARY ENTERPRISE

Meantime, Quintard and his wife had participated in the whirl of religious and social activities which accompanied the Lambeth Conference. He had been one of a number of American bishops receiving honorary degrees at Cambridge.

> At 4 P.M. seven Bps of ye American Ch—Whitehouse, Atkinson, Lee of Iowa, McIlvaine, Lay, Kerfoot, & myself assembled in a room in King's Old Court—& there . . . were habited in scarlet cloaks—ye Vice Chancellor . . . proceeded with us to ye Senate House—where we were received with ye greatest applause by ye Undergraduates and Fellows—Ye Senate House was full. A number of ladies were on ye floor of ye House. Ye address was made by ye Public Orator Mr. Clarke in Latin—& after it we were presented by him to ye Vice Chancellor each one separately—

We stepped forward—received ye hand of ye V. C. & were made in yt simple act L. L. D.'s [sic]).[97]

Quintard embarked on a tour of English pulpits. His first address in England on behalf of the University of the South was on All Saints' Day at the Cathedral of Ely. The small congregation was drawn from four continents and included the Metropolitan of South Africa, bishops of Ely, of Labuan and Sarawak in Borneo, of Perth, Australia, of Ontario, Canada, and of Pittsburgh, Pennsylvania.[98] Of this occasion Quintard wrote:

> At a Provincial Council . . . after ye sermon ye Missionary meeting was held in ye north transept—Ye Bp of Ely made an excellent address & was followed in turn by all ye Bps—After ye addresses Canon Schwyn moved yt £15 of ye collection be given to ye Bp of Capetown [the Metropolitan of South Africa] & £15 to ye Bp of Tennessee for ye University of ye South. Ye motion was seconded by Lord Arthur Hervey & unanimously carried.[99]

In his initial contest with peers, the Lord Bishop of Tennessee tied for first in a field which included some of the best missionary talent of the Anglican world. After this, invitations to preach came from all quarters. "Nearly every Sunday I was solicited to present the claims of the University in parish churches where the offertory was devoted to the work."

Larger gifts came slowly. By Christmas, Quintard thought it advisable to prepare the folks back home for disappointment. "Nothing can be done just now. Ye pressing demands of ye poor at home and ye season of ye year are alike unpropitious."[100]

The Bishop enjoyed his excursions into upper-class society. His diary at the time carried some pleasant notations:

> Went down to . . . Kent, ye seat of A. J. B. Beresford Hope, Esq. Mrs. Hope's carriage met us at ye Etchingham station . . . Lady Blanche Balfour with her son & two daughters was of ye party—Mr. & ye Hon. Mrs. Hussey of Scotney Castle joined us. . . . Lady Mildred drove me over to Kildown Ch. . . . Two spanking gray ponies with a couple of grooms in top boots, buff tassels & cockades mounted on a second pair of beautiful grays, with a light & elegant carriage—made a showy appearance—but was perfectly gentil. Lady Mildred drove with ye skill of an experienced whip.[101]

IDEAL REVISITED 105

In stark contrast was Bishop Green's report to Quintard on conditions in the South:

> It gratifies me no little to think that you are enjoying yourself as you no doubt are among our hospitable English brethren and cannot see the poverty and distress that reigns throughout our beloved South. Bad as things were at the close of our late struggle, they were not to be compared to the general suffering at the present time. The whites are groaning under the task of making a bare subsistence for their families and the blacks are compelled to steal or die of pure want. 'Lord, how long!'[102]

Subscriptions then began to mount. Among the donors were the bishops of London, Lincoln, Chester, Salisbury, Capetown, Gibraltar, Derry, Barbados, Exeter, Worcester, Bombay, St. Asaph, Rochester, Llandaff, Moray and Ross, Perth, New Zealand, Gloucester, and Bristol. Among prominent laymen contributing were the Duke of Buccleuch, the Marquis of Lothian, the Earls Beauchamp, Nelson, and Stanhope, the Earls of Dartmouth, Harrowby, Shaftsbury, and "many others distinguished in social life, in the world of science and letters, and in the work of the Church."[103]

The universities at Oxford and Cambridge made grants of books—approximately 1,000 volumes. The vice-chancellors, heads of colleges, provosts, wardens, and masters contributed. From Oxford the controversial Dr. Edward B. Pusey sent a gift, as did "Professor Adams, the Astronomer Royal." Sewanee's constellation was in the ascendant.

Meantime, a matter of utmost importance developed quite unexpectedly. During the Lambeth council in September Quintard confirmed Commodore Maury, who had been present seven years before at the laying of the cornerstone. This naval officer, rising from midshipman in the days before Annapolis, became one of the best-known Americans in the world by his study of ocean currents. Stationed in Washington after a crippling stagecoach accident, he made statistical compilations of ships' courses from the logs filed there. The saving of days and millions of dollars in shipping time by using "paths of the ocean" placed his *Physical Geography of the Sea* in 1855 almost equal in popular esteem to Charles Darwin's *Origin of Species,* published four years later.[104] His London home was Tremlett's rectory. By December Quintard was convinced that Maury was his man. He wrote Fairbanks:

> I feel it is most important to secure Captain M. F. Maury as our vice-chancellor. His literary renown, his world-wide reputation, his devotion to ye South, his early life in Tennessee, and education by Bp Otey, his having been ye choice of Bp Otey for ye place . . . and ye unanimity with which his appointment would be hailed, make it most desirable for us to act promptly. He is now here (London) and if ye place is offered him, will not only accept, but go at once to Oxford to prepare for ye work. . . . We should . . . get a yes or no from so many of ye Trustees . . . as may give him something definite to act upon. . . . I shall press his appointment by all means in my power, and beg you to join me. *He is immediately available.* And I think your house should be secured for him.[105]

This last was a typical Quintard touch. Willing to make any sacrifice himself, he did not hesitate to ask the same of others. Some persons might have been daunted by being asked to move out of their homes, but not Fairbanks. He and Quintard prosecuted vigorously the campaign for Maury's services.

On January 2 Quintard had supper with Lord Charles Hervey, Maury, and others. The conversation so inspired Maury that he wrote a two-page summary of the steps which he would take if he were setting up the University of the South.[106] But Bishop Green did not want to be precipitate. By March, Quintard was concerned. "Of course I am feeling very anxious about Commodore Maury's appointment. If we lose him, I shall almost despair. And I do beg and pray you to be very *persuasive* with the dear bishop of Mississippi."[107]

Maury was not mentioned in the printed minutes of the trustees' meeting of April 1 in Savannah but he was elected vice-chancellor by the executive committee after that meeting. Green wrote to him a detailed letter defining his ideas of the functions of the vice-chancellor. On April 21 Maury declined. His explanatory letter to Quintard with its sardonic subtlety must have been heartbreaking.

> The Board appears to think of me more highly than I deserve. For I am not possessed of the ability required to take charge of the Junior Department proposed, to organize it, to perform the duties of a professor in it, and then find time to plead the cause of the University as it ought to be pleaded before the public, which last I suppose to be one of the main objects for which a vice-chancellor is at this time required. . . . Think of the work which is chalked out for your vice-chancellor. . . . Moreover, I am afraid I should turn out to be an indifferent headmaster.[108]

The loss of Maury might have been a critical blow. On the other hand, Bishop Green may have known that Maury had the reputation of being an opinionated man. As a lieutenant he had declined to take part in an exploring expedition because he disapproved of the way in which the ranking officers were conducting the preparations. As a naval officer of the Confederacy he was kept in England by superiors who felt that he might cause dissension. His theory of education emphasized science as opposed to classical studies. He considered the West Point plan the best in American education and he joined the faculty of a military school, the Virginia Military Institute, shortly after he declined the vice-chancellorship at Sewanee. He remained at V.M.I. until his death in 1873.[109]

BRITISH FRIENDS RESPOND

Although Quintard's disappointment in the Maury affair must have been keen, he made no acknowledgment of it to his diary. With characteristic resilience he continued his appeal for funds, preaching at every opportunity. "At night I preached in St. Paul's Cathedral . . . under ye great dome . . . 55 minutes. . . . It was a sight full of awe to look down from a pulpit upon ye sea of upturned faces—Over 1,000 persons were in ye congregation."[110] A clipping which reported the service said: "The sermon was preached by the Right Rev. the Bishop of Tennessee, U. S., a learned and eloquent divine, whose appearance in canonicals and whose earnest delivery are not rendered less impressive by his lordship's un-Anglican peculiarity of wearing a well-grown black beard."[111] On another occasion: "Special service at St. Mary's Haggerston at 7½ P.M. Splendid service. I preached in behalf of ye University fund."[112] "Held communion at St. Peters . . . Second service at 11 o'clock. . . . [At St. Gabriel's, Pimlico] I preached at night. Offertory £26."[113] Not all of his appeals were in churches:

> I delivered an address in King's College, London on ye 'Results of Secular Education in America.' If a report of it gets across ye ocean, I shall expect some hard things to be said of me. But I can stand that very well. I made a point at ye close of my address for ye University. I am invited to repeat it both at Oxford and at Cambridge. . . . It is most important that Bishop Lay or yourself should be at work at home, north and south.[114]

Quintard's efforts were not all on behalf of the University. "At ye beautiful little Church at Stoke I preached and made appeal for Church Restoration Fund."[115] He confirmed seventy boys at Red Hill Reformatory School.[116]

Meanwhile, Tremlett was using every approach to gain funds. He addressed a letter of appreciation to Bishop Hopkins on January 15, 1868, just six days after that good man died in Vermont. It was quoted in part by an American paper. Tremlett's letter said that England could not do much at present because of "unusual visitations which have this year befallen so many of our Colonies" and the unprecedented distress at home caused by stagnation of trade. But Tremlett hoped that the North might "be able to supply what is lacking on our part." The article closed editorially with the vain though charitable wish that "our Northern Churchmen" would take hold of this enterprise and give the help that "brothers have the right to expect of brothers."[117]

Absence from his diocese was causing Quintard much concern. His treasurer wrote that he was in debt $1,000 and no money was coming in. "What am I to do?" Quintard asked Fairbanks. "What are ye clergy and laity thinking about? I shall not . . . return home until money is sent me to pay my passage."[118] He was not destined to languish in England, for at its April 1 meeting the Sewanee trustees authorized him to withdraw from his collections enough to pay for his return.[119] Quintard sailed from England on May 5 and after a rough passage landed in New York May 20.[120] By July the results of his trip had reached £1,500 [121] and the final total was £2,500. Fairbanks had said he needed only that many dollars to open the school.

NOTES FOR CHAPTER TWO

[1] Edgar L. Pennington, "The Battle of Sewanee," *Tennessee Historical Quarterly* (Nashville), IX (September, 1950), No. 3, 217-43; Reynolds, "Sewanee and the Cumberland Plateau in the Civil War" (Sewanee Archives); Robert W. Daniel, "The Battle of Sewanee," *Sewanee Alumni News* (Sewanee), XII (August, 1946), 13.

[2] "All of the buildings, with the exception of an old log cabin, were burned by the Federal army while encamped on the ground." Charles T. Quintard, "Convention Address," Tennessee Diocesan *Journal, 1866*. The cabin "still exists as a part of the residence of Mr. MacKellar." "After the War, 1866," Baker *et al.* (eds.), *Sewanee,* 32 n. The rear portion of Mr. MacKellar's residence, now owned by the writer, is built around a log cabin 14 x 20 feet.

[3] "E. Kirby Smith," familiar in Confederate dispatches, had become "Edmund Kirby-Smith" by the late 1880's, the hyphenation appearing on his tombstone at Sewanee.

[4] Walter L. Fleming, *The Sequel to Appomattox* (New Haven, 1919), 2-10.

[5] E. Merton Coulter, *The South During Reconstruction* (Baton Rouge, 1947), 257.

[6] Walter L. Fleming, *Documentary History of Reconstruction*, 2 vols. (Cleveland, 1906), I, 9-24.

[7] General Philip Roddey, CSA, probably missed the last chance to destroy it in October, 1863, when on a cavalry raid to Tantalon, the south end of the tunnel, he merely blocked it as best he could with rocks, having no dynamite with him. Reynolds, "Sewanee and the Cumberland Plateau in the Civil War" (Sewanee Archives), 16.

[8] Noll, *History of the . . . Diocese of Tennessee,* 146 n. See also Tennessee Diocesan *Journal, 1867.*

[9] Louisiana Diocesan *Journal, 1866,* p. 22.

[10] M. Bowyer Stewart, *The Work of the Church in the South during the Period of Reconstruction* (Chicago, 1913), 28, 29.

[11] With Otey and Polk dead, the surviving members were Pise and Fairbanks, both present at the Tennessee convention, and L. N. Whittle and Daniel Griffin of Georgia. *Proceedings, 1861,* pp. 11, 12.

[12] Tennessee Diocesan *Journal, 1865,* p. 14.

[13] Vice-chancellors respectively, 1867-1872, 1872-1878, and 1879-1890.

[14] Stewart, *The Work of the Church in the South during the Period of Reconstruction,* 21-25.

[15] John H. Hopkins, Jr., to Hodgson, March 22, 1884 (Sewanee Archives).

[16] [Hopkins], *Life of the Late Right Rev. John Henry Hopkins,* 347.

[17] Thomas Atkinson, "Address of the Bishop," *Journal of the Fiftieth Annual Convention of the Protestant Episcopal Church in the State of North Carolina* (Fayetteville, 1867), 9. Hereafter cited as North Carolina Diocesan *Journal*. Titles vary.

[18] Guerry, *Men Who Made Sewanee,* 29.

[19] [Hopkins], *Life of the Late Right Rev. John Henry Hopkins,* 349.

[20] Charles T. Quintard, *An Address Delivered in St. Augustine's Chapel, Sewanee, Tenn., at the Meeting of the Board of Trustees of the University of the South, on Thursday, July 31st, 1890* (New York, 1890), 5.

[21] Quintard Family Bible (Sewanee Archives).

[22] William T. Payne [a nephew] to Charles T. Quintard, November 26, 1877, inserted in Quintard Diary, December 1, 1877.

[23] Guerry, *Men Who Made Sewanee,* 34-48.

[24] Virginia Orkney, "The Origin of the University of the South and Bishop Quintard's Part in Making it a Reality," unpublished honors paper, Mary Washington College, May 1, 1952 (Sewanee Archives).

[25] J. Berrien Lindsley to Quintard, May 31, 1879 (Sewanee Archives).

[26] These were in 1952 in the possession of the Bishop's great grandson, C. T. Quintard Wiggins, Jr., of New Orleans.

[27] Arthur H. Noll (ed.), *Doctor Quintard* (Sewanee, 1905), 4.

[28] The surviving thirty-six volumes are in the Sewanee Archives, thirty-three of them the gift of Charles Todd Quintard Wiggins, Jr. Lost are most of the Civil War diaries, from which the memoirs were written, and several volumes between 1865 and 1872 which Quintard used in preparing his address of 1890.

[29] Interview with David A. Shepherd, November 18, 1951.

[30] Newspaper clipping (n.p., n.d.), Quintard Diary, February 15, 1879. "George W. Quintard . . . lives in New York City, and owns a line of steamships and is very wealthy. . . . Edward . . . is now in Europe. There are four sisters who live in New York state."

[31] Interview with Queenie Woods Washington, January 26, 1952.

[32] Interview with Sarah Hodgson Torian, January 3, 1952.

[33] Quintard Diary, June 24, 1866.

[34] *Ibid.*, April 16, 1879.

[35] Thomas F. Gailor, "Address on July 27, 1899" (Sewanee Archives).

[36] Bishop Atkinson to Quintard, December 14, 1872, inserted in Quintard Diary: "I see by a newspaper that you purpose to visit this City . . . to procure aid for the University of the South. . . . It seems to me an act of questionable propriety for one Bishop to go into the diocese of another. . . . I cannot give my consent."

[37] "All" may have encompassed T. Frank Sevier, in whose removal Quintard was instrumental, John McCrady, who thought the Bishop's churchmanship too ritualistic, and possibly Caskie Harrison, who frequently was a dissenter. John McCrady Diary, May 9, 1878, *et passim* (in possession of his grandson, Vice-Chancellor Edward McCrady, Jr., Sewanee).

[38] Frank E. Vandiver, *Ploughshares Into Swords: Josiah Gorgas and Confederate Ordnance* (Austin, 1952), 304.

[39] Amelia Gorgas to William Gorgas, June 20, 1879, *ibid.*, 311, 312.

[40] Guerry, *Men Who Made Sewanee*, 48-54.

[41] Francis P. Fleming (ed.), *Memoirs of Florida*, 2 vols. (Atlanta, 1902), I, 526.

[42] William P. DuBose, "George R. Fairbanks," *Sewanee Review* (Sewanee), XIV (October, 1906), 502.

[43] James G. Glass, biographical sketch of Fairbanks in "Pamphlets," Fairbanks-Glass Papers (Sewanee Archives).

[44] Knight (ed.), *Library of Southern Literature*, XVI, 22; XV, 141.

[45] Quintard wrote in his Diary, May 15, 1877: "Ye non-election of Maj. Fairbanks as a deputy to ye Genl. Convention I greatly deplored, as he is ye best man in ye Diocese to represent ye Church in its great council." Fairbanks, however, was elected deputy by the diocese of Florida and at the general convention of 1904 he was the oldest delegate in point of service, having attended every triennial since the organization of Florida as a diocese in 1851 except the war convention of 1862. John B. Henneman, "George R. Fairbanks," *Sewanee Review*, XIV (October, 1906), 493-98.

[46] DuBose, "George R. Fairbanks," *Sewanee Review*, XIV (October, 1906), 502.

IDEAL REVISITED 111

[47] *Ibid.*, 503.

[48] Fairbanks, *History of the University of the South*, 72-75.

[49] Quintard-Fairbanks correspondence, *passim;* Fairbanks-Glass Papers (Sewanee Archives). Principal gift toward Otey Hall was a thousand dollars from "Mrs. Barnum of Baltimore." Guerry, *Men Who Made Sewanee*, 44.

[50] Fairbanks, *History of the University of the South*, 76.

[51] *Proceedings, 1867*, p. 25. Otey Hall burned in 1881 while occupied by John McCrady and his family.

[52] Tennessee Diocesan *Journal, 1866*, p. 89.

[53] *Ibid.*, 51.

[54] Quintard, "Convention Address," Tennessee Diocesan *Journal, 1866*, p. 51.

[55] Quintard Diary, June 5, 1866. Fulford was named for the Canadian bishop who was one of the consecrators of Quintard.

[56] The Fairbanks home in 1952 was occupied by his daughter, his granddaughter, and great granddaughters.

[57] Fairbanks, *History of the University of the South*, 81.

[58] Quintard Diary, June 8, 1866.

[59] *Ibid.*, September 3, 1866.

[60] Gonce to Underwood, January 1, 1923 (Sewanee Archives). University officials have never considered the 1866 class at the Winchester school to be the first class entering the University and no records of the school exist which include the title "University of the South." Only partial lists are available of students and faculty of the Sewanee Collegiate Institute and Sewanee College.

[61] H. H. Sneed to B. F. Finney, May 25, 1923.

[62] Bishop Gregg did not traverse the vast distance from Texas. Bishops Atkinson of North Carolina and Wilmer of Alabama were absent, Davis of South Carolina had gone blind, Rutledge of Florida died the next month, and Louisiana had no bishop. Clerical trustees present were Pise, Curtis, and William C. Williams of Georgia. Whittle and Fairbanks represented the laymen.

[63] Quintard Diary, October 12, 1866.

[64] Fairbanks, *History of the University of the South*, 80.

[65] "Kendal" was named for the English home of his ancestors. In Mississippi his headquarters were the home of his son, the Reverend Duncan C. Green of Canton. Burger, "William Mercer Green," *Historical Magazine of the Protestant Episcopal Church*, XIX (December, 1950), 340-54.

[66] In 1871 Green presented the portrait of Bishop J. S. Ravenscroft to the University. *Proceedings, 1871*, p. 28.

[67] William S. Perry, *The Bishops of the American Church* (New York, 1897), 111.

[68] Burger, "William Mercer Green," *Historical Magazine of the Protestant Episcopal Church*, XIX (December, 1950), 354.

[69] Green opened an ill-fated theological seminary at Dry Grove, Mississippi, in the 1870's which was wiped out by yellow fever in 1878. *Ibid.*, 352.

[70] *The Influence of Christianity Upon the Welfare of Nations* (Hillsborough, 1831) and *Memoir of Rt. Rev. James Hervey Otey, First Bishop of Tennessee* (New York, 1885) were his major works.

[71] Burger, "William Mercer Green," *Historical Magazine of the Protestant Episcopal Church,* XIX (December, 1950), 351.

[72] Had he lived two months longer, he would have been presiding bishop of the Episcopal Church. Morehouse (ed.), *The Living Church Annual, 1950,* pp. 51, 395, 396.

[73] Spencer Judd, "Miss Lily Green," Baker *et al.* (eds.), *Sewanee,* 135, 136.

[74] Franklin L. Knight, "Report of the Rector, Sewanee Divinity School," Tennessee Diocesan *Journal, 1867,* p. 71.

[75] Tennessee Diocesan *Journal, 1869,* p. 39.

[76] *Proceedings, 1867,* pp. 14-21. Unfortunately no Peabody money came to Sewanee until 1905.

[77] *Journal of the Proceedings of the Thirty-Sixth Annual Convention of the Protestant Episcopal Church in the Diocese of Alabama, May 8-11, 1867* (Mobile, 1867), 40. Hereafter cited as Alabama Diocesan *Journal.* Titles vary.

[78] *Proceedings, 1869,* p. 19.

[79] Fairbanks to J. H. Cornish, Fairbanks, *History of the University of the South,* 86-88.

[80] *Proceedings, 1867,* p. 26.

[81] Fairbanks, *History of the University of the South,* 86.

[82] James M. McAllister to Quintard, July 30, 1867 (Sewanee Archives).

[83] Fairbanks, *History of the University of the South,* 86.

[84] Charles P. McIlvaine to Rutherford B. Hayes, June 19, 1867 (Hayes Memorial Library, Fremont, Ohio, typescript in Sewanee Archives).

[85] Only Green and Quintard represented the bishops, Pise and Williams the clergy, but three new laymen joined Fairbanks and Whittle: F. C. Dunnington of Tennessee, Thomas E. B. Pegues of Mississippi, and Smith Simkins of Florida. *Proceedings, 1867,* p. 22.

[86] *Ibid.,* 23-25. The convention of the diocese of Tennessee in May had urged Quintard's attendance at the first Pan-Anglican conference of bishops at Lambeth Palace in England, September 24-27, 1867, to which bishops of the churches in communion with the Church of England were invited.

[87] The University of Alabama, virtually destroyed by Federal cavalry, received 46,000 acres of land from Congress in 1884 by way of restitution. It reopened for instruction in 1869. Denny, "Universities and Colleges of the South," Mitchell *et al.* (eds.), *South in the Building of the Nation,* X, 246. William and Mary also received reimbursement. *Ibid.,* 239.

[88] *Proceedings, 1867,* pp. 26-28. Not until 1953 was a University dormitory named Elliott Hall.

[89] Fairbanks, *History of the University of the South,* 93. The chapel was named for St. Augustine's School for boys at Canterbury, visited by Quintard in 1867. *Cap and Gown,* 1907, quoted by Baker *et al.* (eds.), *Sewanee,* 37. The school, St. Augustine's College for training young men for the mission field, had operated since 1848 in buildings of ancient St. Augustine's abbey. The ruins of the abbey had been bought for the Anglican Church by Quintard's friend, J. Beresford Hope. In 1952 the central theological college of the Anglican communion, St. Augustine's, was opened in the

IDEAL REVISITED 113

abbey buildings. James W. Kennedy, "St. Augustine's College Preserves Canterbury's Ancient Traditions," *Forth* (New York), Vol. CXVIII (October, 1953), 6-8, 28, 29.

[90] Fairbanks, *History of the University of the South*, 93.

[91] Quintard, *Address Delivered in St. Augustine's Chapel . . . July 31st, 1890*, p. 3. This document is not a reminiscence but was written by the bishop from his diary.

[92] Gailor, *Some Memories*, 79.

[93] C. T. Cantuar to Francis W. Tremlett, Ocober 15, 1867 (Sewanee Archives). The Archbishop thus declared a gift to Sewanee a testimonial of Anglican appreciation for the surprising appearance of so many American bishops at the conference. This fortunate turn in the soliciting approach was used adroitly by Quintard and Tremlett.

[94] Quintard, *Address Delivered in St. Augustine's Chapel . . . July 31st, 1890*, p. 9.

[95] "The Lord Archbishop of York, the Earl Carnarvon, the Viscount Cranborne, the Lord Bishop of Oxford, the Rev. Lord Charles Hervey, the Earl Nelson, the Lord John Manners, W. E. Gladstone, M.P., A. J. B. Beresford Hope, Esq., M.P., Rear Admiral Ryder, R.N., W. H. Pool Parew, Esq., the Dean of St. Andrews," and others. *Ibid.*, 6, 7.

[96] *Ibid.*, 7.

[97] Quintard Diary, October 12, 1867.

[98] Quintard, *Address Delivered in St. Augustine's Chapel . . . July 31st, 1890*, p. 11.

[99] Quintard Diary, November 1, 1867.

[100] Quintard to Fairbanks, December 26, 1867 (Sewanee Archives).

[101] Quintard Diary, November 23, 1867, *et passim*.

[102] Quintard, *Address Delivered in St. Augustine's Chapel . . . July 31st, 1890*, pp. 26, 27.

[103] Quintard, *Address Delivered in St. Augustine's Chapel . . . July 31st, 1890*, p. 10.

[104] Cameron Plummer to the writer, February 2, 1952.

[105] Quintard to Fairbanks, December 26, 1867 (Sewanee Archives).

[106] Matthew F. Maury to Quintard, January 4, 1868 (Sewanee Archives).

[107] Quintard to Fairbanks, March 12, 1868 (Sewanee Archives).

[108] Maury to Green and Maury to Quintard, both dated April 21, 1868 (Sewanee Archives).

[109] H. A. Marmer, "Matthew Fontaine Maury," Allen Johnson, Dumas Malone, and Harris E. Starr (eds.), *Dictionary of American Biography*, 21 vols. and index (New York, 1928-1944), XII, 428-31.

[110] Quintard Diary, January 5, 1868.

[111] Unidentified, undated clipping in Quintard Diary, inserted at January 10, 1868.

[112] Quintard Diary, April 14, 1868. The printed program for this service hangs on the south wall of All Saints' Chapel, Sewanee.

[113] *Ibid.*, April 12, 1868.

[114] Quintard to Richard H. Wilmer, January 8, 1868 (Sewanee Archives).

[115] Quintard Diary, February 9, 1868.

[116] *Ibid.,* April 15, 1868.

[117] Unidentified, undated clipping in Quintard Diary, April 25, 1876. Probably given to him on his second trip to England by Tremlett.

[118] Quintard to Fairbanks, March 12, 1868 (Sewanee Archives).

[119] *Proceedings, April 1, 1868,* p. 32.

[120] Quintard Diary, May 5-20, 1868.

[121] Quintard to Fairbanks, July 22, 1868 (Sewanee Archives).

CHAPTER THREE
OF WILL AND WAY
1868-1872

THE DECISION of the trustees to open the University with the scant funds collected by Quintard was a brave one. A faculty had to be brought together, the ornate curriculum of the statutes reduced to the essentials which the limited resources afforded, the students enrolled, and the community established in important matters like municipal government, elementary schools, and parish churches, and in minor matters like whitewashing the fences. Two factors were favorable. The circumstances of Reconstruction made available a faculty of a calibre ordinarily unobtainable as disfranchised participants in the war sought a livelihood.[1] The interruption by four years of war of the education of young men of the South made available potential matriculants at all levels of preparation.

The trustees next met at a provincial gathering in Savannah in April, 1868, where the consecration of Bishop John W. Beckwith of Georgia insured a good attendance.[2] It was decided to open the junior department[3] of the University of the South in September, and the executive committee[4] was authorized to secure a headmaster and teachers. The board voted to name the first permanent edifice Tremlett Hall in honor of the University's indefatigable English friend. The board ratified the actions of the two previous meetings, at which there had been no quorum, and reduced the minimum attendance requirement from fifteen to nine "provided each order [bishop, clergy, and laity] shall be represented."

The executive committee spent six busy months between April and September, 1868. Empowered to do whatever was necessary, it proceeded with commendable dispatch. Green and Fairbanks carried the brunt of the work until Quintard returned in the latter part of May. On April 3, at the same time that Maury was invited to accept the vice-chancellorship, the Reverend J. H. Coit of New Hampshire was named rector of the junior department and the Reverend Hall Harrison elected professor of classics. Both declined. G. Berkeley Green, son of the chancellor and a graduate of the University of Mississippi, was pressed into service as instructor in mathematics. Green entered the Confederate army in May, 1861, with a group of his classmates. He was wounded and captured at Gettysburg and imprisoned at Fort Delaware until the close of the war. After he left Sewanee, he was a banker in Vicksburg. He died in 1893.[5]

The executive committee offered the post of headmaster of the junior department to General Josiah Gorgas[6] at a salary of $2,500 and a dwelling.[7] Down in Brierfield, Alabama, the Confederacy's brilliant chief of ordnance had become convinced by June, 1868, that he could not continue to operate the foundry which he and friends bought in 1866.[8] He was virtually penniless.[9] Gorgas' appointment was confirmed on June 15. He accepted the following month but did not move to Sewanee until a year later. During the winter he began to have misgivings and decided not to come to Sewanee after all. Quintard prevailed on him to reconsider. "Nothing should be said on ye Mountain of General Gorgas' resignation until I hear from him again."[10]

JOSIAH GORGAS

Gorgas was born at Running Pumps, Pennsylvania, on July 1, 1818, the delicate youngest of ten children. At seventeen, with what education the family circumstances allowed, he went to live with a sister in Lyons, New York. Hard work in a law office, the influence of his employer, and his burning desire for more education combined to win for him an appointment to the Military Academy in 1837.[11] He chose a career in ordnance and served in Mexico. He married the accomplished and charming Amelia, second daughter of Governor John Gayle of Alabama.[12] They had met at Mount Vernon, she a fugitive from yellow fever in Mobile.[13] When Amelia came to Sewanee, she brought a social grace nurtured in a governor's mansion, in Washington, where her father had been a member of Congress, and in a series of army posts at which she and Josiah were stationed during his "old army" and Confederate careers. Her talent as hostess and his grave and punctilious courtesy left their mark on Sewanee. "Every officer, professor, stranger was saluted; every lady was greeted with a lifted cap."[14]

He appeared a fortunate choice for headmaster. Although his reputation was exceeded by that of dozens of field officers,[15] a few men in high places knew that, probably next to Lee himself, Gorgas had contributed more to Confederate arms than anyone else.[16] He was recommended most highly. General W. S. Walker, fellow soldier of Mexican War days, General John B. Gordon, division commander under Lee, Lee himself, Jefferson Davis, Confederate Navy Secretary Stephen R. Mallory, and General William J. Hardee were among those giving warm endorsement.[17] Quintard had written, "General [Francis A.] Shoup . . . speaks in ye most unqualified terms of General Gorgas, and I do think he will accept ye position. He is evidently ye man we need."[18] A university without faculty or students, classrooms or curriculum, would need the services of the "best organizing member of the Confederate Department of War."[19] A Sewanee faculty member of the 1870's paid tribute to the "clear head, the wise spirit and temper, and the strong hand" of Gorgas in the transition from military school to university which took place at Sewanee in those years. The general was elected vice-chancellor in 1872 and served through six years of increasing financial stringency for the institution. He resigned in 1878 at the request of the trustees and was president of the University of Alabama until his last illness began in 1879. He died in 1883.

The headmastership should not be confused with the vice-chancellorship. The executive committee was still actively trying to find a vice-chancellor. In September, acting upon the rumor that he was unhappy at Washington College,[20] the committee offered the post to Robert E. Lee. With characteristic grace he declined.[21] Quintard had regularly offered his resignation but at this turn of events he was persuaded to continue as vice-chancellor until a successor could be found.

Construction and beautification went on during the summer at Sewanee. Quintard wrote to Fairbanks: "I do beg you, my dear Major, to have ye undergrowth cut out in front of your house. It will give that quarter such a *civilized* look. And with whitewashed fences, we shall be able to show a vast advance in morals as well."[22] By August 12 when twelve trustees [23] met at Sewanee, the imminent opening of the institution was a certainty. Gorgas sat with the board. There was much deliberation, little action. Financial plans were the principal concern of the trustees.

A TIME DISCONSOLATE

From the vantage point of the years, the scene appears pathetic. It is not as difficult to understand why the University in those years had little support as it is to understand why it had any support at all. From the donor's point of view, money was being asked for something physically isolated. An incipient urban school or at least its prospective location could be seen physically. It would make a direct economic return to the community. Whatever investment was made in it would remain as a civic asset even if the school itself were unsuccessful. But money given to an enterprise on a wild mountaintop was money gone. If the school failed, the investment would be irretrievable.

Still hopeful, the trustees worked out a four-point approach to the problem of fund-raising. First, they would ask all parishes, with bishops approving, for a "University Offering" the third Sunday in Advent (shortly before Christmas).[24] Next, trustees were asked to obtain individual subscriptions of $20 per annum for five years, payable on Easter Monday, for the support of the theological program.[25] Third, Bishops Young and Beckwith were asked to solicit funds in the North. Finally, Bishops Quintard and Wilmer of Louisiana were asked to solicit in the South. Quintard alone was moderately successful.[26]

When the University of the South opened in 1868, it depended for support almost entirely on the Episcopal churches of the ten participating dioceses, adding only whatever *lagniappe* might be forthcoming from England, from the North, and from non-Episcopalians. Where were these southern churches and how many of them were there? In order of number of clergy, the southern dioceses were as follows:

Diocese	Clergy	Bishop
South Carolina	72	Thomas F. Davis
North Carolina	51	Thomas Atkinson
Louisiana	37	Joseph P. B. Wilmer
Alabama	31	Richard H. Wilmer
Georgia	27	John W. Beckwith
Mississippi	27	William M. Green
Tennessee	27	Charles T. Quintard
Texas	20	Alexander Gregg
Florida	10	J. Freeman Young
Arkansas	10	Henry C. Lay
Total	312	

None of the deep southern dioceses was as large as Virginia, which under Bishop John Johns and his coadjutor Francis M. Whittle had 117 clergy. Kentucky under Bishop Benjamin B. Smith and Assistant Bishop George D. Cummins had 37 clergy.[27] There were 46 bishops, 2,736 clergy, and 194,692 communicants in the 34 dioceses of the United States. The total contribution to the Episcopal Church in the nation in that year was $4,457,888.28.[28] Theoretically Sewanee could call on 10 bishops and 312 clergymen to assist in procuring students, faculty, and money. As events developed, three bishops were consistently helpful, and they and about a dozen clergy and a half-dozen laymen carried the load with help from the resident faculty and staff.

Dark as conditions were at Sewanee as opening day drew near, they appeared more promising when examined in the general context of education in the South. William and Mary had been damaged by the 5th Pennsylvania Cavalry during the Civil War.[29] Though repairs had been made, its main college building was still unfinished and the board of visitors voted to continue the suspension of the collegiate department.[30] There were three faculty members and in two years only 53 students matriculated.[31] The University of Alabama had hardly begun to repair the almost complete destruction of its campus before it was beset with political controversies.[32] At Chapel Hill, the University of North Carolina, physically unharmed by the war, had five faculty members and 105 students in 1868.[33] Taken over that year by a board composed principally of partisan Republicans, the university was closed from 1870 until 1875.[34] South Carolina College was revived as the University of South Carolina in 1865, but it would suffer from reorganization by the legislature in 1869 and the controversy resulting from the enrollment of Negro students and the importation of a new faculty.[35] In Louisiana the legislature cut off funds because the state university would not admit Negroes.[36]

The private colleges of the South, while sharing the poverty of the region, were less affected by political measures than were the state universities. At Washington College in Lexington, Virginia, Robert E. Lee was proving that a man sufficiently great can do anything well. The advertisement of that institution was difficult to resist.

> Faculty, R. E. Lee, President, with professors of Latin, Greek, Mathematics, Modern Languages, Moral Philosophy, History, English Language and Literature, Applied Mathematics, Natural Philosophy, Chemistry, Law and Equity . . . also professional diplomas of Civil Engineer, Mining Engineer. Full corps of assistant professors. All necessary expenses need not exceed $325.[37]

In the North, Yale had a faculty of 53 administering to a student body of 699.[38] It was awarding about 100 degrees a year. Its library contained some 50,000 volumes. It had one postwar building, the Art School, finished in 1866. Annual tuition was $60.[39] Princeton that year had a faculty of 17 and 3 visiting lecturers teaching 280 students.[40] Its full professors received $2,100 plus rent. The Princeton library contained 14,000 volumes.[41] At Harvard 71 faculty members taught 1,050 students.[42]

If the northern educational façade was more prepossessing than the southern, it hid an almost equally rickety structure. There was little graduate work and almost no research in the country.[43] In 1868 Harvard offered graduate work only in science. At Yale and Columbia professors taught as many as four different subjects. The worn-out recitation method dulled both students and teachers who quarantined themselves from each other outside the classroom. Medical instruction was a disgrace and engineering, despite isolated improvement at new technical schools, was little better. Harvard led in combatting the prevailing low entrance requirements and Sewanee found its solution by registering deficient matriculants in its grammar school. A full offering of remedial courses was next door.

By 1868 several trends were discernible which would alter the course of American higher education. Reaction against religion was underway. Darwinism was beginning to be digested. Sewanee would resist secularization, would take an early lead in teaching science, and would join Princeton's James McCosh in his contention that Genesis and geology were compatible.[44]

SCHOOL BEGINS

The University of the South opened its first session on September 18 with solemn services conducted by two bishops. Three Tennessee clergy joined in the ceremonies. "We had four professors [45] and nine students," Quintard recorded, "and as the procession entered the modest little chapel, I stepped aside to allow the plasterer to pass out with his mortar board and trowel."[46]

Knight was the first of the teaching personnel with the title of acting chaplain and instructor in Greek and Latin. He resigned after the first term and so did the mathematics instructor, Berkeley Green.

Dr. Robert Dabney of Virginia was the only faculty member of that first term who remained for the organization of the University proper in 1870. He was on hand for the opening of the school and served as acting headmaster until the arrival of Gorgas the next summer.[47] He was typical of the personnel sought at the start by the executive committee. He was a native of Powhatan County, Virginia. He graduated at Hampden-Sydney in 1851, received his master's degree and doctorate in law at the University of Virginia, where he came under the influence of Professor William H. McGuffey.[48] As a member of the Virginia legislature, he was considered an authority on constitutional history and interpretation. He lost his personal fortune during the war. He became instructor in metaphysics and English literature at Sewanee at thirty-six and taught there until he died of pneumonia seven years later. Dabney was a teacher unusually beloved by his students and neighbors.[49] He gave the name Powhatan to the residence later occupied by General E. Kirby-Smith and then he and his family lived in what was later known as the "Redwood House" near the present military academy.[50] He became Sewanee's first fully accredited ghost, shuffling along in his carpet slippers with no less personages than Major E. A. Green, commandant of the military battalion, and headmaster (later bishop) Charles Beckwith.[51]

The first student to matriculate was Charles Massey Fairbanks, son of the Major. Another of the first nine students was Franklin W. Knight, son of the acting chaplain. Three were Florida boys sent by the reverend trustee J. Jackson Scott, the Dorr brothers, Hawkes Barkley and C. Hawkes, and James Edwin Creary, all of Milton. The other students were Joseph C. Nash of Nashville and R. W. Sherwood of Clarksville, Tennessee, Nicholas J. Cruger of Albany, Georgia, and John Adair Skipwith of New Orleans, stepson of Bishop Polk's daughter.[52] All apparently came on personal solicitation, there having been no catalogue or newspaper advertisement printed. The boys ranged in age from Skipwith and Cruger, who were 12 and 13 respectively, to two who were 19. They lived with their parents or boarded at Otey Hall under the eye of the matron, Mrs. Sarah Eliza Wright Cotten, who had come to Sewanee in the spring of 1867. During the first term which ended in December, five additional students enrolled,[53] but one did no class work until the next term.

Classes were at the college preparatory level. The chapel having been extended thirty-two feet, its two side rooms were used for recitation and study. South Wing, just about completed, Tremlett Hall, and Powhatan Hall, under construction, were not needed until the second term began after the first winter vacation.[54] The college community then consisted of the log houses of Quintard and Fairbanks, the "mansion"[55] of Bishop Green, and the dwelling of Dr. Knight. Down a slight hill a half mile away, the "village" consisted of the home of the postmaster, W. H. Tomlinson, the freight depot which also housed the Tomlinson store, two cabins, and nothing more. The total population was fifty or sixty.[56]

Shortly after the first term began, the trustees met for a third time that year between general convention sessions in New York, October 13-21. The ten Sewanee bishops were together for the first time. With five clergymen and six laymen, the best attendance was recorded since the laying of the cornerstone. Still hopeful of attracting Kentucky, the trus-

Of Will and Way

tees authorized the Vice-Chancellor to seek participation of other dioceses. They formally designated Dr. Tremlett commissary of the University of the South in England and approved a joint address restating the claims of the University, reporting progress, and appealing for funds and students.[57]

The winter of 1868-1869 may well have been the loneliest vacation in the history of the University. Probably never during the winter did columns of smoke issue at one time from more than half of the eight or ten scattered buildings. Fairbanks and his family remained on the mountain. The weather was unpropitious for building: when there was no snow and ice, there was fog and rain. Even with the trees bare of leaves it was impossible to see all the way from Fairbanks' house at one end of University Avenue to Bishop Green's at the other, for there was a heavy growth of underbrush except around each building.[58] Quintard and Green came and went. Sunday services were held regularly in the little chapel, with Knight, Quintard, or Green in charge, but otherwise it was a time for writing letters and reflecting on what was to be done.

From Memphis Bishop Quintard wrote: "A great number of people have visited me, and among them Gen. Joseph E. Johnston ... my first choice for ye vice-chancellorship. ... I proposed his name when Bishop Elliott threw ye burden on me (1865). I still think he would fill our requirements, but ye proposition must come from ye malcontents in ye Episcopate."[59] Little by little, the *impedimenta* of learning assembled. Quintard wrote again: "I sent today two maps to be hung in ye schoolroom and have a copy of ye Latin Vulgate 300 yrs old,"[60] and "I enclosed you this morning a draft for $250. I now enclose one for $200. ... I trust this will relieve ye pressure."[61] The executive committee thanked former trustee Daniel Griffin for "a very large terrestrial globe."[62]

SECOND TERM BRINGS OPTIMISM

On February 10, Ash Wednesday, the second term of the junior department opened with ceremony.[63] On hand or arriving shortly afterward were Bishops Green and Quintard, Instructors Knight, Green, and Dabney, Major Fairbanks, five visiting Tennessee clergy, and about thirty students. At least six of the original thirteen students re-enrolled.

Lists of students who matriculated in 1868, 1869, and 1870 are available, but exactly when they entered and withdrew is not known.[64] By May, when Fairbanks reported to the annual convention of the diocese of Tennessee, there were about fifty.[65] By November, when time came for the winter vacation, eighty-six new students had matriculated.[66] Nineteen came from Georgia, seventeen from Alabama, thirteen from Tennessee, eleven from Florida, ten from Texas, five from Mississippi, four from Arkansas, two from Louisiana, and one each from North Carolina, Kentucky, Missouri, Virginia, and Illinois. During the Lent term of 1869 the executive committee's recommendation on dress was carried into effect and students wore "a grey sack coat, grey pants with black stripes."[67] Total charges for the year were $300 plus a matriculation fee of $10.[68] Payments were made three months in advance to Fairbanks, acting treasurer.[69]

All was not serene among the staff that year if a letter signed "Robert" can be believed.

> [I am] among . . . rebels . . . they are only overcome and not subdued. . . . In *Spirit, language, conduct, feeling,* in all essential things they are *rebels* as really today as when the *Arch-traitor* Jeff Davis was on the *throne* of their bogus Confederacy. The com[m]on *Cognomen* of all Northerners is "Northern Infidels," "Mercenary Vandals," "Scum of the Earth" etc. etc. These are our beautiful titles and you can judge how delightful a situation a man with a *true, loyal* heart beating in his bosom must be in among such a people. They are Bombastic, ignorant, lazy & defiant, and the women are the very personification of His Satanic Majesty. . . . I was urged in New York to take the situation of Musical instructor in a boys school titled with the big sounding name of University of the South—a bigger humbug for such a name was never known, and I must say that I am not happy in it, and it is exceeding doubtful if I remain longer than a few months.[70]

Sectional feeling apparently did not extend to the executive committee, for in February the Reverend J. A. Bolles, D.D., of Boston, was invited to join the theological department. He, like Coit and Hall Harrison, declined without seeing the University.

In the late spring, with the arrival of Bishop Young of Florida, the first musical training recorded in the University annals began. The Bishop volunteered to coach the choir and take charge of the musical

OF WILL AND WAY 125

services. The Chancellor boasted late in the summer, "At no institution of like character . . . can there be found a set of youths better trained in the chants and anthems of our . . . worship."[71]

INSTRUCTION AND DISCIPLINE

Instruction, given at levels varying with the preparation of the student, was on a personal basis. There was no pretense that advanced college work was being done, and no one in school in 1869 was ready for a degree four years later. With an assortment of bishops on the periphery, there was an attitude of seriousness. General Gorgas let it be known that "the study hours are hours of *work* . . . those who will not work in their rooms must do so at the chapel under the eye of the master."[72] There may have been a little pulling in opposite academic directions with the staunch classicists Dabney and Knight, and later Harrison, Elliott, and DuBose on one side and the West Pointers on the other. Gorgas said: "We must try to satisfy in some degree the tendency to the *practical* which is now so general—It is possible we have too many Latin and Greek authors on our list."[73] The apprehension of the General was justified, for by 1890 the classicists had routed the militarists. In the compromise, drilling and uniforms went to the grammar school, which in 1908 became Sewanee Military Academy.

At first the younger boys were assigned indiscriminately to Otey, South Wing, and newly finished Tremlett Hall. A separate discipline was established in July in which the students who were doing some college work were exempted from certain rules governing the grammar school.[74] By August it was decided to teach the younger boys in separate buildings.[75] On the recommendation of Gorgas and Dabney, the executive committee organized the grammar school as a distinct department with the master in control of all forms of discipline except dismissal. His objectives would be college preparatory work, texts would be selected in consultation with the faculty of the junior department, but, for all other purposes of administration, the master was responsible only to the vice-chancellor.[76]

Colonel T. Frank Sevier was appointed master of the grammar school. He was an important figure in the community for the next eight years. He served as proctor of the University [77] and was responsible for student discipline. He was peace officer for the domain, with the title of marshal. With the organization of a student drill corps, he became commandant. For a time he was acting professor of commerce. He was distantly related to John Sevier, hero of King's Mountain and first governor of Tennessee.[78] He served through the Civil War in the regiment to which Quintard had been principally attached. He was fearless in dealing with occasional lawbreakers of the community,[79] and brought to the University a rigid military discipline which by 1875 was under criticism by a minority group of faculty members. At the time of his resignation in 1877, Quintard wrote: "Another most important change has been effected by ye resignation of Col. Sevier, ye Proctor. He would have been dismissed had not his resignation been presented to ye Board."[80]

SAME GOAL BUT SLOWER PACE

A meeting of the trustees, the first to be held at Sewanee after the opening of the University, convened August 11-16, 1869, with twenty-two present, the most since the laying of the cornerstone nine years before. Every diocese was represented, seven by bishops. Quintard's report as vice-chancellor showed careful attention to the constitution and to the prewar planning.[81] There would be no deviation from the plans of the founders but the pace would be slower. He was optimistic over academic achievement. "Having grown from nine to ten times nine, and presenting a regular organized system, with which for order, decorum, diligence, well behavior and gentlemanly bearing of its members, we challenge comparison." He was optimistic over financial prospects. "Last year the cotton crop of the Southern States sold for two hundred and fifty millions. . . . We may hope that there are many who are sufficiently alive to the educational interests of the South, to contribute liberally toward the full development of the University."[82] Bishop Quintard cited recent gifts: "Mrs. Cyrus Mason, of New York, . . . stone font . . . Mr. Sharp, of New York, a handsome stained glass window . . . Messrs. Masury and Whiton . . . three hundred pounds of paint . . . Messrs. Pott and Amory's liberal contribution of books. . . . Mrs. Mary Clarke . . . one hundred ten pounds sterling, as the nucleus of a Mis-

OF WILL AND WAY 127

sionary Scholarship." Other income included receipts from England for the past year, $8,711.56; collections in the South by Bishop Quintard, $1,388.50; church offerings, $272.51; donations collected by a Baltimore clergyman, $106.75; and leases, $299.00.[83]

Fairbanks' report as commissioner of buildings and lands encouraged leasing lots to "suitable church families . . . to make their residence here, and erect upon their own account, boarding houses for the . . . students."[84] He listed immediate needs as a wooden study hall, twenty by forty, which could be built for $700 in sixty days, and a steam laundry and mangle with bathing rooms attached. He hoped that a $30,000 stone building could be started at once, to be paid for as the construction progressed, about $10,000 per year. He thought that a hotel erected at Sewanee would attract many vacationers going to cool places in the summer. The last two hopes, temporarily, were vain.

Not all trustees shared the determination of Quintard and Fairbanks to keep ever in view the now distant vision of the founders. Less vigorous adherents of the University project shared in varying degrees the comfortable rationalization expressed by the Bishop of Louisiana.

> There will be little cause to lament the change in its fortunes if the effect will be to substitute a silent steady growth, for a sudden, untried maturity. Commencing with a few scholars, discipline will be more readily enforced, the early traditions of the place will assume a more healthful tone, rival institutions will be disarmed of jealousy and opposition, the mistakes and errors inseparable from all incipient institutions will be circumscribed and more easily rectified, and the public confidence being fairly earned rather than purchased, will prove a sure and lasting boon of more value than the more ample endowment from public or private munificence.[85]

No more subtle reasoning could be employed for insuring the collapse of all but dribbling financial help from Louisiana. The record, alas, sustains this judgment. By his successor's evaluation, Polk's original accomplishment was at best a sturdy step in the wrong direction.

HOLLOW FISCAL STRUCTURE

The finance committee's statement presented from Fairbanks' figures was unrealistic. Assets were listed at $160,637. The domain was valued at $100,000, its improvements at $21,450, and the remaining $39,187 included miscellaneous real estate, bonds, and rail securities, all at their prewar valuations. A forced sale of those assets beyond the domain and its improvements might bring $10,000.[86] Liabilities were listed at $10,899. It was bad to be bankrupt but worse not to know it. Or was it better? Had the true condition been understood, had the next few years been foreseen, even those stout-hearted men might have surrendered.

The board concerned itself with financial problems.[87] Total student fees for the first term in 1869 had come to $3,165, enough to pay two teachers. This amount was equivalent to the income from about twenty students paying in advance for a half year. Some were not paying the full fee; some were attending on credit. Board and lodging, but not tuition, of "several young men" was being paid by the Society for the Increase of the Ministry.[88] The executive committee directed at the opening of the term that half tuition be charged the first ten sons of clergymen who should apply.[89] The board voted to renew effort on the Advent offering plan by sending a printed appeal to the parishes. The Reverend Owen P. Thackara of Florida was elected agent to solicit the ten dioceses for cash subscriptions or notes like those Polk had sought, with interest to be paid annually by donors. Thackara's efforts proved disappointing. Fairbanks was relieved of his duties as treasurer, retained as commissioner of buildings and lands at $1,000 per year, and charged with the special responsibility of recovering what he could from the Louisiana prewar pledges. H. M. Anderson, M.D., trustee from Rome, Georgia, whose wife was Mrs. Quintard's sister,[90] was named general treasurer. Sevier became resident bursar to collect fees until the new treasurer arrived.

The board conferred the first honorary degree of the University upon Tremlett, still soliciting abroad. At Quintard's suggestion the degree was designated Doctor of Civil Law, after Oxford's custom, and according to him, unique at that time in American universities.[91] The trustees offered prizes for student achievement, and a prize for gentlemanly deportment was set up by an unnamed Louisianian.

The trustees again left wide powers in the hands of the executive committee now composed of only Quintard and Gorgas. The authority

OF WILL AND WAY

was not left unused. The committee directed Fairbanks to erect signboards to show exactly where the buildings in the Hopkins plans were to be placed. It directed that the chaplain wear an academic hood with his vestments and that professors wear cap and gown when on duty.[92]

FACULTY ENLARGED

In September the executive committee offered the post of resident physician and instructor in chemistry to twenty-eight year old John Barnwell Elliott, M.D., who came to Sewanee and began work the month of his election. Of the fourteen men who held faculty status in the first ten years of the University's operation, he was one of the most influential. After he severed his connection with Sewanee in 1885, he was awarded one of the two honorary doctorates of philosophy in the University's history.[93] Fairbanks thought hardly anyone had accomplished as much to raise standards and to enlist the enthusiasm of the students.[94]

Elliott, the third son of the late Bishop of Georgia, attended South Carolina College before the war, served as lieutenant in the Confederacy, and in 1868 graduated first in his class at South Carolina Medical College in Charleston. His brother Robert Woodward Barnwell Elliott in 1874 became first bishop of West Texas and trustee of the University. When Dabney died in 1876, Dr. Elliott became senior professor and when Gorgas left Sewanee in 1878, he served a year as acting vice-chancellor.

When he died in 1921 after a brilliant career at Tulane Medical School,[95] he left some notes which were printed posthumously by one of his seven children, Huger.[96] In these notes he classified the thinkers to whom he was most indebted: Immanuel Kant, Johann Fichte, Georg Hegel, and others. He discussed philosophical concepts of space, time, and cognition, and concluded, "We may truly say that modern science from the side of physical research has restored to the world the doctrine of the Immanence of God in his Creation."[97] One of Elliott's students, years later, remembered him as the wisest teacher he ever had.[98]

Before the close of 1869 the executive committee made three more appointments. Quintard and Gorgas named the Reverend Francis A.

Juny to teach modern languages. Native of France and alumnus of Louvain,[99] this Episcopal clergyman was an accomplished linguist. His four sons helped swell the rolls of the grammar school and junior department for the two years that he remained at Sewanee before going to the University of Mississippi in 1872.

Much more important was the appointment of Francis Asbury Shoup as mathematics instructor and acting chaplain. Shoup was born in Indiana and graduated from West Point shortly before the war. He resigned his commission because of southern sympathies [100] and moved to St. Augustine to practice law. In 1861 he was commissioned major and rose to the rank of brigadier general, serving on the staffs of Bragg and Joseph E. Johnston.[101] During the war he knew Polk and Quintard and was baptized on the battlefield by Bishop Elliott.[102] After the war he taught mathematics at the University of Mississippi, entered the Episcopal ministry, and joined the Sewanee staff in 1870. Here he married Esther Elliott, daughter of the University's third chancellor. One of his students described him as "Handsome as Plato, indolent, until aroused to mental coruscation, mathematician, engineer, Confederate general, and last metaphysician."[103] In 1875 he left Sewanee to engage in parish work. He remained for a time in Waterford, New York, and while there interested an Episcopal family in giving the University in the late 1880's its most famous architectural landmark, Breslin Tower, modeled after Magdalen Tower at Oxford. Shoup returned to Sewanee in 1883 and continued intermittently on the faculty until his death in 1896. An idea of his versatility may be gained from the titles of four books written by him: *Infantry Tactics* (Little Rock, 1862); *Artillery Division Drill* (Atlanta, 1864); *Elements of Algebra* (New York, 1874); and *Mechanism and Personality* (Boston, 1888).

The third faculty appointment was also of a high order. Caskie Harrison was a student at Cambridge when Quintard visited England. The two dined together [104] and talked with Maury about the University. Harrison was invited by the executive committee to teach Latin and Greek. The youthful Virginian was described by contemporaries as handsome and charming, "remarkable in every way."[105] For twelve years he was a "severe but brilliant teacher."[106] In controversy he always took the side of higher academic standards and less military discipline.

His chair of classics was "long ... the most important in the university; a natural result of church control and of the avowed following of English traditions."[107] His translation of the first book of the Horatian odes into English verse [108] received tolerably good reviews.[109] He resigned in 1882 and established a successful classical preparatory school in Brooklyn, where he died in 1902.[110]

Construction continued during the winter vacation of 1869-1870. Gorgas' genius for detail early became evident. On a trip home to Brierfield he wrote Sevier: "What about the new grammar school? Any lumber yet on hand for it? I want the work to be done by contract on specifications and a *belfry* for the bell. Don't forget that. I think a great deal about that bell and hope no accident will befall it."[111]

ACADEMIC EVALUATION

Academically, 1870 was a key year. When the Lent term opened, astonished authorities counted 95 new students for a total enrollment of 125, the largest increase and the largest number of new matriculants in the first twenty-five years of the University's history. New accommodations were rushed to completion—four dormitories and eight single-room cottages called Oxford Court and located on University Avenue across from Bishop Green's. A wooden school building was erected on the north side of the chapel at a cost of $1,250. Bishop Gregg and Bishop Young erected with funds given by themselves and their friends a "neat library building built of wood." In it was placed the "considerable library ... accumulated by gifts from England, [Reverend] Dr. Carder, and others."[112] There were 4,000 volumes in 1872.

By contemporary southern standards, the faculty was formidable. General Gorgas taught engineering and physics; General Shoup taught mathematics and served as chaplain; Caskie Harrison taught Greek and Latin; Juny offered French, German, and Spanish; Dabney taught English literature and metaphysics; and Elliott taught chemistry. In the grammar school, tutors John Locke Cooper, who doubled as registrar, and the Reverend Lucian Holmes, assisted Sevier. The fifty students doing college work received adequate instruction; the younger boys did not fare quite so well.

Supporting the formal teaching staff was a small but notable community. The two resident bishops, Green and Quintard, established close relations with the students. During the summer they were joined by a third bishop, Alexander Gregg of Texas, who was a vital part of the Sewanee scene from the founding of the University at Lookout Mountain until his death in 1893. He built a home near Bishop Green's,[113] and spent the greater part of twenty-five summers there. He was the first elected chancellor of the University, succeeding Bishop Green upon his death in 1887.

Gregg was born in 1819 at Society Hill, South Carolina, the son of the remarkable and eccentric David Gregg. At Winnsboro Academy the young descendant of clan McGregor acquired a reputation for diligence. His mother's approval prevailing over his father's suspicion, he attended South Carolina College, came under the influence of Chaplain Stephen Elliott, and graduated first in his class in 1838 at the age of nineteen. Against the advice of his father, who preferred for him a mercantile career, Gregg studied law, was admitted to the bar in 1841, and in the same year married dark-eyed Charlotte Wilson Kollock, grandniece of Governor John Lyde Wilson of South Carolina.[114] Her Episcopal preference so completely prevailed over his Baptist background that in April, 1843, he experienced one of the sudden conversions characteristic of the "great revival" period and determined to become a candidate for the ministry. He was ordained in 1846 and took the aristocratic St. David's Parish, Cheraw, in the heyday of the planter civilization. By 1859, when he was elected bishop of Texas, he had a far-flung reputation for conscientiousness. Devotion to the University became a conspicuous factor in Gregg's life.[115] He continually brought Sewanee to the attention of his parishes with the result that Texas sent more students than any other state except Tennessee and Mississippi and almost every year in the 1870's contributed more to the University than any other diocese.[116] Indeed, an evaluation of effort for the University in this most remote of the owning dioceses shows that the Sewanee plan of diocesan sponsorship was sound. Had half of the dioceses matched the record of Texas, Sewanee might well have had a secure financial position. Instead, the comfortable words of Bishop Wilmer were distressingly

OF WILL AND WAY

prophetic and Sewanee's claim to distinction had to be made in other realms than those of material success.

REPORT TO A CONSTITUENCY

Gorgas and Fairbanks represented the University at the annual convention of the diocese of Tennessee on May 11, 1870. Their encouraging report estimated that upwards of two hundred applications could be expected for the next year and stated that accommodations were a pressing problem. They made a disturbingly naive comment that the University could look forward to supporting itself from student fees. This state has been attained only rarely by educational institutions before or since and certainly was not a condition contemplated by the founders. Before many months had passed, the University's administrators saw that a university is, almost by definition, a deficit operation. Gorgas and Fairbanks asked for five-year subscriptions of $100 to $500.[117] They were factual in their report, but the diocesan committee on educational institutions rhapsodized, "The University... has leaped, as it were, by a single bound, from a mere germ into vigor and high promise."[118] Three of the six signers of this report were Jefferson Davis, Jacob Thompson, and Richard S. Ewell, respectively president, legislator, and lieutenant general in the Confederacy. Later the same month Bishop J. P. B. Wilmer of Louisiana made a brief appeal for the University in an address to his annual convention.[119]

Two trustees thought that the ninth postwar meeting of the board, held July 11-16, 1870, with a record attendance of twenty-four, was probably more important than any since the founding of the University.[120] "The success of this institution has been singularly flattering," they reported to their diocesan convention. Bishop Green recalled in the address of the chancellor that "nearly twenty years had passed before that now noble Institution—the 'University of Virginia' could boast a hundred pupils."[121] Quintard and Gorgas were continued as the executive committee. Quintard presented his resignation as vice-chancellor but was induced to continue.

Construction was underway on all sides. Existing accommodations would care for 190 students.[122] Thirty-nine leases had been granted in the previous year and more applications were in the offing. Unfortunately the hotel which Fairbanks and Quintard had envisioned at Green's View failed to materialize when the prospective builder let his lease lapse. The most pressing needs of the University were declared to be an additional school building, $1,500; headmaster's residence, $2,500; laundry, $1,000; bathing rooms, $300; dormitory, $1,250; infirmary, $800; bakery, $300; and temporary water closets, $100.[123] Fairbanks was authorized to build as money came in.

THE FIRST BEQUEST

Financial matters again absorbed much of the trustees' attention. The first legacy to the University was announced, $1,000 from the estate of Mrs. Frances T. D. Taylor of Baltimore, "and she a stranger."[124] Raising funds by mathematical computation, a favorite device of tyros in the business, was not neglected. This time each of the ten dioceses was to obtain one hundred subscriptions of $100 each.[125] The only implementation of this plan was the election of Bishops Quintard and R. H. Wilmer commissioners for endowment.[126] The Reverend Mr. Thackara, whose services as fund agent were discontinued, reported collections of $6,143.26, but when salary and expenses were deducted, the University received only $3,940.81.[127] Fairbanks predicted that only a fractional part of the remaining $20,215.44 in Louisiana securities would materialize. He had made a careful survey and found almost all the original donors well disposed toward the University but bankrupt or poverty-stricken. Many had died insolvent. Two pieces of property worth a few thousand dollars might be salvageable. The most favorable fiscal news given the trustees was that the income from the Lent term, $10,200, had exceeded expenses by $737.[128]

One fact was clearly emerging in the financial picture—namely, that the founders' idea of collecting and investing money to be held in the dioceses for the University was being superseded by the direct appeal of the University to parishes and individuals. In 1871 Charles T. Pollard of Alabama, one of the original trustees, sent a request to the diocesan convention that "the shares of ... Railroad stock donated by him to the University of the South and now held by the treasurer of the diocese

... be sold and the proceeds ... remitted to the treasurer of the University to be used in the erection of buildings."[129]

FROM SCHOOL TO COLLEGE

The formal organization of the University into the schools contemplated by the prewar statutes was authorized by the board, although Fairbanks and other trustees thought this action premature in view of the uncertain financial stability of the institution.[130] Seven schools—ancient languages, modern languages, mathematics, metaphysics (including English literature, rhetoric, and composition), civil engineering, chemistry, and moral science and the evidences of the Christian religion—were named. Six professors were elected [131] and given five-year contracts. Only the chaplaincy with its accompanying chair of moral science was vacant. The average salary of the professors was $1,500 with $300 for house rent, the largest stipend to be paid for many years.

The transition from junior department to university was completed when nine trustees remained for a session with senior faculty members.[132] They discovered that the 114 students enrolled in college work for 1870 were taking courses as follows: mathematics 108, Latin 87, Greek 41, French 40, chemistry 38, physics 32, English literature 24, German 15, metaphysics 6, Spanish 6, rhetoric 4, and theology 2.[133] They determined grammar school requirements,[134] approved a latitude of choice in subjects for the advanced students, discussed the tutorial system, ruled on pronunciation of Latin and Greek, and listed texts for various courses. The work of this committee of trustees and faculty remained essentially unchanged for many years. The period of initial transition was brought to a close: Sewanee was now a college, with a coordinate grammar school.

The academic offering of the University of the South, in its first decade of existence as an institution of higher learning, justifies study in historical context. In the middle ages the seven liberal arts included the Trivium (grammar, rhetoric, logic) and the Quadrivium (arithmetic, astronomy, geometry, music). In the 1640's Harvard College prescribed courses for a four-year bachelor's degree which included grammar, rhetoric, logic, arithmetic, astronomy, and geometry, with metaphysics, ethics, natural philosophy, Greek, Hebrew, and ancient history added. If preparing for the ministry, the student spent three more years studying theology and philosophy.[135]

In the 1870's at Sewanee, the four-year B.A. degree required, as at Harvard in 1640, grammar, rhetoric, logic, arithmetic, astronomy, geometry, metaphysics, ethics, philosophy, Greek. Added in the curriculum were chemistry, physics, Latin, English literature, and a modern language, with Hebrew held over for study in the three-year theological course.[136]

That far-reaching academic development, the elective system, found Sewanee cautious. As early as 1865 Harvard adopted a University of Virginia custom allowing the student some choice in the subjects he would take. Harvard's newly inaugurated president, Charles W. Eliot, in 1869 increased electives, and by 1875 seniors at Harvard had only one required course and juniors three.[137] Sewanee made a concession to flexibility by declaring its degrees "are adapted to the varying tastes and capacities of students. The Degree of *Bachelor of Arts* embraces nothing in Mathematics beyond the Junior course, and avoids the domain of Science and Natural Philosophy. That of *Bachelor of Science* embraces only intermediate Latin, omitting Greek entirely, embracing instead a full course of Mathematics with Political Science, History, Chemistry, Geology and Mineralogy."[138] At a time when Yale offered no political economy and Columbia no French and little history, Sewanee students could elect courses in these and also civil engineering, bookkeeping, commercial law, banking, and elocution. When the teaching of sciences was rare, Sewanee offered physics, chemistry, biology, mineralogy, and geology, but in the main clung to the hard core of the classical curriculum.

THEOLOGICAL TRAINING

The present school of theology at Sewanee considers its date of founding as 1878 when St. Luke's Hall was built and the Reverend Telfair Hodgson became dean, but theological training began much earlier. Two students in theology, T. J. Morris and P. G. Rucker, are listed in the student body of 1870. In 1871 DuBose, Shoup, and Juny offered courses in theology.[139] The following year six students were listed as ministerial candidates.[140] The courses offered in 1872 were systematic divinity, moral science and evidences of revealed religion, and Hebrew. Greek and Latin were included in the college curriculum. Fortunately the University did not become involved in the internecine strife which in the 1870's plagued other parts of the Episcopal Church. At Kenyon College in Gambier, Ohio, the tractarians and the entrenched evangelicals struggled for control of the Kenyon seminary, Bexley Hall. "The effect of this theological outbreak was calamitous. . . . Both seminary and college enrollments began to decline in 1868. . . . In 1872 there were no students at Bexley."[141]

Despite the academic progress at Sewanee, Gorgas disclosed in a letter to Quintard that the financial situation was precarious. He wrote shortly after moving into his partly finished home across from St. Augustine's Chapel:

> Our financial difficulties press so heavily on us that I cannot let you & Bishop Wilmer rest in peace. . . . Unless we can raise more money I must suspend the completion of my house. It needs . . . about $500 more. . . . I was gratified to learn from . . . Bishop J. P. B. Wilmer, that two churches in N. O. had raised $300 each, & a Scholarship for their Advent Offering. It makes one regret that a Bishop who *can* do so much for us had not heretofore understood us, & has therefore done little, *materially*. He will do it now, I think. . . . Major F. [Fairbanks] has just gone on his annual trip to Florida. . . . Barbaud [Barbot], the Winchester Tailor is making arrangements to live here.[142]

For the rest of the Quintard administration, the pattern established by the 1870 trustees was followed. The executive committee, in 1871 composed of Quintard, Gorgas, and Fairbanks, used the large powers given them by the trustees. More and more Gorgas assumed responsibility for the management of the University, and Quintard spent more time in the diocese.

The trustees' meeting of July 12-18, 1871, was informed that the grammar school seemed able to support itself but that the University could not. The trustees took cognizance of municipal needs, passing suitable ordinances. The Bishop of Florida was requested to prepare a design for the Seal of the University.[143] Academic attire was prescribed: uniforms for cadets, caps and gowns for college students and professors, a crimson robe for the vice-chancellor, and a royal purple one for the chancellor. A move to restrict leases to Episcopalians was defeated. It was decided to continue emphasis on the Advent offering, better this year than before, and to continue seeking coupon subscriptions of $100 each.[144]

The 1872 meeting was held at Sewanee July 10-15 with a record attendance of twenty-eight. The fund-raising responsibility was given specifically to Quintard, who was to seek a thousand subscriptions of $500 each.[145] For the first time the ominous note of debt obtruded itself, and the treasurer, Dr. Anderson, was authorized to borrow up to $10,000 to meet current expenses. Quintard reported a decrease in the Advent offering. Jefferson Davis addressed the board, urging a plan of endowment by insurance with the Carolina Life Insurance Company of Memphis. Though favorably reported by the committee, the proposal was held over until the next meeting but never adopted. Degree requirements were debated although no prospective graduates were in the offing. Hoods for twelve degrees were approved in the same designs and colors used in 1952.

The most important action was the acceptance of Quintard's third resignation and the election of Gorgas as second vice-chancellor.[146] The retiring president Quintard made a critical mistake in his report when he suggested that the executive committee be abolished. The committee on constitution dissented, urging that it be retained for whatever incidental purpose it might serve.[147] All the bishops supported Quintard and the motion passed; Fairbanks was among the opposition. The ultimate failure of the Gorgas administration can probably be traced to this resolution, for thereafter the vice-chancellor faced the august trustees alone. Quintard thought that the action would give Gorgas a freer hand, but the new Vice-Chancellor was not another Quintard.

THE COMING OF DUBOSE

In July, 1871, the Bishop of Tennessee brought to the attention of the trustees the pressing need for a full-time chaplain to relieve Shoup, who had been acting chaplain since 1869.[148] The Reverend William Porcher DuBose of South Carolina was well known by Bishop Green and especially admired by Sewanee's new lay trustee from South Carolina, Major General Joseph Brevard Kershaw, a relative under whom Du-Bose had served in the war. He recently had been defeated in a close diocesan election for assistant to the blind Bishop Davis. DuBose was nominated for Sewanee's chaplaincy by the bishops, elected by the board, and advised by telegram.[149] He accepted and later said that, had he been elected bishop, "It would have been the great misfortune of my life."[150] During the next half century he established himself as the greatest Sewanee teacher.

DuBose was a Huguenot, born in 1836 near Winnsboro, South Carolina, of wealthy parents, Theodore Samuel Marion DuBose and Jane Porcher. William was reared at Farmington, a model patriarchal plantation, scientifically combining agricultural, mechanical, and industrial processes.

He had a gift for classical languages but mathematics baffled him. At Mount Zion Academy he memorized an algebra book in order to begin military training at the Citadel. His vacations were spent riding his horse Bagatelle on visits to the plantations of his kin. He revealed late in life that during his third year at The Citadel he experienced the midnight visitation of a "presence" which changed the course of his life.[151] In 1856 he graduated first in his class and the next fall went to the University of Virginia, where he received an M.A. degree. In the fall of 1859 he began ministerial training in the second class of the new seminary at Camden. When war came he served with Lee in Virginia in the most approved fashion, accompanied by a blooded mount and his faithful body servant, Stephen. He was twice wounded, reported dead, captured, exchanged, furloughed, married, sent back to action as a chaplain, and finally mustered out at the end of the war. He took charge of a mission in Abbeville, and moved there with his wife, Anne Barnwell Peronneau.[152]

From Abbeville he went in 1871 to the chaplaincy at Sewanee. He brought his widowed sister-in-law, Mrs. McNeely DuBose, and her two sons, his brother Robert, his cousin, Miss Porcher, and his wife and their three children. Three frame houses were built by them from the scant remains of the family fortune: the rectory, Palmetto Hall, and

Magnolia.[153] While construction was in progress, DuBose lived with the Gorgases, forming a close attachment to that family.

Before leaving his native state the young minister made a recruiting trip through South Carolina. Whereas two students had come to Sewanee from that diocese the previous year, twenty-four registered in 1871-1872.[154] From the nucleus of those whom he had personally enlisted, a tenth of the student body, his influence permeated the entire institution. Dances were held in his dining room, penny readings in the parlor, ice-cream parties on the lawn outside.[155] He told the students that although learning was important, training in character and conduct was more important.[156] He thought that a man's dress helped to shape character,[157] and he encouraged the custom of wearing coat and tie to class. He was chaplain for twelve years and continued to teach undergraduates after the end of his chaplaincy.

In 1873 his wife died, and five years later he married the talented Mrs. Maria Louise Yerger, founder of the Fairmount School for Young Ladies at Monteagle.[158] When St. Luke's Hall for theological students was finished that year, the DuBoses moved in and for ten years the lives of these two extraordinary teachers were closely identified with those of the students.[159] Meantime, DuBose had "developed his Christology which . . . initiated an Epoch in the interpretation of the New Testament."[160]

His *Soteriology of the New Testament* (New York, 1892) was reprinted repeatedly. Other theological works were *The Ecumenical Councils* (New York, 1896); *The Gospel in the Gospels* (New York, 1906); *The Gospel According to St. Paul* (New York, 1907); *High Priesthood and Sacrifice* (New York, 1908); and *The Reason of Life* (New York, 1909).[161] An autobiography, *Turning Points in My Life*, was published in 1911. His works attracted wide attention.[162] He was among the first of the theologians to articulate a recovery from the impact of nineteenth-century skepticism, in language which breathed an awareness of the present. "The New Testament no more gives us doctrine than nature gives us science," said DuBose.[163] This was revolutionary. The Reverend General Shoup talked of a trial for heresy.[164]

His pupil, Bishop William T. Manning of New York, said, "DuBose [has] received far too little attention here.... Our country has produced few first-rate theologians, no other whose contribution to theological thought and to Christology has made such an impression abroad."¹⁶⁵ The Reverend George B. Myers called DuBose "the foremost thinker in the Episcopal Church in America," but quoted the less conservative Professor William Sanday of Oxford as saying DuBose was the "wisest Anglican writer . . . on both sides of the Atlantic."¹⁶⁶

DuBose "accepted the moral, philosophical, and psychological presuppositions of his age . . . embraced wholeheartedly the new form of apologetic, beginning with man's evaluation of the human life of the Savior."¹⁶⁷ Standing for a reconciliation between science and religion when such a position was almost untenable, he possessed "a passion for Reality and . . . absolute loyalty to Truth."¹⁶⁸ Although DuBose's influence reached into every part of the Episcopal Church in the South and traveled far beyond, by his death in 1918 he was still thought of at Sewanee as one who could answer a student's question, "How do you explain the Book of Revelation?" with "I wish I knew."¹⁶⁹

As one "born mentally and spiritually honest,"¹⁷⁰ Chaplain DuBose brought a new concept of discipline to Sewanee. He felt that students could be influenced to discipline themselves. In 1873 he secured the exemption of juniors and seniors from military drill and, the black Oxford gown already being the prescribed academic dress of faculty and students, he organized the Order of Gownsmen. Composed of the more advanced undergraduates and graduate students, this group developed a tradition of leadership and provided an aristocracy of talent on the campus for governing student affairs.

OTHERS OF THAT COMPANY

For a few months in 1872 Charles Landon Carter Minor was professor of Latin and headmaster of the grammar school. He was president of the Maryland Agricultural and Mechanical College before he came to Sewanee and he left because he felt it his duty to return to Virginia, as Lee and Maury had done. He helped organize the Virginia Agricultural and Mechanical College at Blacksburg (now the Virginia Polytechnic Institute), served as its president, and then was owner and principal of the Shenandoah Valley Academy at Winchester.¹⁷¹

By 1872 the faculty for the first decade was complete except for the arrival of General Edmund Kirby-Smith and the Reverend George T. Wilmer in 1875 and John McCrady in 1877. Dabney, Gorgas, Shoup, Elliott, Harrison, and DuBose—they were the men who established the early tradition. Bishop Green and Bishop Quintard must be added to their number because the peculiar circumstances of the community made them as influential in shaping the careers of the students as the teachers themselves. Others came later to add their influence, but until the 1890's when the liberalism of the Oxonian tradition had definitely relegated the West Point characteristics to the grammar school, the pattern established by the first group was fixed. William Crawford Gorgas assessed the work of that faculty in his 1912 Commencement Oration:

> The environment was such as had never occurred before.... Our great war had just been finished and we were thus able to get for our faculty such men as General Kirby-Smith [who] ... had commanded an army, General Shoup [who] had been chief of artillery of an army, and my father [who] had just laid aside ... the Ordnance Department of the Confederacy. We had also on the Mountain many of the first ladies of the land who had been impoverished by the war. The combination was ideal for the work in hand, and the results at the time speak for themselves....[172]

Notes for Chapter Three

[1] More than half of the faculty members in the first four years of the University's operation were former Confederate officers: Brigadier Generals Josiah Gorgas and Francis A. Shoup, Captain William Porcher DuBose, Lieutenant John B. Elliott, and Second Lieutenant Berkeley Green, as were the three principal officers of administration, Chaplain Charles T. Quintard, vice-chancellor; Major George R. Fairbanks, commissioner of buildings and lands; and Colonel T. Frank Sevier, proctor. In 1875 Sewanee's highest ranking officer, General Edmund Kirby-Smith, became professor of mathematics.

[2] All bishops were present except Quintard, who was in England, Lay of Arkansas, and Gregg of Texas. Beckwith began his twenty-two-year trusteeship at this meeting and John Freeman Young of Florida, who had sung with Quintard at the laying of the cornerstone, was also present for the first time as bishop. Only Curtis of North Carolina and Secretary Williams of Georgia represented the clergy, but the laymen boasted the best turnout since the war. Smith Simkins came from Florida with another new member, J. J. Williams. John Wilkes and Armand J. deRosset were on hand from North Carolina, Pollard from Alabama, Whittle from Georgia, and Fairbanks from Tennessee. *Proceedings, April 1, 1868,* pp. 30, 31.

[3] The term "junior department" of the University of the South instead of the more accurate "high school" or "preparatory school" was used "that there be no questions as to the formal beginning of the operations of the University." Thus it never became necessary to defend the conditional clause in the land title from the Sewanee Mining Company. Fairbanks, *History of the University of the South,* 96, 97.

[4] Green, Quintard, J. P. B. Wilmer, Banister, Williams, Whittle, Dunnington, and Fairbanks. *Ibid.,* 97.

[5] William E. Mickle, *Well Known Confederate Veterans and Their War Records* (New Orleans, 1915), 51, 149.

[6] Next choice, had Gorgas declined, would have been General Samuel Jones. Fairbanks, *History of the University of the South,* 98.

[7] Robert E. Lee at Washington College was receiving $3,000. Henry A. White, *Robert E. Lee and the Southern Confederacy* (New York, 1897), 452. The three highest paid ministers in the diocese of Tennessee were receiving respectively $3,000, $2,500, and $2,100. Tennessee Diocesan *Journal, 1866,* p. 9.

[8] Vandiver, *Ploughshares Into Swords,* 285.

[9] Josiah Gorgas to T. Frank Sevier, December 2, 1869 (Sewanee Archives).

[10] Quintard to Fairbanks, January 23, 1869 (Sewanee Archives).

[11] Vandiver, *Ploughshares into Swords,* 4 *et passim.*

[12] Garrett, *Public Men in Alabama,* 458, 459.

[13] The same disease was destined to bring his son William both a wife and immortality.

[14] Guerry, *Men Who Made Sewanee,* 88.

[15] Montgomery, Alabama, *Church Register,* August 20, 1868.

[16] Vandiver, *Ploughshares into Swords,* 3.

[17] *Ibid.,* 287, 288; and Sewanee Archives.

[18] Quintard to Fairbanks, July 2, 1868 (Sewanee Archives).

[19] William Porcher DuBose, *Turning Points in My Life* (New York, 1911), 4.

[20] Douglas S. Freeman, *R. E. Lee: A Biography,* 4 vols. (New York, 1934-1936), IV, 370.

[21] Robert E. Lee to William M. Green, September 23, 1868 (Sewanee Archives).

[22] Quintard to Fairbanks, July 2, 1868 (Sewanee Archives).

[23] Bishops Green, Gregg, and Quintard; clergymen Curtis, Williams, J. M. Banister of Alabama, and G. H. Hunt of Tennessee; laymen Whittle, Pegues, deRosset, Fairbanks, and newcomer H. M. Anderson of Georgia. *Proceedings, August 12, 1868,* pp. 5-8.

[24] Support of the University by church collections has failed consistently except for the annual church-wide offering on Theological Education Sunday in recent years.

[25] This failed at the time but five-year subscriptions begun again in 1940 with amount specified by donor have been successful.

[26] *Proceedings, August 12-14, 1868,* pp. 5-14.

[27] Parker's *Church Calendar and General Almanack, 1868* (Oxford, 1868), 35. In 1953 the University is supported by 22 dioceses with 1,035 clergy.

[28] Morehouse (ed.), *Living Church Annual, 1950,* pp. 46, 47.

[29] Fisher, *Church Colleges,* 15-21.

[30] William and Mary Faculty Minutes, July 10, 1868, quoted by Herbert L. Ganter to the writer, January 2, 1952.

[31] Ganter to the writer, January 2, 1952.

[32] Fleming, *The Sequel to Appomattox,* 216.

[33] Robert W. Madry to the writer, January 3, 1952.

[34] J. G. deRoulhac Hamilton, *Reconstruction in North Carolina* (New York, 1914), pp. 622-30.

[35] Francis B. Simkins and Robert H. Woody, *South Carolina during Reconstruction* (Chapel Hill, 1932), pp. 418, 440-42.

[36] Fleming, *The Sequel to Appomattox,* 216, 217.

[37] New Orleans *Daily Picayune,* September 9, 1868.

[38] Richard C. Lee to the writer, November 29, 1951.

[39] Franklin B. Dexter, *Sketch of the History of Yale University* (New York, 1887), 91 *et passim.*

[40] O. R. Hoffman to the writer, January 2, 1952.

[41] Thomas J. Wertenbaker, *Princeton, 1746-1896* (Princeton, 1946), 300, 311.

[42] William M. Pinkerton to the writer, December 27, 1952.

[43] Allan Nevins, *The Emergence of Modern America* (New York, 1927), 282.

[44] *Ibid.,* 264-89.

[45] Quintard was counting Gorgas, who was present but did not begin teaching until the following July. In 1869 Fairbanks was listed as instructor in history but there is no indication that he taught in 1868. Teaching the first term were Franklin L. Knight, Robert Dabney, and Berkeley Green.

[46] Quintard, *Address Delivered in St. Augustine's Chapel . . . July 31st, 1890,* 6. The Bishop nowhere indicates that the University of the South was a continuation of Sewanee College. The Winchester school operated until 1871.

[47] Fairbanks, *History of the University of the South,* 99, 100, 121, 160.

[48] *University News,* April 5, 1876, II, 13, 4. Independently published by William Harlow.

[49] *University Record,* April, 1876, 1. A publication of the University.

[50] Rose D. Lovell, "The Redwood House," Baker *et al.* (eds.), *Sewanee,* 144.

[51] W. M. Patterson, "Shades and Shadows," *ibid.,* 146.

[52] Rainsford Glass Dudney and Helen A. Petry, "Matriculation Register, University of the South, 1868-1953," unpublished manuscript in Registrar's Office, University of the South.

[53] *Ibid.*

[54] *The Progress of the University,* a circular probably issued by Gorgas in 1872 (Sewanee Archives).

[55] Fairbanks, *History of the University of the South,* 82, 98.

[56] *University Record,* March, 1874, I, 71.

OF WILL AND WAY 145

[57] *Proceedings, 1868,* pp. 14-16.

[58] Rose D. Lovell, "In the Beginning," Baker *et al.* (eds.), *Sewanee,* 38, 39.

[59] Quintard to Fairbanks, January 23, 1869 (Sewanee Archives). This letter throws light on the willingness of Quintard, even before he became a trustee of the institution in 1865, to assume personal responsibility for its welfare. Apparently Bishop Elliott asked him to take the initiative. This letter reveals also Quintard's reaction to the failure to secure Maury. For him to call his brother bishops "malcontents in ye Episcopate" is strong language.

[60] Quintard to Fairbanks, March 2, 1869 (Sewanee Archives).

[61] Quintard to Fairbanks, January 26, 1869 (Sewanee Archives).

[62] Fairbanks, *History of the University of the South,* 101.

[63] Never again as long as the winter vacation was observed did the University open so early. In June, 1869, the executive committee ruled that school years should consist of forty weeks, to begin in March and close the second week in December, with a vacation of one week at the close of the first twenty weeks. Students were not to leave the mountain except with parents' permission.

[64] Dudney and Petry, "Matriculation Register, 1868-1953," reconciles the discrepancies between student lists and enrollment figures in Fairbanks, *History of the University of the South,* Arthur Howard Noll, *Sewanee Alumni Directory* (Sewanee, 1913), and the *Calendars* of the University. Since 1884 each student has signed "The Matriculation Book of the University," but the names in the book for the years 1868-1884 were entered from secondary sources. After the 1868 term the date of entrance of each student is known but the date of withdrawal is not recorded for the early years of the University. Mrs. Petry and Mrs. Dudney are preparing a revised Alumni Directory.

[65] Tennessee Diocesan *Journal, 1869,* pp. 21-22.

[66] *Calendar of the University of the South, 1870-1871* (Sewanee, 1871), 17-19. Hereafter cited as *Calendar, 1870-1871.* Titles vary. The *Calendar* is in error in listing John S. Rowland in this term, according to the "Matriculation Register, 1868-1953."

[67] Fairbanks, *History of the University of the South,* 101.

[68] Washington College in 1868 charged $325. New Orleans *Daily Picayune,* September 15, 1868.

[69] William Mercer Green, May 1, 1869 (Sewanee Archives). This folder, one page printed and three pages blank, was the forerunner of the University *Calendar, 1870-1871.* Faculty, aims of the school, and other information are given.

[70] Robert [?] to John [?], May 2, 1869, Glass-Fairbanks Papers (Sewanee Archives). The origin of this letter is unknown, and it has been impossible to identify "Robert" among the persons known to have been at Sewanee in 1869.

[71] Green, "Chancellor's Address," *Proceedings, 1869,* p. 44.

[72] Vandiver, *Ploughshares into Swords,* 289.

[73] Gorgas to Dabney, September 28, 1868, *ibid.*

[74] Fairbanks, *History of the University of the South,* 102.

[75] *Ibid.,* 107.

[76] *Ibid.,* 101, 102.

[77] *Proceedings, 1869,* p. 32.

[78] Nashville *Banner,* June 16, 1945.

[79] Lovell, "In the Beginning," Baker *et al.* (eds.), *Sewanee,* 39.

[80] Quintard Diary, August 4, 1877. Sevier's son was christened "Quintard" in 1870. When the Seviers moved from Sewanee, the boy's name was changed to "Granville." Queenie Woods Washington to the writer, November 2, 1951. When Granville Sevier died January 31, 1944, he left the University $100,000. *Sewanee Alumni News* (Sewanee), X (May, 1944), 2.

[81] *Proceedings, 1869,* pp. 7-13.

[82] *Ibid.,* 10. The bishop's optimism and his general attitude toward the fiscal problem are shown in a letter two months before the meeting of the trustees. "Ye Rev. Dr. Reid, a Presbyterian minister . . . had been on a begging tour through ye South, and had raised $15,000 to rebuild a Presbyterian meeting house in Richmond. And yet *we* can do nothing but sit down and suck our thumbs. . . . I will . . . go with you to Chicago and Detroit. . . . Or you may go South while I visit ye above named places. . . . Or I will go to Georgia with you, or anywhere, or do anything that you may deem best." Quintard to Fairbanks, May 22, 1869 (Sewanee Archives).

[83] *Proceedings, 1869,* p. 26.

[84] *Ibid.,* 16.

[85] Joseph P. B. Wilmer, "Address of the Bishop," Louisiana Diocesan *Journal, 1869,* pp. 27, 28.

[86] This estimate is based on a study of the depreciation of similar securities, 1865-1875, in the bishop's fund of the diocese of Alabama, taken from diocesan journals.

[87] *Proceedings, 1869,* pp. 25-40.

[88] Tennessee Diocesan *Journal, 1869,* pp. 21, 22.

[89] Fairbanks, *History of the University of the South,* 100, 101. Later no tuition was charged sons of clergy, a practice continuing in 1953.

[90] Interview with Queenie Woods Washington, November 15, 1951.

[91] *Proceedings, 1869,* p. 7.

[92] Fairbanks, *History of the University of the South,* 108.

[93] *Calendar, 1887-1888,* p. 81. Caskie Harrison received the other in 1889. *Calendar, 1889-1890,* p. 83.

[94] Fairbanks, *History of the University of the South,* 122.

[95] Telephone interview with Dr. Rudolph Matas, November 12, 1951.

[96] Lucy Pinckney Elliott Cunningham to the writer, December 12, 1951.

[97] John B. Elliott, *Philosophical Notes for My Children* (n.p., n.d.), 9.

[98] Interview with Dr. J. Leo Burthe, December 9, 1951.

[99] *University Record,* June, 1872, I, 1, 4.

[100] Knight (ed.), *Library of Southern Literature,* XV, 398.

[101] Fairbanks, *History of the University of the South,* 121, 331.

[102] Charlotte St. John Elliott to the writer, September 5, 1953.

[103] William Norman Guthrie, "Veni, Vidi, Vici," Baker *et al.* (eds.), *Sewanee,* 75.

[104] Quintard Diary, March 15, 1868.

OF WILL AND WAY 147

[105] Interview with Queenie W. Washington, November 17, 1951.

[106] Thomas F. Gailor, "The Faculty in 1882," Baker *et al.* (eds.), *Sewanee*, 60.

[107] Charles F. Smith, "The South's Contributions to the Classical Studies," Mitchell *et al.* (eds.), *South in the Building of the Nation*, VII, 156.

[108] Published by Ginn and Heath, Boston, 1877.

[109] Quintard Diary, October 26, 1877.

[110] *Proceedings, 1903*, p. 44.

[111] Gorgas to T. Frank Sevier, December 2, [1869] (Sewanee Archives). About 1910, when All Saints' Chapel was opened, the Meneely bell from St. Augustine's was moved to Breslin Tower. In the 1930's it was recast and hung in St. Luke's Chapel at the School of Theology.

[112] Fairbanks, *History of the University of the South*, 110. The library stood on the present site of the Alpha Tau Omega fraternity house.

[113] Still standing in 1952 on the road to Sewanee Military Academy.

[114] Arthur H. Noll (ed.), *Alexander Gregg, First Bishop of Texas* (Sewanee, 1912), 12, 13.

[115] Fairbanks, *History of the University of the South*, 298, 299.

[116] Quintard, "Memorial Sermon on Alexander Gregg" (Sewanee Archives).

[117] Tennessee Diocesan *Journal, 1870,* pp. 52, 53.

[118] *Ibid.,* 31.

[119] Louisiana Diocesan *Journal, 1870,* p. 23.

[120] Reverend J. M. Banister and N. H. R. Dawson, Alabama Diocesan *Journal, 1871,* Appendix, 91-94. This was the first report on Sewanee in the Alabama journal since the war.

[121] *Proceedings, 1870,* p. 68.

[122] Fairbanks, *History of the University of the South*, 113.

[123] *Proceedings, 1870,* p. 34.

[124] *Ibid.,* 36. In 1872 a bequest was left the University by Bishop Green's kinsman James Hill of Mississippi. The principal was not received until 1893 when his widow died. The amount, about $40,000, was one of the largest received by the University in the first fifty years of its existence and the significance of the bequest is that it was made by the donor at so early a stage in the University's career.

[125] *Proceedings, 1870,* p. 34.

[126] During the ensuing year trustees responded to this $100,000 plan by sending $2,623 in cash and $13,587 in pledges. Fairbanks, *History of the University of the South*, 128.

[127] *Proceedings, 1870,* p. 31.

[128] Fairbanks, *History of the University of the South*, 112.

[129] Alabama Diocesan *Journal, 1871,* p. 15.

[130] Fairbanks, *History of the University of the South*, 117.

[131] *Proceedings, 1870,* pp. 32, 33, 42. Professors elected for the schools were Harrison, ancient languages; Juny, modern languages; Shoup, mathematics; Dabney, metaphysics; Gorgas, civil engineering; and Elliott, chemistry.

[132] Fairbanks, *History of the University of the South*, 126, 127.

[133] *Calendar, 1870-1871*, pp. 22-24.

[134] The grammar school minimum course of study included sacred studies, spelling, reading, writing, composition, geography, history, arithmetic, algebra, bookkeeping, chemistry, physics, science, Latin, and Greek. Fairbanks, *History of the University of the South*, 127, 128.

[135] Thomas J. Wertenbaker, *Puritan Oligarchy* (New York, 1947), 142.

[136] *Calendar, 1872-1873*, p. 24.

[137] Nevins, *Emergence of Modern America*, 264-89.

[138] *Calendar, 1876-1877*, p. 22.

[139] *Ibid., 1870-1871*, pp. 13, 14.

[140] *Ibid., 1872-1873*, p. 13. They were I. O. Adams, Alabama; C. M. Gray, Tennessee; John Kershaw, South Carolina; Milnor Jones, South Carolina; T. J. Morris, Texas; W. G. W. Smith, Connecticut.

[141] George F. Smythe, *Kenyon College, Its First Century* (New Haven, 1924), 198.

[142] Gorgas to Quintard, January 12, 1871. Inserted loose in back of Quintard Diary, 1875-1876.

[143] The seal was designed by Reverend John Henry Hopkins, Jr., son of the Bishop of Vermont and author of a hymn, "We Three Kings." His first draft of the seal, submitted in 1872, was redesigned without essential change in 1877. It was piscina shape with "the initial letters of the dioceses in the links of a catena on the inside of the legend University of the South, a dove with rays of light descending on a Latin cross in the center." Fairbanks, *History of the University of the South*, 138.

[144] *Proceedings, 1871*, p. 39.

[145] *Ibid., 1872*, p. 39.

[146] His salary was $2,500, with an extra $500 for the current year. *Proceedings, 1872*, p. 38.

[147] *Ibid.*, 13, 14, 42.

[148] Reverend Samuel S. Harris of Columbus, Georgia, declined the appointment as chaplain in 1870. He was later Bishop of Michigan. Fairbanks, *History of the University of the South*, 129.

[149] *Proceedings, 1871*, p. 51.

[150] Bratton, *An Apostle of Reality*, 77.

[151] *Ibid.*, 24.

[152] Guerry, *Men Who Made Sewanee*, 81.

[153] In 1952 the oldest building in use by the University.

[154] *Calendar, 1871-1872*, pp. 15-17.

[155] Rose D. Lovell, "The Rectory," Baker *et al.* (eds.), *Sewanee*, 54, 55.

[156] John McCrady Diary, March 27, 1878.

[157] George B. Myers, "William Porcher DuBose," *Dictionary of American Biography*, V, 472-73.

[158] Then called Moffat, five miles distant by rail.

OF WILL AND WAY

[159] Interview with May P. DuBose, November 17, 1951.

[160] Bratton, *Apostle of Reality,* 86.

[161] *Ibid.,* 118.

[162] In the Sewanee Archives are book reviews from London, Edinburgh, Dublin, Liverpool, Brisbane, Sydney, Paris, Berlin, and Copenhagen.

[163] Bratton, *Apostle of Reality,* 118.

[164] William N. Guthrie, "The Doctor as I Knew Him," *The Churchman,* December 5, 1936, pp. 16-18.

[165] William T. Manning, "An Apostle of Reality" (review), *The Living Church* (Milwaukee), October 24, 1936, pp. 457-59.

[166] Myers, "William Porcher DuBose," *Dictionary of American Biography,* V, 472-73.

[167] John Stewart Lawton, *Conflict in Christology* (London, 1947), 280.

[168] John S. Marshall, *The Word Was Made Flesh, The Theology of William Porcher DuBose* (Sewanee, 1949), vi.

[169] Myers, "William Porcher DuBose," *Dictionary of American Biography,* V, 473.

[170] Bratton, *Apostle of Reality,* 13.

[171] Cameron McR. Plummer, his grandson, to the writer, December 28, 1951.

[172] *Sewanee Alumni News,* XVII, 1 (February 15, 1951), 24.

CHAPTER FOUR

PLOUGH AND SCYTHE
1866-1872

IN A small institution "the faculty" and "the university" are almost synonymous. The quality of the institution varies with the quality of the faculty. What the institution stands for is what the faculty represents. Obviously there are other factors. Fine teachers can be inhibited by unsatisfactory conditions, a shortsighted educational plan, or poor students, but fine teachers under bad auspices are likely to achieve better results than poor teachers under any circumstances. Trustees set policy, provide money at times, pass motions which are implemented and motions which are not, but if the principal purpose of an educational enterprise is education, then the faculty is the most important consideration. The student thinking on his college days seldom remembers what the trustees did for him. He remembers his teachers.

This was as true of the University of the South as of any small school, but at Sewanee there was something more. Ranged beside the professors were a supporting cast, the residents of the community. This was not an obtrusive element; all players had bit parts and knew it. Still, their cumulative impact on the lives of students was considerable. The ladies came first. Some were wives of faculty or staff, some were daughters. Some were widows with sons to educate or with daughters needing husbands. All were subjected to the community entrance examination. They must qualify by the intangible criteria of southern society. "Family" helped but was not definitive.

THE VILLAGE

The tradespeople had an important if somewhat stratified position and their influence impinged upon the lives of students. Below them the laborers also seemed to feel a part of the school. A wagoner attempted to clarify the interrelationship of town and gown when he answered a puzzled stranger's query, "Where is the University?"

"You's in [it] now. We all's the University. Everybody's the University. That's all there is—just folks and boys what stays with the folks."[1]

If the wagoner's tale was typical, there was a nearly complete identification of all elements of the community with the central purposes of the institution. Such certainly was the ideal and there is evidence that it was partially fulfilled.

The community underwent the most rapid expansion of its history during the Quintard administration, principally in 1871 and 1872. Up to July, 1870, only thirty-nine leases had been granted by the University.[2] At the end of 1872 three times that many were on the records. In the next six years only twenty-five more were added.[3] The commissioner of buildings and lands reported to the trustees in 1872 that Sewanee had "the appearance of a prosperous and well established community."[4] By fall that year Gorgas could summarize:

> The chapel was enlarged, and embellished. Aided by the liberality of Judge Gray of Texas,[5] a most comfortable and commodious Grammar School was built, capable of seating 130 to 140 pupils. Handsome dwellings rose on all sides. . . . until now we can count by the dozen cottages, halls and houses, whose many lights, on the summer evenings, gleam thro' the trees. . . . At the village . . . forty or fifty shops, stores, and dwellings are formed into streets, or perched upon the adjacent hills.[6]

In the thirty months following January, 1870, twenty-four private dwellings were erected in the campus area. Ten of them had a value of over $5,000 each, seven averaged $3,000, and the rest about $2,000.[7] The monthly newspaper boasted in its third issue that four hundred students could now be accommodated.[8] Some $200,000 had been invested in non-University construction. Thirty-six families were living in the college community and the estimated village population was between five hundred [9] and eight hundred [10] living in a hundred buildings. The first small store, established by Pleasant Gilliam [11] in 1867,[12] was now far surpassed by Tomlinson's, "probably the largest and best stocked in the county."[13]

Bishop Quintard sought to form a model village around the University. In his travels he encouraged skilled workmen, especially those of foreign birth, to settle at Sewanee. Herr F. Fischer, a fine cabinet worker, came from Germany by way of Canton, Ohio, and nearby Winchester about 1872.[14] Henry Schneider was an equally talented craftsman and William Philpot was an English upholsterer. Harvey O. Judd, who ran the laundry,[15] was one of a numerous family which moved to Sewanee in 1871.[16] C. S. Judd became the University photographer.[17]

Charles Wadhams, who ran the bakery,[18] was nicknamed "The Bishop" by youngsters who made his ice-cream arbor at the top of the hill a pleasure spot. He was a tall, ruddy-faced Scot and had been a member of Queen Victoria's Coldstream Guards.[19] Pierre Barbot came to Sewanee from Winchester in 1871 to establish a tailor shop. Later joined by a fellow Frenchman, L. Pillet,[20] he made not only uniforms for the students but formal and informal attire of such elegance that Dr. DuBose, recalling his first impressions of Sewanee in 1871, said, "It was only a grammar school, and it was already known . . . [by] the elegant fit of [the students'] dress."[21] Some of the advertisements of Barbot and Pillet deserve reproduction:

> The outward form, the inner man reveals,
>   We guess the pulp before we eat the peel;
> One single precept might the whole condense:
>   Be sure your tailor is a man of sense.
>
> Barbot and Pillet have plenty of sense, and they have additionally a large stock of clothes—doeskin, cassimers, vestings, grey cloth for uniforms . . . linen ducks, fine shirts. . . .[22]

Henry Schlapback, Swiss butcher, was joined in 1874 by a fellow countryman and competitor, C. Reuf of Berne. They distinguished themselves respectively by playing the accordion at Sewanee's first dance hall above the laundry and by reading Schiller in German to meat customers.[23] Among other early advertisers in the *University Record* were W. A. Gibson, dry goods; T. M. Forbes, shoemaker; Hoge and Miller, groceries; H. H. Roberts, hacks and horses; H. N. Caldwell, bookstore and pharmacy; George A. Mayhew, merchant; W. H. Johnson, shoemaker; Joseph F. Bork, tinsmith and hardware dealer.[24] The

Roberts public hack was "a long ambulance with narrow slanting seats running lengthwise." Earlier there had been only ox-wagons to haul freight from the station and, for fancy affairs, Major Fairbanks' small carriage with his sleek mule, Joe.[25] In 1872 a coal mine was opened on the domain having "an incline with stationary power . . . built by the University." It furnished coal to residents at fifteen cents per bushel.[26] Lime-burning and brick-making establishments were operated by Gillespie and Kennedy.

BENEFACTOR UNSUNG

Much of the rapid development of the village community was due to the remarkable interest of Jabez W. Hayes of New Jersey.[27] He had heard of the educational project through his connection with the Episcopal Church in Newark.[28] Its plans coincided with what he had long considered a logical idea for Christian education.[29] In 1867 he leased one hundred acres of land on the southeast spur of the mountain two miles from the station,[30] planted fruit trees, grapevines, and vegetables, keeping careful records of progress made by the different varieties. He supplied the community with produce previously unknown to the area.[31] In 1870, after the death of his wife, he began spending more of his time at Sewanee. He set up a steam sawmill with lathe and shingle machines, extended credit to persons wishing to build residences and halls for the students, and in 1872 built for himself a mansion overlooking the valley.[32] He contributed generously to the University from the "ample fortune earned by his own industry."[33] After his death his home and lands at Sewanee were sold to the Sisters of St. Mary, an order of Episcopal nuns, who in 1885 opened a school for underprivileged girls of the coves. The "investments" of this beneficent capitalist were so many and so injudicious as profit-making ventures that he may well deserve the title of first large [34] benefactor to early Sewanee.

Sewanee in 1872 had these components of civilization: a church, a school, and a jail. In November, 1871, Shoup organized St. Paul's-on-the-Mountain [35] for the village community [36] and by the next year a church building seating 250 was under way. Within six months the Sunday school had a hundred pupils. Faculty families technically were members of this parish though they more often attended the services in the University chapel. Hayes built a school beside the village church and, by 1875, it had seventy-five pupils under the volunteer tutelage of Miss Flora Fairbanks and Miss Charlotte Elliott,[37] the daughters of Major Fairbanks and Bishop Stephen Elliott. The calaboose, a project of Major Fairbanks, served as temporary shelter for one prisoner, a native liquor purveyor;[38] otherwise its long career was of dubious usefulness.

Leases for businesses were not granted in the campus area, a thousand acres being reserved exclusively for the use of the schools and persons immediately connected with them. Leases forbade cutting of trees, maintaining a nuisance, or conflicting with the best interests of the students as interpreted by the commissioner of buildings and lands, the vice-chancellor, or the trustees.[39]

HOMOGENEITY

Polk said that Sewanee would create its own society. And so it did. The three dozen families living within five hundred yards of the chapel were a homogeneous group. Many were related by blood or marriage. Almost all had the common interest of religion and the common circumstance of poverty. All were sympathetic with the southern cause, and most had well-developed cultural, literary, and scientific interests. There was much communal entertainment centering around the church, the student activities, and the various homes. At Sewanee were ladies who had known southern society at its zenith and several were sufficiently ingenious to improvise a social life of graciousness.

During the summer of 1870 the faculty formed a club whose name, the E.Q.B., was suggested by Gorgas from *Ecce quam bonum,* the first words of the 133rd Psalm.[40] It was organized in Fairbanks' parlor and met fortnightly at members' homes. For nineteen years meetings included supper but when a clubhouse was erected refreshment deteriorated to wine, punch, or beer. The "lead" was a formal paper to which one or more previously designated persons answered.[41] Then followed lively discussion from which affairs of the University were excluded.[42]

Judge John D. Phelan was first president of the E.Q.B. Club. He personified the sort of resident Bishop Elliott had in mind for peopling the plateau. For almost a decade he was an important figure of the community. Before the war Phelan was prominent in Alabama as sometime editor of the Huntsville *Democrat,* member of the state legislature, speaker of the house, circuit judge, and member of the supreme court. In 1857 he lost the nomination for governor.[43] When he was removed from public office by the Reconstruction government, he came to Sewanee in 1870 and took paying guests into his large home, "The Forks." Phelan was a lay trustee from Tennessee and an occasional lecturer in the University. After his marriage [44] in 1872 to Maria Shelby of Nashville,[45] he spent winters at his wife's fine establishment "Fatherland" in Nashville, where he died in 1879.[46]

The *University Record* must be regarded as an organ of propaganda since it was edited in its first three years by faculty and reflected administration views. Nevertheless it gives, albeit exuberantly, some of the atmosphere of the early community.

> The society of the University is unsurpassed. The Bishops of Mississippi, Tennessee, Alabama,[47] and Texas have summer residences, and others of the southern bishops spend a portion of the summer here. There are meetings of the E.Q.B. every two weeks and also a meeting every two weeks open to all the community interested in reading or musical entertainment. There is no hotel but visitors can board in the families of Mr. Green, Mrs. Polk, Mrs. Wilkinson, Mr. Gibson, Mr. Tomlinson, and others at $30 to $50 per month. There is daily mail and money order service, and there are express and telegraph offices.[48]

Miss Sarah Barnwell Elliott, Sewanee's most prolific novelist, pointed out that Sewanee's manner of living was not indigenous to the primeval plateau or even the recent frontier but had been transplanted from many places. Speaking of those who came to Sewanee between 1866 and 1871, "Miss Sada" gave this eyewitness report:

> Bishop Quintard brought enough enthusiasm for an army—he introduced the Oxford cap and gown—also all manner of beautiful flowers; and Mrs. Quintard's *Recipes* were from Georgia. Bishop Green and his daughter, Miss Lily, . . . kept open house; and their *Recipes* came from Mississippi. Major Fairbanks brought tropical flowers, had his first "pit" for flowers; and Mrs. Fairbanks' *Recipes* came from Florida. Colonel

Sevier introduced cauliflower and business methods; and Mrs. Sevier's *Recipes* came from Kentucky. Judge Phelan (and his daughters, all of them handsome and young) was the first to throw open his house as a stopping place for strangers . . . and Judge Phelan's *Recipes* came from Alabama. General Josiah Gorgas introduced celery, and military discipline; and Mrs. Gorgas' *Recipes* were collected from many sources, as she had gone from post to post in the old army. General Shoup brought mathematics . . . and a very advanced church service . . . he was not married then. . . .

Professor Robert Dabney—a gentle soul dearly loved of all—brought metaphysics; and Mrs. Dabney's *Recipes* came from Virginia. Okra was introduced by Mrs. Stephen Elliott, who planted it in her own garden and distributed seed among the friendly farmers; to them she also suggested that cantaloupe be not planted along with squash and cucumbers. Mrs. Elliott's *Recipes* came from South Carolina and Georgia. Professor Caskie Harrison, fresh from Cambridge, England, placed classics at the head of the curriculum and set going and guided the movement that gave us "Old Forensic."[49] . . . Doctor John Elliott brought chemistry to the front; . . . further, as health officer he insisted on a public baker. . . . And this decision . . . brought in Mr. Wadhams, a Scotchman, who once served in the "Coldstream Guards," which meant that he was very tall and very straight, and who, in the twinkling of an eye, it seemed, became the friend of everyone—and . . . the patron saint of every student and every smallest child in the community. Mr. Wadhams' *Recipes* came from Scotland and England.

. . . They were necessarily enthusiastic gardeners, and there were great rivalries in this matter, and generous exchange of seed and roots. . . . There were still greater rivalries . . . among the housekeepers as to the suppers provided for the Faculty Club—the E.Q.B. that met in turn from house to house—for here it was that all the *Recipes* rising up from out of a sea of troubles fought their way to the very front of the community stage.[50]

ACADEMIC DIVERSION

By 1872 the influx of summer visitors was creating academic problems. For afternoons and week-ends there were "the walking parties, the ox-wagon picnics, the exploring expeditions down into the caves and valleys, the professors and students all walking and talking and laughing in company."[51] Every home was crowded with paying or nonpaying guests and more and more of the guests were young ladies. Many of them came for a summer which began in May and ended in October and created a gay atmosphere which added to the social development of the students but probably affected their studies adversely. Nevertheless, the summer girl proved a hardy perennial and was only uprooted in 1909 when Sewanee conformed to the prevailing college term beginning in September and closing in June.

To insure the intimacy which they felt essential for the sort of intellectual and spiritual growth which they contemplated, the original planners had expressly limited to twelve the number of students in each hall. When the new chaplain, DuBose, built Palmetto Hall for *thirty* students there was murmuring. "It was *so* large! . . . Yet it was so close to the Rectory, and under such good influences, that it was soon pronounced all right, and other people who had houses began to add outstanding cottages."[52] From two to eight students lived in each of the outbuildings, ten or twelve with the family, and all ate in the big house [53] which bore the designating name of the cluster.[54]

Letters written home by John Gass in 1874 give some idea of the board provided in the halls. He received "splendid fare, turkey twice a week, dessert three times."[55] Molasses on the table at every meal was standard. There were fruits and vegetables in seasonable profusion from the valley and from the Hayes farm. Wild huckleberries grew on the mountain. Almost every vegetable-vending farmer brought two or three warm rabbits, shot from the wagon seat as his rickety conveyance lurched up the mountain. One little girl achieved immortality by greeting a group of unexpected visitors at mealtime with the announcement, "Mama's not here. She saw you coming and went for another rabbit."[56] Hot breads were the rule. Chicken, eggs, beef, lamb, and pork were plentiful and cheap. By 1872 Hayes had two ice houses in operation,[57] insuring refrigeration for meats.

THE HALLS

Great rivalry developed between the halls and on occasion discipline was difficult. Once a raid on Powhatan was repulsed with sticks and baseball bats.[58] Palmetto, Magnolia, Kendal, Bellewood, Powhatan, Tremlett, Otey, South Wing, Oxford Court, Mrs. Cotten's, Mrs. Polk's, Mrs. Rutledge's, Mrs. Elmore's, Mrs. Anderson's—these are the names which would evoke echoes in the memories of early students.

It seemed then, said a resident of those days, "that all the halls were kept by the widows of the Confederacy, saddened, impoverished and genteel women of the South, who had found a refuge in the community of 'simple living and high thinking' as someone called Sewanee."[59] Living in family groups, the students and residents developed close ties. Each lady felt herself responsible for the manners, appearance, and social unfolding of her charges. Frequently a student arrived bearing letters of introduction to Sewanee residents, and the routine of the formal call, the invitation to a meal, the party call, was taken seriously. A young gentleman who failed promptly to make his manners with his hostess could expect an earnest lecture from the matron of his hall, raised eyebrows from his dancing companions, admonition from a gownsman, and likely enough an indignant letter from his parents.[60]

> [From] colonial mansions, with wide piazzas and open-hearted hospitality . . . Miss Maria L. Porcher came to Sewanee, and gave the house that she built . . . a name that would connect it, wistfully, with . . . South Carolina. . . . With orphaned nephews to educate, and her property and theirs swept away by the Civil War, Miss Porcher with characteristic courage, energy, and sound judgment, undertook the great adventure of making a home in what her South Carolina friends called "the wilds of the mountain." . . . Not only her nephews but many other boys came. . . . No one will ever know how many boys were taken in Magnolia for half-pay or none at all.[61]

Gorgas advocated a modification of the original housing plan. He was willing that "the University students might . . . be allowed the privileges . . . contemplated by the statutes,"[62] but he thought that the younger boys should room together in homes or dormitories supervised by instructors. This arrangement would have allowed the poorly paid instructors to supplement their $500 to $1,000 salaries. The ideas of Cobbs and the founders prevailed, however, and ladies rather than instructors supervised most of the living quarters, though students might board in the homes of faculty members.

A denizen of one of the halls thus described them: "Sewanee's old houses [were] expansive and rambling, made for students to race about in. . . . The gracious charm of these first Sewanee homes contributed no small share to the characters of the first students. . . . These old Houses . . . did duty for home, dormitory and fraternity in one."[63] Regardless of its romantic, idealistic, or sentimental implications, the student hall system had its practical advantage for the University, for by 1872 Fairbanks was able to announce that there was "no necessity for additional dormitories being erected, as the requirements of the University were fully met by the increase of resident families licensed to board students."[64]

STUDENT LIFE

When a student arrived at Sewanee he came by train southeast from Nashville or west from Chattanooga to Cowan. If he were not met by a hack from Sewanee or did not want to walk the five miles from Cowan, he waited, occasionally overnight in the old Franklin House, for the Sewanee coal train. If the passenger car was on, he rode in comparative comfort; if not, he piled his bags into an empty coal gondola and enjoyed views of the valley while he collected an encrustation of cinders on the tortuous nine-mile ascent.

Disembarking at the tiny station in a cluster of village shops a half mile from the edge of the mountain, he rode by hack to his hall. If he had followed the instructions of the University Calendar, he unpacked a pair of blankets, three single sheets, two pillow cases, six napkins and a napkin ring, six towels, a clothes bag, two pairs of strong shoes, and clothing marked with his name.[65] Gray uniforms [66] at $25 were purchased by grammar school cadets and, after 1871, by undergraduates not yet entitled to the $15 academic gown. It was reserved for the older students.[67] If he was paying the full year's fees, his parents sent $330 to the treasurer.[68]

Student life was primitive in many ways but not dull. When Enfield rifles [69] were stacked after an early morning drill,[70] breakfast was waiting, served in most halls between 7:00 and 7:30 a.m. Then followed morning chapel at 8:00. Here gathered faculty and students for the regular prayer book service with only such modifications as were approved by the trustee-bishops. A student choir reminiscent of English schools [71] sang chants from the nave while the faculty adorned the chancel, an exposed position irreverently called "the crow's nest."[72]

Dogs were frequent visitors to chapel.[73] The service lasted from fifteen to twenty-five minutes with no sermon except on Sundays or special occasions. Recitations followed, lasting until 1:00. Dinner came and then another two hours of recitation. Afternoon chapel services at 4:00 lasted about fifteen minutes. All students were expected to attend morning and evening chapel. Sports took precedence over studies in the free time which followed. Supper was customarily served at 6:30 p.m. and then only special events displaced studies. University students could keep lights on in their rooms after 10:00. On Wednesdays and Saturdays grammar school boys were free from 1:00 to 7:15 p.m. Juniors or undergownsmen of the University were free on Saturday only.[74]

The letters of John Gass give an idea of student activities. He joined the Hardee baseball team and a debating society, walked to Rutledge Point, and visited a coal mine. "One great comfort is the tank," he told his family back in South Carolina. His class could use the swimming pool [75] only at hours which indicated a crowded schedule, 6:00 to 7:00 a.m. and 9:00 to 10:00 p.m. "Ice cream has commenced," he said, "but I have not regaled myself in that luxury for my pocket fund is rather low." Young Gass talked of torchlight processions and fireworks after the Hardees won their first series in three years. His uniform, made by Miss Sue Peronneau, had a white shirt with red shield on the breast, a large white "H" in the shield, tape around the sleeves, red collar and cuffs, and red knee breeches.[76]

ATHLETICS

The only organized sport among the first students was baseball. In 1869 a club called the Sewanees succeeded an earlier team known briefly as the R. E. Lees.[77] More spirited even than the rivalry between the halls was that between the two baseball clubs which by 1870 had become "traditional" foes, the Sewanees and the Hardees, wearers of the blue and red. The Hardees were named for the lieutenant general who with Joseph E. Johnston had seen Polk fall at Pine Mount.[78] Each club fielded a half-dozen teams. The only expenses were for balls and bats, for lady supporters made the brilliant uniforms. Monday was the weekly holiday and everyone turned out to watch the games in front of Tremlett Hall. Most of the crowd sat on logs, while small boys and Negroes climbed into treetops. The crippled Professor Cooper, master of the grammar school and registrar, umpired from his wheel chair.[79] Silver baseballs and a cup went to the winners. In 1872 a medal for the most gentlemanly student went by popular ballot to the captain of the winning team because he was captain of the winning team. Hero-worship of athletes is not a twentieth-century phenomenon. New boys were met at the train by partisans asking them to join the Hardees or Sewanees. "The feeling was more intense than any other, until we began to play Vanderbilt."[80] From time to time the R. E. Lees and the Independents would appear for a season or two but it was the Sewanee-Hardee rivalry which continued steadily for two decades, threatened but never obscured by the hall teams, Tremlett, St. Luke's, Devils, Angels, Kendal, Magnolia, Right Bower, and Hell Cats.[81] Off-campus baseball began in 1875.

Other sports included gymnastics, croquet in Bishop Quintard's back yard [82] and football. The football club appears in only one *Calendar,* and little is known of its early history at Sewanee, but by the turn of the century it completely eclipsed baseball and the Sewanee-Vanderbilt game became the pivotal point of the year's extracurricular activity.

EXTRACURRICULAR

There were occasional dramatic presentations under Caskie Harrison's sponsorship. A cornet band organized in 1872 persisted through the next decade.[83] One of the earliest student organizations was the Guild of St. Mark, organized by Dr. Knight in 1869. It had three purposes: religious advancement of its members, improvement of moral tone of the student body, and missionary work in the surrounding country.[84]

Overtones of seriousness characterized many student activities of the day. Forensics was very popular. Three societies were founded in the first four years, all named with Greek initials of the founders of the University. Sigma Epsilon (Stephen Elliott) was started in 1869.[85] Pi Lambda (Leonidas Polk) and Omega (Otey) got underway the next year. Each had senior and junior divisions. At the close of 1872 Pi

Lambda and Omega combined as Pi Omega which, with Sigma Epsilon, remained vigorous until World War II. On July 10, 1872, Jefferson Davis presided at a three-way oratorical contest.[86] Declamation, debate, essay, original oration, and poetry were accorded places on the programs of the public exhibitions. The presidency of a society was a campus honor almost equal to the captaincy of a baseball nine. The literary societies received the benign editorial smile of the faculty-sponsored *University Record*. Following the death of a Cornell student in 1873 hazing at Ithaca, this publication nodded approval at the absence on the Sewanee campus of secret organizations.[87]

Many elaborate prohibitions associated with denominational colleges[88] were lacking at Sewanee. The younger students were forbidden the use of tobacco but older students could smoke if not on the streets or school grounds. Alcohol could not be bought, sold, possessed, or used by the students.[89] There were no reasons at Sewanee for rules against visiting horse races, cock fights, and saloons. Dancing was encouraged, rather than frowned upon, and parties were given a formal atmosphere by the participation of ladies resident upon the mountain and their young summer visitors. Cultivation of social graces in mixed groups was the desideratum of Sewanee's female mentors.

TWO OF THE BOYS

The record of young Willie Gorgas[90] gives a cross-section of student activities. He matriculated in 1869 as a student in the junior department. In 1870-1871 he studied Latin, Greek, mathematics, and French, and received the Alabama medal for scholarship, one of several state medals awarded. The next year he became a gownsman and continued his courses in Latin, Greek, and mathematics, substituting metaphysics for French. He served as first sergeant of Company B of the Sewanee Cadet Corps. In 1872-1873, Greek, Latin, chemistry, and moral science were his studies, and he was awarded diplomas in the schools of mathematics, metaphysics, and English literature. He was president of the Sewanee football club, librarian of Pi Omega literary society, and director and captain of the first nine of the Hardee baseball club. He continued to direct the Hardees in 1874, though emphasis was on his studies, with courses in Greek, Latin, French, chemistry, and physics. At Commencement, 1874, he received diplomas in chemistry, physics, and Greek. Final diplomas were obtained at the 1875 Commencement in French, Latin, and moral science, and on August 5, 1875, he received the degree of bachelor of arts.[91]

A more intimate view of student life is furnished by matriculant number thirty-three, John S. Bradford, Jr., from Springfield, Illinois, who entered the junior department in the second term, February, 1869. Bradford was the only Yankee student. As he recalled at ninety, Sewanee was then "a wagon track through the brush with old Tremlett at the end, Otey Hall opposite the Fairbanks' home."[92] Bradford lived on the second floor of Tremlett above the temporary quarters of Gorgas, who was a "most rigid disciplinarian . . . the personification of dignity." Schoolboy pranks and practical jokes were high in student and low in professorial favor. Bradford relates:

> In the rear of Tremlett a broad path led down the hill to the Spring. Part of the way down, another path led over to a small house in the brush. . . . For a little excitement, I stuck a piece of paper under the shingles and set it afire. It made only a small blaze and I thought it had gone out. I went up the hill and some boys behind me yelled "fire, fire!" Others came rushing over and instead of putting out the small blaze, they turned the house over. I had to plead guilty to Col. Sevier and got what his name would indicate.[93]

At Sewanee there were no student affrays with carpetbaggers or Negroes such as harassed General Lee at Washington College the same year.[94] Of carpetbaggers there were none, and all of the Negroes remained on the nether side of the line set by the doctrine of the "superior" race. One incident of trouble was reported: desperadoes from the village set upon one of Professor Dabney's Negro servants and left him near Otey Church severely cut.[95] There is no report of a strike or riot involving students.

INTIMATION OF IMPORTANCE

In essential routine, student life at Sewanee had changed little from that of the denominational colleges of the Old South.[96] The typically secluded campus, carefully shielded from moral contamination; compulsory chapel twice daily; rigorous discipline—all these were hallmarks of the prewar church-sponsored school. Missing from the mild Episcopal atmosphere were the powerful revivals which swept some campuses.

Life at Sewanee, far from the political tensions of the day, was pleasant for resident and student. Homogeneous backgrounds and similar ambitions bound the early Sewanee people together and made them forget there was not a stone building on the domain. A process of natural selection weeded out of the community the person whose first thought was personal gain, for it was obvious that greater material success could be achieved elsewhere. The same process eliminated the thrill-seeking student. There were no bright lights at Sewanee and excursions to nearby cities were major undertakings. At Sewanee there was an intimation of importance, a feeling that the institution had a mission; there was an atmosphere of promise.

Notes for Chapter Four

[1] Fannie E. Selph, *The South in American Life and History* (Nashville, 1928), 107, 108.

[2] Fairbanks, *History of the University of the South*, 123.

[3] "Leases: The University of the South," 7 vols. (Treasurer's Office, Sewanee), I, passim.

[4] *Proceedings, 1872*, p. 15.

[5] P. W. Gray, trustee from Houston.

[6] Josiah Gorgas, *The Progress of the University* (Sewanee Archives), a soliciting piece used by Quintard on his trip through the South in the winter of 1872-1873.

[7] *Ibid.*

[8] *University Record*, November, 1872, I, 3, 11.

[9] *Ibid.*

[10] Gorgas, *Progress of the University* (Sewanee Archives).

[11] Lovell, "In the Beginning," Baker *et al.* (eds.), *Sewanee*, 38, 39. Miss Lovell spells the surname "Gillem" instead of "Gilliam."

[12] Pleasant Gilliam was holder of Lease No. 2. "Leases: The University of the South" (Treasurer's Office, Sewanee).

[13] *University Record*, September, 1872, I, 2, 1. W. H. Tomlinson had kept the "hotel" before the war.

[14] Died of injuries received while building the A.T.O. fraternity house. Rose D. Lovell, "Artisans of Sewanee," Baker *et al.* (eds.), *Sewanee*, 55, 56.

[15] *University Record*, June, 1872, I, 1, 2.

[16] "Leases: The University of the South" (Treasurer's Office, Sewanee), Lease No. 85.

[17] His brother Spencer succeeded him as photographer at Sewanee. The Sewanee Archives contain several hundred examples of Spencer Judd's art, painstakingly assembled by a series of collectors. His original files were destroyed by fire after his death. Spencer Judd's compositions of Sewanee scenery have never been surpassed.

[18] Sarah Barnwell Elliott, "The Evolution of Sewanee," Baker *et al.* (eds.), *Sewanee*, 106-108.

[19] Rose D. Lovell, "Bishop Wadham's," *ibid.*, 46-49.

[20] Rose D. Lovell, "Barbot and Pillet," *ibid.*, 39-42.

[21] William P. DuBose, "The Romance and Genius of a University," *Sewanee Review*, XIII (October, 1905), 499.

[22] *University Record,* October, 1875, II, 10, 8.

[23] Lily Baker, "The Meat Shop," Baker *et al.* (eds.), *Sewanee*, 53, 54.

[24] *University Record,* June, 1873, I, 4, 20.

[25] Elliott, "The Evolution of Sewanee," Baker *et al.* (eds.), *Sewanee*, 106.

[26] *University Record,* November, 1872, I, 3, 12.

[27] Newark *Daily Journal,* April 24, 1873.

[28] Quintard Diary, February 22, 1877.

[29] Fairbanks, *History of the University of the South,* 131.

[30] *Plan of the Lands of the University of the South* (Sewanee Archives). This map, scale 4,000 feet to the inch, undated but drawn about 1870, was lithographed in Philadelphia. It shows ten buildings in the campus area, eleven around the station, and three on the Hayes tract.

[31] *University Record,* November, 1872, I, 3, 12.

[32] Troy Beatty, Jr. (his great grandson) to the writer, August 7, 1952.

[33] *University Record,* March, 1874, I, 11, 71.

[34] Hayes probably spent $100,000 at Sewanee between 1870 and 1880.

[35] Fairbanks, *History of the University of the South,* 129.

[36] *University Record,* November, 1872, I, 3, 12.

[37] Lily Baker, "Sewanee's First Missionaries," Baker *et al.* (eds.), *Sewanee*, 110. Miss Elliott married Sewanee alumnus Charles McDonald Puckette. Miss Fairbanks and Miss Green, especially the latter, had a number of children in the village named for them, not just "Lily Green Jones" but on occasion "Miss Lily Green Jones."

[38] Fairbanks, *History of the University of the South,* 156. In 1953, the calaboose still stood on the leasehold of William J. Hamilton.

[39] *Ibid.,* 123, 138, 149.

[40] These words were written by Henry C. Lay on the title page of the *Proceedings* of the 1857 meeting at Lookout Mountain. *Ibid.,* 129.

[41] Lyman Wells, "The E. Q. B. Club," Baker *et al.* (eds.), *Sewanee*, 102, 103.

[42] The E. Q. B. continued its fortnightly meetings in 1953. Early minutes and files of papers of the organization were destroyed in the Supply Store fire of 1899.

[43] Garrett, *Public Men in Alabama*, 114-16.

[44] Gorgas to Quintard, December 20, 1872 (Sewanee Archives). "Judge Phelan married last night, so that we are without a President for the E. Q. B. Club."

[45] Interview with Queenie Woods Washington, December 1, 1951.

[46] Quintard Diary, September 21, 1879.

[47] Bishop R. H. Wilmer spent several summers at Sewanee but his interest waned. By the late 1870's he came only for trustees' meetings, if at all. On these occasions he usually arrived with his cousin, Bishop J. P. B. Wilmer of Louisiana, and they stayed at "Kendal" with Bishop and Miss Lily Green. Interview with Mary W. Cotten, April 15, 1947. Bishop Young of Florida was granted a "perpetual lease" in 1869 "near Proctors Hall on Young's Cliff," but did not carry out his plans for organizing a religious sisterhood there. Bishop J. P. B. Wilmer was granted a lease in 1871. Both leases were later cancelled. "Leases, The University of the South," 7 vols., I (Treasurer's Office).

[48] *University Record*, August, 1874, II, 1, 1.

[49] Where students and residents met for parties and dances. Erected 1873. Fairbanks, *History of the University of the South*, 155.

[50] Sarah Barnwell Elliott, "Introduction," Mrs. George A. Washington (ed.), *The Sewanee Cook Book* (Nashville, 1926), 6, 7.

[51] Elliott, "The Evolution of Sewanee," Baker et al. (eds.), *Sewanee*, 108.

[52] *Ibid.*, 107.

[53] Before the war Bishop Cobbs had said, "No student should sit down at a table unless there is a lady at the head of it." Fairbanks, *History of the University of the South*, 319.

[54] Bishop Green's "Kendal," built in 1867 with its three cottages added soon after, is still standing in 1953, looking much as it did in the 1870's.

[55] John Gass, "Old Letters," Baker et al. (eds.), *Sewanee*, 49.

[56] Interview with Queenie W. Washington, December 10, 1951.

[57] *University Record*, June, 1872, I, 1, 2.

[58] Harry Easter, "Early Days," Baker et al. (eds.), *Sewanee*, 45, 46.

[59] Queenie W. Washington, "Memories," *ibid.*, 61-63. Mrs. Washington names, among others, Mrs. Herndon of "Bellewood," who educated three sons at Sewanee, and Mrs. Anderson, a relative of Jefferson Davis, whose wife visited her. Another widow was Mrs. Hugh Aiken, the sister of Mrs. Gorgas, who was matron at Tremlett Hall. Mrs. Stephen Elliott, widow of the presiding bishop of the Confederate Episcopal Church, lived at Sewanee, and, later Mrs. Susan Dabney Smedes spent her last days there.

[60] David A. Shepherd, statement to writer, January 4, 1952.

[61] Louise Finley, "Magnolia Hall," Baker et al. (eds.), *Sewanee*, 100-02.

[62] Fairbanks, *History of the University of the South*, 112.

[63] Maristan Chapman, "Wyndcliff Hall," Baker et al. (eds.), *Sewanee*, 137-40.

[64] Fairbanks, *History of the University of the South*, 139.

[65] *University Record*, June, 1872, I, 1, 4.

[66] *Calendar, 1871-1872*, p. 26.

[67] The gowns were frequently homemade. Mrs. Mattie DuBose made Professor McCrady's gown. McCrady Diary, September 22, 1877.

[68] Fees were raised from $300 in 1870. The new charge included board, tuition, washing, mending, fuel, lights, matriculation, and surgeon's fee. *University Record,* June, 1872, I, 1, 4. Confederate orphans were accepted for $25 per term plus room and board. *Ibid.,* September, 1872, I, 2, 7.

[69] *Ibid.,* November, 1872, I, 3, 12. These were furnished by the State of Tennessee, the first "state aid to education" at Sewanee.

[70] Easter, "Early Days," Baker *et al.* (eds.), *Sewanee,* 44. The students in 1870 requested permission to form a military company. Fairbanks, *History of the University of the South,* 126.

[71] *University Record,* August, 1874, II, 1, 1.

[72] Interview with Sarah H. Torian, November 17, 1951.

[73] *University Record,* November, 1873, I, 9, 57. And continue so to this day.

[74] *Ibid.,* August 1874, II, 1, 1.

[75] Size 76 x 15 x 6 feet. *Ibid.,* June, 1872, I, 1, 2. Gass gave the dimensions as 60 x 15 x 5.

[76] Gass, "Old Letters," Baker *et al.* (eds.), *Sewanee,* 49.

[77] Sarah Hodgson Torian, "Sewanee-Hardee," *ibid.,* 105, 106. This source refers to an earlier one, the *Cap and Gown,* 1885.

[78] Joseph E. Johnston to Quintard, October 9, 1885 (Sewanee Archives); and resolution of Hardee Baseball Club expressing sympathy to family of General W. J. Hardee, November 11, 1873, *University Record,* December, 1873, I, 10, 64. Hardee was also a close friend of the Gorgas family: a special bed had been built for his long frame at Brierfield. Vandiver, *Ploughshares into Swords,* 278 n.

[79] Easter, "Early Days," Baker *et al.* (eds.), *Sewanee,* 45.

[80] Torian, "Sewanee-Hardee," *ibid.,* 105, 106.

[81] *Ibid.*

[82] Quintard to Sevier, August 27, 1870 (Sewanee Archives).

[83] *Calendar, 1871-1872,* p. 27.

[84] *University Record,* June, 1872, I, 1, 3. Three of the five officers listed in this article were theological students. Ultimately the guild was taken over by the seminarians. By 1910 more than a dozen Sunday preaching missions were operated on the plateau and in the coves near the University. The name of the guild is preserved in the mission church of the Negro community at Sewanee, St. Mark's.

[85] Quintard Diary, June 8, 1879, refers to tenth anniversary.

[86] *University Record,* September, 1872, I, 2, 6.

[87] *Ibid.,* December, 1873, I, 10, 67. The first fraternity, Alpha Tau Omega, came to the University in September, 1877. *Ibid.,* March, 1879, I, 1, 1.

[88] Godbold, *Church College of the Old South,* 108-12.

[89] Fairbanks, *History of the University of the South,* 102. There were no rulings on alcohol among faculty and staff. References to toddies are found in the diaries of Bishop Quintard and John McCrady and the social drink crops up in stories of General Kirby-Smith and Dr. DuBose. Fairbanks was an ardent prohibitionist and largely through his influence the State of Tennessee later passed a "four-mile law" making illegal the sale of liquor within that distance of certain educational institutions. *Ibid.,* 167-69.

[90] William Crawford Gorgas, son of Josiah Gorgas, late surgeon general of the United States army, knighted by George V.

[91] The *Calendars, 1870-1871, 1871-1872, 1872-1873, 1874,* and *1875* list the courses in which each student was enrolled and the officers of student organizations.

[92] John S. Bradford to writer, May 20, 1946 (Sewanee Archives).

[93] Bradford to writer, June 6, 1946 (Sewanee Archives).

[94] Freeman, *R. E. Lee, A Biography,* IV, 351-62.

[95] Lovell, "In the Beginning," Baker *et al.* (eds.), *Sewanee,* 39.

[96] Godbold, *Church College of the Old South,* 187, 188.

CHAPTER FIVE

FIRST FRUITS
1872

By 1872 the University had attained a major objective. It had prepared one clergyman for the Episcopal Church. No one can better understand the academic achievement of those first four years than a modern industrial technician. The cost of producing the first bomber runs high. And high too was the cost of ordaining to the Episcopal ministry the first student trained at the University of the South. If the founding of the University is placed in perspective, it is seen that the need for a theological seminary was the primary impulse which set in motion its establishment. In the 1830's when Otey and Polk first planned an interdiocesan institution, there was a scarcity in the deep South of Episcopal clergy. Most of the southern dioceses were newly organized and bishops had difficulty finding ministers for their congregations.[1] Towns in need of clergy were increasing in the new West—Mississippi, Louisiana, and Texas. Many plantations owned by Episcopalians were able to support chaplains. Polk's letter to the bishops in 1856 stressed the fact that a southern seminary would increase a native ministry.[2] The ordination in 1872 of Charles McIlvaine Gray of Tennessee [3] was the culmination of forty years of successively greater efforts directed toward that act.

When Gray received the sacrament of ordination—the apostolic laying on of hands—he represented the fruit of an elaborate cultivation. Leading up to that moment when he entered the Episcopal ministry was a material investment of more than a hundred thousand dollars, the voluntary labor of many able men and the extraordinary sacrifice of a few, the wholesale transplanting to a virtual wilderness of dozens of families, the gathering of a small but talented faculty.

The gala Commencement of 1872 provided a fitting climax to the administration of the first vice-chancellor. The record attendance of trustees, the presence of Jefferson Davis, the prospect that Gorgas would be elected to succeed Quintard,[4] the awarding of many prizes [5] and the first diplomas [6] all combined to engender optimism. The conservatism of the hebdomadal board in not yet awarding degrees was praised in an editorial.

> Everybody knows that, with some exceptions, the diplomas, degrees, and honors generally, of most of our American collegiate institutions are not held in high regard. The temptation to follow popular wake is strong, but it is the avowed determination of this University to give no evidence of accomplishment in any department of letters or science, unless fully won.[7]

FANFARE WITH TRUMPETS MUTED

It was the first commencement at which so much physical improvement was evident on the campus. A half-dozen frame buildings clustered around the ever-expanding chapel, not counting the library built by Bishops Young and Gregg across the street. Bishop Quintard, resplendent in scarlet vice-chancellor's robes and ermine hood sent by friends at Cambridge,[8] congratulated the gownsmen on their appearance in new caps and gowns.[9] With its vested choir, surpliced clergy, robed and hooded bishops, capped and gowned faculty and students, and uniformed grammar school boys, the academic procession earned the admiring inspection of summer girls, local and visiting matrons, sisters, and parents. For many the pathos of the situation—the flimsy homes, some of them hardly better than shanties for all the glowing accounts, the clapboard classrooms, the mounting debts—may well have been forgotten when the Meneely bell pealed for the baccalaureate and almost as many marched in the procession as watched it. Bishop Quintard, with his love of formality in the Anglican tradition, made sure that this commencement would be a worthy progenitor of those that would follow.

When the trustees' meeting of 1872 closed in a flow of enthusiasm, when all the favorable aspects of the project were proudly and redundantly enumerated, when Quintard was praised and thanked for his "unsparing devotion . . . gratuitously rendered,"[10] the balance sheet had a favorable appearance. Four hundred matriculants in the first four years was "probably unexampled in this country for an unendowed school, independent of state patronage."[11] To trustees who visited Sewanee only once a year it seemed almost a miracle that an orderly and even attractive community had grown up in the wilderness.

REALIST IN THEIR MIDST

There was one who assessed the situation differently. The new Vice-Chancellor had completed only a semester in office when he wrote to his predecessor, who even then was on his most extensive fund-raising trip throughout the South:

> You will be surprised and overwhelmed to learn that the $10,000 are already more than exhausted, and that our debts are not all paid! I am sick at heart tonight. . . . I write to you rather to relieve my own thoughts, knowing your ready sympathy with our troubles. . . . The only consolation . . . is that without [the $10,000] we should have been unable to continue the school. It has saved us, at least for the moment, from ruin. . . . It is difficult for me to avoid blaming the gentlemen who unwittingly covered up this ruinous condition and actually made the Board of Trustees think we were in a flourishing condition. Now that we are attempting to pay our debts, we begin to find out how hollow is our financial condition.[12]

In this message Gorgas indicts the preceding administration. The *apologia* is simply that the Bishop was not an executive in the modern sense, not an organizer of detail as Gorgas was. He traveled almost continuously, dashing off letters by hand as they occurred to him and keeping records in his diary. He had no executive office or centralized records at Sewanee. His determined optimism prevented him from exercising what is referred to as sound business judgment. To him an obstacle was not a sign for caution or for investigation but a personal challenge to his ability and his faith. His solution for the problem of a deficit was to raise more money, not to economize. Throughout his administration he was a temporary vice-chancellor, who continued in the position only as a last expedient after the refusal of Maury and Lee, and he thrice offered his resignation.

Yet Quintard was the man for the day. He did not recognize or would not admit defeat. He had a genius for improvization. He went from action to action with keen insight into most situations, with intuitive grasp for long-term strategy. As the University owed its origin "to the clear and comprehensive mind" of Leonidas Polk,[13] it owed its existence in 1872 to "the courageous faith and invincible zeal" of Charles Todd Quintard.[14] He seemed to be the only man available for doing what was necessary to revive the University after the war. Could Bishop Green have done it? Would Bishop Gregg have done it? These questions cannot be answered categorically, but it can be stated that Bishop Quintard could do it and did.

CONCLUSION

The four years after the opening in 1868 brought three clear achievements to the University: the plans of the original founders were fixed as the ideal, the feasibility of a regional venture in higher education by the Episcopal Church was established, and five specific cultural patterns were woven together to form the University's character.

FOUNDERS' PLANS SURVIVE

The idealism of Polk, Otey, and Elliott fixed for their successors the excellence which emerged as criterion for the teaching and community life at Sewanee. Without the careful, complete, and compelling prewar plans it is impossible to conceive at all the opening of a university in the South by southern Episcopalians after the devastating war. The University of the South is today the only accredited institution of higher learning in the former Confederate states which opened under southern auspices for white students in the six years following the war.[15] Even with the founders' plans as inspiration, the refounders barely managed to continue the University. William Porcher DuBose described those years:

> To have set out with the largest, completest, and most ideal conceptions, and with the possession and expectation of the amplest means for executing and realizing them; and to have come down to the paltriest beginnings and the total absence of any means at all; to feel the needs,

intellectual and spiritual, greater and more pressing than ever, the conceptions truer, the ideals more vital and more matter of life and death with us in our adversity than ever they had seemed in our prosperity; and then year by year to be made to experience more and more the inadequacy of faith and endurance alone for the achievement of results that of necessity must be more tangible and material, if their ends were ever to be accomplished; —all this may have been very needful discipline for results as yet hidden in the impenetrable future; but they were not easy to endure or survive at the time.[16]

Without the prewar preparations, elaborate hopes and perfectionist standards in such a wasted land would have been impossible. The imaginative quality of the plans and preparations of 1860 and the postwar residue of enthusiasm and determination prevented those plans being forgotten, ignored, or shelved for less idealistic ones. What induced the trustees to send forth Fairbanks to mark the sites of the buildings planned by Hopkins? The situation was much like the early days of World War II when soldiers maneuvered in jalopies painted "This is a tank." Tremendous confidence and great faith were required to render such play-acting heroic rather than ridiculous.

According to Bishop Gailor, who came as a young teacher in 1882, "They set a standard of scholarship and life at Sewanee which influenced the whole South. For ten long years, from 1869 to 1879, she was the forlorn hope for higher education in the South ... when State Governments were paralyzed with the desolation of war and when private benefactions had not reached the prostrate South."[17] It is possible that the isolation of the University played a part more important even than predicted by the founders in 1857. The civil turmoils of Radical Reconstruction left no recorded effect on the new community. There were no dissident elements: no missionaries from the North, no carpetbaggers, no scalawags.

The theory that history is a process of evolution is less applicable at Sewanee than other institutions because of the advanced nature of the original conception. Sewanee history has been one of striving toward a clearly drawn pattern rather than moving from experiment to experiment. The basic purposes of the University remain much the same after ninety years. Bishop Quintard expressed Sewanee's educational philosophy in a rough memorandum written in 1873.

Education . . . must . . . be commensurate with ye whole man. Ye body must be trained by healthful exercise, ye mind . . . drawn out & strengthened, & . . . ye heart . . . sanctified & ye will subdued. It is ye aim . . . of ye University of ye South to develop a harmonious & symmetrical character, to fit & prepare men for every avocation in ye life that now is . . . & to teach all those things which a Christian ought to know & believe to his soul's health.[18]

The University Senate today declares the function of Sewanee's liberal arts college to be "the training of youth in Christian virtue, in personal initiative, in self-mastery, in . . . intellectual integrity" and adds "in aesthetic appreciation . . . and in scientific methods of inquiry."[19] At no time has the University been concerned only with a man's mind or a man's vocation.

BEFORE ITS TIME, THE REGIONAL IDEA

Proving the feasibility of a regional venture in higher education by the Episcopal Church was the second clear achievement of the first four years. Great as was the service of Bishop Quintard, he cannot be regarded as the sole reason for the survival of the University. In sending the institution on its way, he was joined by Fairbanks of Florida, Gorgas of Alabama, Green of Mississippi, Gregg of Texas, DuBose of South Carolina, and John B. Elliott of Georgia. Sewanee was never the project of any one diocese except during the brief interval in 1865 and 1866 when Tennessee initiated its revival. Of interest to the historian, if not to the educator and the cleric, is this early example of a regional development in education. A century later interstate planning and concentration of resources had come into vogue. Sewanee, both before and after the war, was in every sense a cooperative venture.

An examination of the enrollment further substantiates the regional character of the University. More than a tabulation of financial support, it is a direct indication of the effort put forth in the University's behalf by its friends, its trustees, and its supporting Episcopal clergy. Students evidently came as a result of personal solicitation since there was no advertising and little promotional literature, not even a proper catalogue until 1871. The four hundred sixty students matriculated in theological, collegiate, and grammar school courses through 1872 came

First Fruits 175

primarily from the owning dioceses. Kentucky and Virginia were much closer to Sewanee than Texas yet together they sent fewer than ten students.

Enrollment and matriculation figures for all departments were as follows:

		New Matriculants[20]				Total Enrollments[21]	
	1868	1869	1870	1871	1872	1870-1871	1871-1872
Alabama	2	17	27	15	7	39	28
Arkansas	—	4	5	5	1	7	5
Florida	3	11	4	5	4	11	11
Georgia	1	19	6	9	4	13	9
Louisiana	3	2	17	14	11	27	23
Mississippi	—	5	18	32	15	47	41
North Carolina	—	1	2	2	2	3	4
South Carolina	—	—	—	2	23	2	24
Tennessee	5	13	26	32	24	57	51
Texas	—	10	13	12	7	27	17
All others	—	4	7	4	5	5	10
Totals	14	86	125	132	103[22]	238	223

The enrollment chart shows the effectiveness of Quintard as a recruiter and the activity of Green in Mississippi. About a dozen of the students matriculated by 1872 were sons of faculty members and an equal number were nephews and cousins of men teaching at Sewanee. As many as twenty were the sons or grandsons of trustees. Texas, considering its distance, was outstanding in the number of students it sent to the University. By contrast, North Carolina—and South Carolina until DuBose joined the faculty—reflected a lack of interest by Bishops Atkinson and Davis.

Not all dioceses took an equal interest in the progress of the University. Alexander Guerry, ninth Sewanee vice-chancellor, said that if the University ever had the enthusiastic support of one hundred men at the same time, it could become the most effective institution in American education.[23] Doubtless he was thinking of the hundred men who are members of the board of trustees. The record of the early trustees is a good example of what Guerry meant. Attendance at meetings is no positive index of effectiveness of trustees in the service of an institution, but it is a helpful guide. In the ten meetings between the war and the close of Quintard's administration in 1872, diocesan representation at meetings was as follows:[24]

	1866	'67	'67	'68	'68	'68	'69	'70	'71	'72	Total
Alabama	0	2	0	2	1	2	1	3	1	2	14
Arkansas	1	1	0	0	0	1	1	1	0	1	6
Florida	1	2	1	3	0	3	4	2	1	4	21
Georgia	3	2	2	3	3	3	3	3	4	3	29
Louisiana	0	2	0	0	0	1	1	2	2	2	10
Mississippi	1	2	2	1	2	3	3	4	3	4	25
N. Carolina	1	1	0	4	2	2	3	0	0	2	15
S. Carolina	0	0	0	1	0	2	1	2	2	4	12
Tennessee	3	2	4	1	3	2	4	4	4	4	31
Texas	0	0	0	0	1	2	1	3	2	2	11
Duplicates[25]	-1	-1									
Totals	9	13	9	15	12	21	22	24	19	28	

Dioceses which sent the most students to Sewanee also had the best attendance at meetings of the board. Tennessee, Mississippi, and Georgia showed the most consistent interest. Only Arkansas, which did not elect clerical and lay trustees until 1872, and North Carolina failed to be represented at every meeting after school opened. One or two men made the 1,500-mile journey from Texas in every year after 1867. The more active dioceses usually elected one or two faithful trustees, then year after year tried vainly to fill the other posts with men sufficiently interested to attend the meetings.[26] The three bishops who were most valuable to the institution, Green, Quintard, and Gregg, had the best attendance.

One of the factors in the survival of the University was the continuity of responsibility which was vested in the office of each southern bishop. Whether he assumed it or not, every southern diocesan, at his consecration, was given a personal responsibility for the several enterprises of his diocese. Of these enterprises, the University of the South was one, rendered so by the action of the council of each diocese. Always there were bishops who were unable or unwilling to accept responsibility for the University, but out of ten, and more as the number of dioceses increased, there always were enough. Always the statutory responsibility was there, always the challenge beckoned. The list of those who responded is a list of great names in Sewanee's history.[27]

Dependable support by the owning dioceses was never achieved in the early days of the University. The optimistic expectations of Quintard and Fairbanks were not realized. Efforts to raise thousands brought hundreds. The prewar fortune had disintegrated under war and Reconstruction. Except for Quintard, one by one the bishops were tried and found wanting as beggars. Gregg of Texas responded nobly in the Advent offerings, Young of Florida raised a few hundred dollars, and that was about all. The total gifts to the University by 1872 had not exceeded $35,000, of which a third came from England, raised by Bishop Quintard, who was responsible for about two thirds of the total. There was no lack of ingenuity in devising plans for raising money. But the sponsors too frequently failed to assist in implementing their own plans. That these deficiencies were understood by some trustees is shown by the report of the committee on ways and means in 1871:

> By thus multiplying agencies, [we] only serve to complicate our efforts at the expense of success. . . . Pastoral letters, appeals to be read to congregations, a general division of responsibility, and second-hand efforts, may do very well in their place and under other circumstances, but will inevitably fail here, as they have ever done in the matter of raising funds. Single, individual, persevering effort, by personal contact, is indispensable. There must be work—earnest, untiring, individual work—or we will ever fail.[28]

A steady income from the Episcopal Church was not forthcoming until the national organization imposed standard budgetary practices on the individual parishes. Even so, the idea of the annual offering should have proved successful. With reasonable promotional methods, with printed appeals, with reminders before the appointed time, the offering might have brought, even in the earliest days, as much as $5,000 to $10,000 per year. But clergymen were forgetful. Bishops failed to give enthusiastic support. Vestrymen were unconvinced of the need. Parishes themselves were needy. The answer to the problem finally came in the 1940's when a systematic drive was made to have the University placed in the annual budget of each diocese and parish.[29]

The record of church support for 1869-1872 shows at once the possibilities and the failings of the voluntary offering. This tabulation is restricted to Advent offerings and does not include other gifts of individuals from those dioceses nor does it include occasional special gifts of parishes other than the Advent offering.

Diocese	1869[30]	1870[31]	1871[32]	1872[33]
Alabama	37.00	130.55	444.75	179.85
Arkansas			17.25	36.70
Florida	33.50	38.00	58.00	7.00
Georgia	46.00	18.10	231.50	393.51
Louisiana	18.80	40.00	403.90	20.00
Mississippi	29.93	91.55	101.50	169.30
North Carolina		81.00		31.00
South Carolina	11.75	43.80	40.60	159.30
Tennessee	6.00	233.65	131.58	315.55
Texas	89.53	352.62	680.49	572.03
	$272.51	$1,029.27	$2,109.57	$1,884.24

THE FIVE-FOLD TRADITION

Much like a person, an institution has a personality of its own. Will Percy intuitively sensed the character of Sewanee and in his poetic *Lanterns on the Levee* gave the best appraisal of its nature which has yet been made. But Sewanee's character lends itself to the analysis of the historian as well as to that of the poet. The third achievement of the Quintard administration was the establishing at the University of a recognizable tradition, or character, which has endured unchanged for almost a century. This tradition had five origins. It was and is a composite of five influences.

THE OXONIAN

An Oxford-Cambridge bent was clear from the first. Polk thought Oxford, of all the world's universities, most worthy of emulation.[34] Nomenclature and organization were borrowed from the English universities: the honorary chancellor, the executive vice-chancellor, the advisory hebdomadal board, proctor, tutor, and hall. Oxford and Cambridge honored Sewanee's vice-chancellor and sent a thousand volumes to the library. The black gown for students and professors was English.

FIRST FRUITS 179

Quintard, Harrison, Dabney, and DuBose were particularly sympathetic to the Anglican tradition in education. This tradition has continued at Sewanee in academic organization, terminology, architecture, and curriculum. The Latin ceremonies of the University are still patterned after those of Cambridge, and the vice-chancellor still wears the scarlet robe.

THE MILITARY

Military influence was strong in early Sewanee. Gorgas and Shoup with their West Point training might have been expected to impose rigid discipline. Sevier was even more militaristic. Nor was this influence unpopular with the students, who requested permission to form drill companies. During the war these students had been hero-worshipping boys. Only two are known to have served in the army.[35] Others regretted having been deprived of the glory of wearing the Confederate uniform. Militarism was not in the thinking of the original founders, but any inconsistency between warlike training and Christianity did not trouble postwar Sewanee. Several benefits of militarism attracted the early administrators. Drill brought healthy and economical diversion, and the accepted pattern of military discipline allowed an academic and social control over the students which would be unthinkable in the normal academic community. The acceptance of the West Point tradition may well have constituted an unconscious bow to the practical. The military feature went to the grammar school in the 1890's and has there continued,[36] while reappearing in the college as a student army training unit in World War I, a navy officer training unit in World War II, and an air force reserve officer training corps since 1951.

THE CLASSICAL

The next great influence in the five-fold tradition might be called the classical mantle. The beginning of the classical tradition at Sewanee is clear. Among the first founders, Graeco-Roman culture was exemplified best by Bishop Elliott. Among those who came afterward it was emphasized by Quintard and DuBose, by Caskie Harrison and John B. Elliott. From them the mantle descended to Basil M. Gildersleeve, William P.

Trent, John B. Henneman, and Henry M. Gass, not to mention the theologians, Charles L. Wells and W. Lloyd Bevan. These men had much Latin and more Greek. They breathed the bracing air of the civilization that was Athens and they kept alive on Sewanee Mountain Socratic wisdom, Platonic idealism, Aristotelian balance—under circumstances which all too often demanded the fortitude of Epictetus.

THE SOUTHERN

The fourth influence entering the Sewanee tradition was the aristocratic influence of the Old South. The blessings, real and imaginary, outlined in prewar southern propaganda had been transmuted into golden ideals by 1870. The good was remembered and the bad forgotten. Sewanee became a repository for the hopes and dreams of the Old South. With the passing of years Sewanee took on some of the attributes of a matriarchy. The widowed ladies with whom students boarded, the mothers who came with boys to educate and who remained to educate others, became *grandes dames.* Every student sat at table with a lady at the head of it and was inculcated with good manners in the southern tradition. The poise of the students noted by William Alexander Percy in his *Lanterns on the Levee* was not accidental. The Old South continues to be venerated at Sewanee. Its customs are perpetuated and its families live on. In 1953 descendants of the first five vice-chancellors were at Sewanee, and the fourteen-man board of regents included great grandsons of Bishop Polk and Bishop Elliott.

THE EPISCOPAL

The fifth and strongest influence was that of the Episcopal Church, one which was not out of harmony with the Oxonian or the planter tradition. The University was avowedly a Christian institution. Its organization was effected and its policy controlled by Episcopalians, though it was supported with restraint. The chapel stood at the center of the campus physically and spiritually. The religious services held twice a day were compulsory for students. No student had to be Episcopalian but many of them were. No faculty member had to be Episcopalian but in the early days all were. Non-Episcopalians were not ex-

FIRST FRUITS 181

cluded from the domain but they had to travel some distance to attend another church. In Episcopal circles the University gave promise of generative qualities, not only producing ministers for the church but also a religiously educated laity. The University has remained under the control of the Episcopal Church and each of the original dioceses is still associated with the institution. Not since 1910 has there been a major effort to remove the University from denominational ownership.[37] In 1953 the University comprised the only four-year men's college directly owned and controlled by the Episcopal Church.

A TALE OF TWO TIMES

The University of the South is the child of two eras—the rich, confident, aristocratic South of the 1850's, and the beaten, emaciated, poverty-stricken South of Reconstruction. The University's institutional personality is formed by the complex confluence of traditions of both eras. The reconstruction of the University bore many outward resemblances to the depressing period in which it took place. The poverty of Sewanee was the poverty of the South, but its leaders were not distracted by the troubles of the times. Reconstruction at Sewanee was not pathetic at Sewanee. The dark prophecy of Bishop Smith of Kentucky was proven false. Manners did not become slovenly nor students boorish, and even ecclesiastical epidemics were kept at a distance. Instead, as we have seen, an institution was created with ideals of excellence, regional foundations, and enduring traditions.

A modern historian looks back to Reconstruction and laments, "Grace and gallantry were more vulnerable to the new climate of push and progress and survived only in sheltered places."[38] Sewanee, not by accident but by design, was one of those places.

NOTES FOR CHAPTER FIVE

[1] There were five priests and three deacons in Tennessee when Otey became bishop. There were eight clergymen in Alabama when Cobbs went there as bishop in 1844. Polk found six clergymen in Louisiana in 1841. E. Clowes Chorley, "The Missionary March of the Episcopal Church," *Historical Magazine of the Protestant Episcopal Church,* XVII (March, 1948), pp. 17-43.

[2] Hodgson (ed.), *Reprints of Documents Prior to 1860,* p. 8.

[3] Charles M. Gray of Bolivar was present at the opening of the Lent term in 1869.

His courses for that year are not recorded but in 1870-1872 he studied Latin, Greek, metaphysics, English literature, philosophy, moral science, theology, and Hebrew. Gray did not receive a degree from the University. The first bachelor of divinity degree was awarded in 1881 to William Klein of England, who came to the United States with Bishop Quintard.

[4] Gorgas had for some time been addressed as acting vice-chancellor. *University Record,* June, 1872, I, 1, 4.

[5] Prizes were given for scholarship, sacred studies, deportment, composition, oratory, dictation, and spelling.

[6] Eight diplomas were awarded to six students by the schools of chemistry, English literature, and metaphysics. *Calendar, 1871-1872,* p. 14. The *Calendar* includes A. M. Avery, Florida, omitted from the list in the *University Record,* September, 1872, I, 2, 5, 6, which names D. F. Hoke, Alabama; T. J. Morris, Texas; and B. B. Myles, F. W. Royster, and D. R. Barnett, Mississippi.

[7] *University Record,* September, 1872, I, 2, 5. The first degrees were awarded August 6, 1874, six years after the University opened, to Thomas Bringhurst of Texas, Joseph R. Gray of Tennessee, and Beverly B. Myles of Mississippi, bachelor of arts, and Edwin C. Steele of South Carolina, bachelor of letters. *Calendar, 1874,* p. 13.

[8] *University Record,* June, 1872, I, 1, 1.

[9] *Ibid.,* November, 1872, I, 3, 12.

[10] *Proceedings, 1872,* p. 44.

[11] *University Record,* June, 1872, I, 1, 1.

[12] Gorgas to Quintard, December 7, 1872 (Sewanee Archives).

[13] Statement of the "History and Location" of the University of the South, *Calendar, 1870-1871,* p. 7, and subsequent *Calendars* through 1875.

[14] *Proceedings, 1893,* p. 16. Resolution adopted by the trustees in 1893 when Quintard declined to be considered for election as chancellor.

[15] A. J. Brumbaugh, *American Universities and Colleges,* 5th edition (Washington, 1948). Also surviving are Trinity University in San Antonio, Texas, a project of the northern branch of the Presbyterian Church, opened in 1869, and thirteen colleges and universities opened for the freedmen. Among these was St. Augustine's, begun as a normal school in Raleigh in 1868 and partly supported by the Episcopal Committee on Missions to the Colored People in the United States. Stewart, *Work of the Church in the South During the Period of Reconstruction,* 57.

[16] DuBose, "Fairbanks," *Sewanee Review,* XIV (October, 1906), pp. 498-503.

[17] Gailor, *Some Memories,* 80.

[18] Untitled manuscript inserted in Quintard Diary, 1873-1874, p. 15.

[19] *Bulletin of the University of the South, Annual Catalogue, 1950-1951* (Sewanee, 1951), p. 20.

[20] These figures include all students in the college and grammar school and are derived from Noll, *Alumni Directory,* and from Dudney and Petry, "Matriculation Register." These sources are essentially in agreement as to year in which a student enrolled but the research of Dudney and Petry in grade books and other records has resulted in the reclassification of many students as "grammar school" or "college."

[21] *Calendars, 1870-1871,* and *1871-1872.* In 1870-1871, 114 were enrolled in the college, and in 1871-1872 there were 125 college students. Dudney and Petry, "Matriculation Register." The terminology of the divisions of the institution is as follows:

First Fruits

September-December, 1868—"Junior Department of the University of the South." Lent term, 1869—"Junior Department . . ." Trinity term, 1869 and Lent term, 1870, "Junior Department . . ." and "Grammar School." In the Trinity term, 1870, the "Schools of the University" were put in operation and the "Grammar School" continued. Undergownsmen of the University continued for many years to be known as "juniors."

[22] There seems to be no special significance in the decline in enrollment of 1872 because it was promptly offset the next year. Until 1872 each year's students filled existing accommodations but not for thirty years after that did the University threaten to overflow.

[23] Interview with Alexander Guerry, June, 1948.

[24] Information here is from *Proceedings* of pertinent years. The first six meetings of 1866-1868 were held at Sewanee, Montgomery, Sewanee, Savannah, Sewanee, and New York. Meetings in 1869, 1870, 1871, and 1872 were held at Sewanee.

[25] Fairbanks in 1866 and 1867 is listed from Tennessee and from Florida.

[26] Only seven men attended more than half of the first ten postwar meetings of the board, 1866-1872: Bishops Green, Quintard, and Gregg, Reverend W. C. Williams of Georgia, Major Fairbanks, L. N. Whittle of Georgia, and Thomas E. B. Pegues of Mississippi.

[27] An example of a bishop who did not respond is Atkinson of North Carolina. He reported to his diocesan council in 1877 that the success at Sewanee evidenced "the lively interest of the dioceses which have combined to maintain it. For this success, however, I cannot claim much credit, either for myself or for the diocese. . . ." He said that the cause for North Carolina's apathy was its "distance from the site of the University." North Carolina Diocesan *Journal, 1877*, pp. 42, 43. He did not mention that he started in 1871 a rival theological seminary with an endowment of $750, or that from the opening in 1868 through 1872 he did not mention Sewanee in his annual addresses to the diocese and the trustees did not report to the annual meetings. Nor did he mention his refusal to allow Quintard to solicit funds for the University in his diocese in 1872.

[28] *Proceedings, 1871*, p. 39.

[29] In 1952 parishes and dioceses contributed over $90,000 to the University through the Living Endowment and the Theological Education Sunday Offering.

[30] *Proceedings, 1869*, p. 26.

[31] *Ibid., 1870*, pp. 55, 56.

[32] *Ibid., 1871*, pp. 73-75.

[33] *Ibid., 1872*, pp. 52-54.

[34] William Giles Dix in an address at the state capitol in 1859 expressed the hope that the University would "be the Oxford of America." Hodgson, *Reprints of Documents Prior to 1860*, p. 151.

[35] Ministerial candidates Van Winder Shields and John Kershaw were veterans. Another veteran, H. O. Judd, is listed in Noll, *Sewanee Alumni Directory*, 41, but was probably one of Dr. Knight's theological students before the opening of the University and not a college matriculant.

[36] Sewanee Grammar School became Sewanee Military Academy in 1908. It remained under the control of the vice-chancellor and board of trustees of the University.

[37] *Proceedings, 1910*, pp. 18-20, 34.

[38] Woodward, *Origins of the New South*, 160.

APPENDIX

EARLY OFFICERS AND FACULTY OF
THE UNIVERSITY OF THE SOUTH
1857-1872

CHANCELLORS

Rt. Rev. James Hervey Otey - - - - - - - - - 1857-1863
Rt. Rev. Leonidas Polk - - - - - - - - - - - 1863-1864
Rt. Rev. Stephen Elliott - - - - - - - - - - 1864-1866
Rt. Rev. William Mercer Green - - - - - - - - 1866-1887

VICE-CHANCELLORS

Rt. Rev. Charles Todd Quintard - - - - - - - - 1867-1872
Gen. Josiah Gorgas - - - - - - - - - - - - - 1872-1878

SECRETARIES OF THE BOARD OF TRUSTEES

Rev. Henry C. Lay - - - - - - - - - - - - - - 1857-1859
Rev. David Pise - - - - - - - - - - - - - - - 1860-1868
Rev. William C. Williams - - - - - - - - - - 1868-1877

FACULTY—1868-1872

John Locke Cooper (1872), grammar school tutor
Robert Dabney, M.A., LL.D. (1868-1876), English and metaphysics
Robert M. DuBose (1871-1878, 1882-1885), grammar school assistant
Rev. William Porcher DuBose, M.A., S.T.D., D.D., D.C.L. (1871-1918), chaplain, moral science, theology
Maj. George Rainsford Fairbanks, M.A. (1869), history
John B. Elliott, M.D., Ph.D. (1869-1885), chemistry, health officer
Brig. Gen. Josiah Gorgas (1868-1878), civil engineering, headmaster of junior department, master of grammar school, vice-chancellor
W. F. Grabau (1871-1878), assistant and instructor in music in the grammar school
G. Berkeley Green, A.B. (1868-1869), mathematics
Caskie Harrison, M.A., Ph.D. (1869-1882), ancient languages
Rev. Lucian Holmes (1871-1872), grammar school tutor
Rev. Francis A. Juny, D.D. (1869-1872), modern languages, Hebrew
Rev. Franklin L. Knight, M.A., D.D. (1868-1869), Greek, Latin, acting chaplain
Charles Landon Carter Minor, M.A. (1872), Latin, master of grammar school
Col. Frank Schaller, M.A. (1872-1878), modern languages
Col. T. Frank Sevier (1869-1877), master of grammar school, proctor, commerce and trade
Rev. Francis Asbury Shoup, M.A., D.D. (1869-1896, intermittently), mathematics, ecclesiastical history, acting chaplain

NOTE: The dates show total tenure on faculty. The subjects are those taught 1868-1872. The degrees include all awarded in the person's lifetime. These data have been compiled by Mrs. Robert L. Petry in preparation for a Centennial Alumni Directory.

ACKNOWLEDGMENTS

Factual data for this book were acquired over a period of seven years. It is impossible to acknowledge all help received. The assembly of this material as a thesis was uncontemplated until 1951 and the information was not accumulated in an orderly way until then.

Major collectors of Sewaneeana are listed in the bibliography but none has done so much to make available the primary source material as the Archivist, Mrs. Sarah Hodgson Torian. Following the example of her father, the third vice-chancellor, in contributing her services to the University, she has assembled a rare collection of documents and publications on Sewanee, the Episcopal Church, and the South.

The writer is indebted to C. T. Quintard Wiggins, Jr., of New Orleans, who made available the diary of his great-grandfather, Vice-Chancellor Charles Todd Quintard, and then placed the diary in the Sewanee Archives. The Reverend Caleb B. K. Weed revealed the possible existence of the diary and General L. Kemper Williams provided for its microfilming. The films are now available for scholars in southern history (1864-1898) at the libraries of North Carolina, Louisiana State, and Vanderbilt Universities. Mrs. Frank Polk and Yale University are responsible for the gift to the Sewanee Archives of the Leonidas Polk Collection. Vice-Chancellor Edward McCrady permitted the examination of the diary, 1877-1881, of John McCrady, his grandfather and predecessor as professor of biology. The diary reveals important information about faculty members of 1868-1872. Mrs. Jessie Palfrey Leake permitted the examination of the diary of Vice-Chancellor Josiah Gorgas, her grandfather, and presented his copy of the *Book of Common Prayer* to the Sewanee Archives. Mrs. Clara Slatter Gaidry permitted access to the files of the Winchester *Home-Journal*. Mrs. Mary McNeal Dilworth gave the Sewanee Archives the McNeal Papers.

The late historiographer of the University, the Reverend Edgar Legare Pennington, was very helpful in the earlier stages of the study, and

Mrs. Pennington loaned material from his library. The Reverend Walter H. Stowe, editor of the *Historical Magazine of the Protestant Episcopal Church,* suggested sources. Dr. J. G. deRoulhac Hamilton's long acquaintance with the documents concerning his *alma mater* was generously shared with the writer. Dr. Niels Sonne, librarian of the General Theological Seminary, loaned volumes of diocesan journals. Susan B. Keane, reference secretary of Tulane University, assisted in research. John Hodges, librarian of the University of the South, offered every cooperation. Dr. James W. Patton, of the Southern Archives of the University of North Carolina, is making available the Otey Papers.

More than two hundred persons answered questions orally or by letter. For information concerning Sewanee and its people the writer is indebted to the following relatives of persons connected with the University 1857-1872: Mrs. Gayle Aiken, Jr., New Orleans; Phelan Beale, New York; Dr. Isaac Croom Beatty, III, Lafayette, Indiana; Troy Beatty, Jr., Memphis; Mrs. Olivia Proctor Benedict, Cincinnati; George Yerger Campbell, Memphis; Mrs. Lucy Pinckney Elliott Cunningham, Scarsdale, New York; Dr. Marye Y. Dabney, Birmingham; Thomas Ewing Dabney, New Orleans; William Green deRosset, Sarasota; W. C. Dowdell, Gadsden, Alabama; W. Dudley Gale, Nashville; Charles McIlvaine Gray, St. Petersburg; Mrs. Mattie Bailey Haywood, Raleigh, North Carolina; Mrs. Hamilton Polk Jones, New Orleans; Sterling S. Lanier, Hopkinsville; Mrs. Margaret Lord Miller, Chattanooga; Dabney Maury Pollard, Beaumont; Charles McD. Puckette, Chattanooga; Cameron McRae Plummer, Mobile; Mary Gayle Robertson, Columbia, South Carolina; Kate Skipwith, Oxford, Mississippi; Mrs. Queenie Woods Washington, New Orleans; Mrs. Aileen Gorgas Wrightson, Chevy Chase; and the following persons from Sewanee: Mary Wright Cotten, Fanny Bowdoin deRosset, Mrs. Rainsford Glass Dudney, May Peronneau DuBose, Charlotte St. John Elliott, Dr. Robert Woodward Barnwell Elliott, Mrs. Eva Fairbanks Glass, Mrs. Polly Brooks Kirby-Smith. Other helpful persons whose family associations began with the University before 1900 were the Reverend F. Craighill Brown, Dora Colmore, Dr. Henry M. Gass, Charlotte Gailor, Dr. Telfair Hodgson, Dr. Reynold M. Kirby-Smith, Mrs. Nell Gildersleeve Kirby, Joseph

Acknowledgments

Brevard Jones, David A. Shepherd, Johnnie Tucker, Douglas L. Vaughan, and the Reverend Cary Breckenridge Wilmer, last surviving faculty member of the 1870's. Mrs. Caro Sedway Perkins, Nashville, Mrs. Lillie Hardin Yates, Macon, Mississippi, and Charles M. Moss of Nashville also were helpful.

Bishop R. Bland Mitchell provided information about his predecessor as bishop of Arkansas, Leonidas Polk, and Bishop Edmund P. Dandridge provided information about diocesan records in Tennessee. The following provided material in addition to their published information: Dr. John S. Marshall on William Porcher DuBose, Nash Kerr Burger on William Mercer Green, and Dr. Frank Vandiver on Josiah Gorgas.

Information about their professors was provided by Doctors J. Leo Burthe and Rudolph Matas of New Orleans, students of John B. Elliott, and by the Reverend George B. Myers, student of William Porcher DuBose. Dr. Arthur J. Nurah examined Tulane records concerning John B. Elliott. Reverend Messrs. R. Emmet Gribbin, Jr. and Robert Hunsicker provided information on specialized aspects of Episcopal Church history.

The following public relations officials provided information about their institutions: Robert B. Brown, Kenyon, Herbert L. Ganter, William and Mary, O. R. Hoffman, Princeton, Richard C. Lee, Yale, Robert W. Madry, North Carolina, and William M. Pinkerton, Harvard. William S. Griffin of the University of Mississippi provided material from the alumni files.

Mrs. Floyd Medford was researcher on the John McCrady diary and on other special problems. Barbara Ann Tinnes assisted in typing and gave an admirable reading for style. Especially appreciated are the marginal notations made by Dean Charles T. Harrison and Dr. Robert W. Daniel. Other valued readings were given by Tudor Seymour Long, Dr. Edward McCrady, Dr. Reynold M. Kirby Smith, Mrs. Henry T. Kirby-Smith, the Reverend John H. and Mary W. S. Soper, Dr. Robert W. B. Elliott, and others.

Three members of the history department at Tulane rendered services which cannot be overlooked. Dr. Fred C. Cole's personal interest from the start was encouraging. The comments of Dr. William R. Hogan on Chapters 1 and 11 were helpful. But the conscientious attention given the manuscript in all its thesis stages by Dr. Wendell H. Stephenson deserves unbounded gratitude.

In a special category is Elizabeth Nickinson Chitty, history major under Dr. Robert S. Cotterill of Florida State University. She transcribed notes, proofread, edited, and made critical comment on all parts of the book, bringing to the task her talent for research and her faculty for connecting names and family relationships.

There are others who must remain nameless. They are the countless persons who have answered questions and letters since 1946. To all of them the author is humbly grateful.

PERMISSIONS

Thanks are due several copyright owners for permission to use direct quotations. In order of their appearance in the book, we acknowledge our gratitude to the following:

Yale University Press for permission to quote from William E. Dodd, *The Cotton Kingdom* Volume 27, *The Chronicles of America,* (New Haven, 1919);

Richard H. Bassett for permission to quote from his father, John Spencer Bassett, *Middle Group of American Historians* (MacMillan, New York, 1917);

Longmans, Green & Co., Inc. for permission to quote from William M. Polk, *Leonidas Polk, Bishop and General* (New York, 1915);

The Rev. Walter H. Stowe for permission to quote from Moultrie Guerry, "Beginnings of the University of the South," *Historical Magazine of the Protestant Episcopal Church,* Volume VII, December, 1938;

Yale University Press for permission to quote from George F. Smythe, *Kenyon College, Its First Century* (New Haven, 1924);

Louisiana State University Press for permission to quote from C. Vann Woodward, *Origins of the New South* (Baton Rouge, 1952).

BIBLIOGRAPHY

This bibliography includes material specifically concerned with Sewanee during the period 1857-1872 or with educational enterprises of the Episcopal Church. It does not list general references in southern history or general encyclopedias, even though there are citations to these sources in the text.

PRIMARY SOURCES
Unpublished Diaries, Letters, Collections
(These are in the Sewanee Archives unless some other location is stated.)

Alumni Biographical Files, University of the South. These files include matriculation data on each student and letters and clippings concerning many students.

Bradford, John, to writer, May 20, June 6, 1946. Recollections of a matriculant of 1869.

Colyar, Arthur St. Clair. Untitled manuscript, a discussion of the relationship between the University and the Sewanee Mining Company (probably rough draft of speech for Sewanee Semi-Centennial, 1907).

deRosset, Frederick A., Papers. Letters, report cards, and other papers of a matriculant of 1872 in the possession of his son, William G. deRosset, Sarasota, Florida.

DuBose, William Porcher, Papers. Letters to DuBose, newspaper clippings about his works, and manuscripts of his sermons.

Elliott, John, Letters. Correspondence from Sewanee, 1869-1874. In Habersham Elliott Papers, University of North Carolina.

Elliott, Stephen, Papers. A few at Sewanee. Others examined were in library of the late Edgar L. Pennington, historiographer of the University.

Fairbanks, George R., and Glass, James G., Collection. Bound volumes collected by two University historiographers, Fairbanks and his son-in-law, Glass. Principal volumes concerned with this period were "Fairbanks-Gorgas-University Letters-Miscellaneous (1861-1908)," "Old Letters-Documents-University-Fairbanks," "Cornerstone Letters-Early Miscellaneous Letters," "The Crisis of 1875-78," "Pamphlets," a volume containing nineteen items pertaining to Fairbanks, and an untitled volume of letters and clippings about the laying of the cornerstone. Other Fairbanks-Glass material is in the possession of Mrs. Rainsford Glass Dudney, Sewanee.

Gonce, John W., to Charles W. Underwood, January 1, 1923. Letter containing description of laying of cornerstone and of Sewanee Collegiate Institute, Winchester, Tennessee.

Gorgas, Josiah, Diary. In possession of Mrs. Jessie Palfrey Leake, his granddaughter, University, Alabama.

Gorgas, Josiah, Papers. Letters to Robert Dabney, T. Frank Sevier, and Charles T. Quintard.

Johnston, Joseph E., to Charles T. Quintard, October 9, 1885. Description of death of Leonidas Polk.

Lea, Albert Miller, to Charles T. Quintard, All Saints' Day, 1879. Description of laying of the cornerstone.

Lee, Robert E., to William M. Green, September 23, 1868. Letter declining the vice-chancellorship.

Maury, Matthew F., to William M. Green, April 21, 1868; and Charles T. Quintard, January 4, April 21, 1868. Letters in regard to the vice-chancellorship.

McCrady, John, Diary, 1877-1881. In the possession of his grandson, Vice-Chancellor Edward McCrady, Sewanee.

McIlvaine, Charles P., to Governer Rutherford B. Hayes, June 19, 1867, Hayes Papers, Hayes Memorial Library, Fremont, Ohio, typescript in Sewanee Archives. Letter concerning disappearance of University documents during the Civil War.

McNeal, Albert T., Papers. Letters and documents collected by McNeal during the forty years he was associated with the University as legal counsel, trustee, and dean of the law department. Given to the Sewanee Archives by his daughter, Mrs. Lawrence Dilworth, West Palm Beach, Florida.

Nauts, William Boone, Collection. Bound periodicals and scrapbooks collected by the late professor of Latin.

Otey, James Hervey, Papers. Principal collection is at the University of North Carolina. Southern Archives and Sewanee Archives have exchanged microfilms of the Otey and Polk collections.

Polk, Leonidas, Papers. Sewanee's considerable material was augmented in 1953 by Yale University's gift of the Frank Polk collection. Mrs. Frank Polk interceded to bring back to Sewanee the most important collection relating to its founding.

Quintard, Charles T., Diary, 1864-1898, 36 vols. Sections in 1865, 1866, 1867, 1868-1872, 1873-1875 are missing. There are notes for April, 1873, to April, 1874, and there are published accounts covering his war experiences and the 1867-1868 visit to England. Placed in the Sewanee Archives by his great grandson, Charles Todd Quintard Wiggins, Jr., of New Orleans. Three volumes are the gift of Charlotte Gailor.

Quintard, Charles T., Papers. Documents and letters to George R. Fairbanks, W. P. Rathbun, T. Frank Sevier, Richard H. Wilmer, et al.

Quintard Family *Bible*.

Sneed, H. H., to Vice-Chancellor Benjamin F. Finney, May 25, 1923. Description of Sewanee Collegiate Institute.

University Records

"Leases, The University of the South." 7 vols. Treasurer's office, Sewanee. Volume I contains a record of the number, approximate location, and lessee of each lease granted in this period.

"Matriculation Book of the University." Registrar's office, Sewanee.

Bibliography

University and Campus Publications, Proceedings, Maps
(All of these are in the Sewanee Archives.)

Calendar of the University of the South, 1870-1871. Sewanee, 1871. Succeeding *Calendars* to the year 1879. The *Calendars* include information usually found in a college catalogue, lists of faculty and students, courses offered, organizations, and historical accounts.

Cap and Gown (Sewanee), I (1881), *et seq.* The student literary magazine in the 1880's and the college annual beginning in 1891. These contain many references to earlier periods of the University's history.

Constitution, Ordinances, and Rules of Order of the University of the South. Sewanee, 1938.

Gorgas, Josiah [?]. *The Progress of the University.* Sewanee, 1872. A fund-raising promotional piece prepared for Quintard's 1872-1873 trip.

Green, William Mercer. One-sheet folder listing faculty and aims of the University, May 1, 1869.

Hodgson, Telfair (ed.). *University of the South Papers, Series A, No. 1* (Sewanee, 1888), *Reprints of the Documents and Proceedings of the Board of Trustees of the University of the South Prior to 1860.* Includes charter, constitution, statutes, account of first six trustees' meetings, laying of the cornerstone, and the principal addresses on those occasions.

McCrady, Edward, Jr. *Map of the University of the South and Environs.* Sewanee, *circa* 1940.

Noll, Arthur Howard (ed.). *Sewanee Alumni Directory.* Sewanee, 1913.

Plan of the Lands of the University of the South. Philadelphia, n.d. Lithographed map *circa* 1870.

Proceedings of the Board of Trustees of the University of the South at Their Sessions Held at Columbia, S. C., October 15-20, 1861. Rome, Ga., 1871. In the Sewanee Archives are collections of proceedings for various years bound by members of the board and presented to the University. Titles vary.

Sewanee Review (Sewanee), I (1892), *et seq.* In its earlier years, especially in the editorship of William Peterfield Trent, the *Sewanee Review* contained historical articles.

Statement of the History, Progress, Present Situation and Wants of the University of the South. N.p., n.d. The copy in the Sewanee Archives bears a penciled notation: "Used 1869-70. Written by G. R. Fairbanks." The pamphlet probably was used as a "Calendar" for that year and as a mailing piece for prospective donors and students.

University News (Sewanee), I, Nos. 1-10 (1875); II, Nos. 1-37 (1876); special edition, July 13, 1876. Then published as the *News,* Vol. V (1877). An independent publication.

University of the South. N.p., 1873. Four-page folder, including list of texts used in college and grammar school.

University Record (Sewanee), I, Nos. 1-4, 6, 8-12 (1872-1873); II, 1-5, 7, 9 (1874-1875); and I (1879). A University publication.

Church Journals and Periodicals

The annual *Journal* of the proceedings of the convention or council of each of the owning dioceses provides information about the University. Used in this study were the journals of the dioceses of Alabama, Tennessee, North Carolina, and Louisiana. Diocesan journals of this period are in the library of the University of the South.

American Quarterly Church Review (New York, 1848-1890). Vols. I-LIX in library, School of Theology, University of the South.

Church Register (Montgomery), 1868.

Church Almanac, 1849-1863. New York, 1849-1863. Bound volume in library, School of Theology, University of the South. Contains list of clergy and statistics on each diocese. Issued annually by the New York Protestant Episcopal Tract Society.

Morehouse, Linden H. (ed.). *The Living Church Annual, 1950.* New York, 1950. Contains statistics and directories of the Episcopal Church. Issued annually.

Parker's Church Calendar and General Almanack, 1868. Oxford, 1868.

Newspapers

Winchester *Home-Journal*, 1858-1860. In the possession of the editor's daughter, Mrs. Clara Slatter Gaidry. This newspaper, published at the county seat, reprinted articles concerning the University from other newspapers all over the South.

Contemporary references to the University are found in the Nashville *Republican Banner* (1860), New Orleans *Daily Picayune* (1860), Newark *Daily Journal* (1873), Nashville *American* (1880).

Historical accounts appear in the Nashville *Banner*, Nashville *Tennessean Sunday Magazine*, and the Chattanooga *Times*.

Published Diaries, Reminiscences, Autobiographies

Baker, Lily, Charlotte Gailor, Rose D. Lovell, and Sarah Hodgson Torian (eds.). *Sewanee.* Sewanee, 1932. Reprints of documents and reminiscences.

DuBose, William Porcher. *Turning Points in My Life.* New York, 1911.

Elliott, John Barnwell. *Philosophical Notes for My Children.* N.p., n.d.

Fairbanks, George Rainsford. *History of the University of the South.* Jacksonville, 1905. Fairbanks must be considered a primary as well as a secondary source. He was present at every meeting of the board of trustees after the first at Lookout Mountain and he includes information found in no other sources.

Gailor, Thomas Frank. *Some Memories.* Kingsport, 1937.

―――. "Reminiscences," Thirteenth *Alumni News Letter* (Sewanee), May 1, 1917, pp. 18-22.

Green, William Mercer. *Memoir of Right Reverend James Hervey Otey, First Bishop of Tennessee.* New York, 1885.

Noll, Arthur Howard. *Doctor Quintard, Chaplain C. S. A. and Second Bishop of Tennessee.* Sewanee, 1905. Based on notes begun by Quintard in 1896.

BIBLIOGRAPHY

SECONDARY SOURCES

Unpublished Manuscripts

de Rosset, William Green. "Index of Graves in University Cemetery." Card file, 1953. Office of Commissioner of Buildings and Lands.

Dudney, Rainsford Glass, and Helen A. Petry. "Matriculation Register of the University of the South, 1868-1953." Registrar's Office, University of the South. The register lists every student with the year and department in which he matriculated.

Gailor, Charlotte. "Skit Presented by Woman's Club at Sewanee Public School October 7, 1950." Sewanee Archives. Scene I of this carefully researched play is set at University Place, October 9, 1860, and Scene II at Sewanee, October 9, 1875.

Gailor, Frank Hoyt. "Sewanee in the Years before the Civil War." N. d.

Hill, James Otto. "Sewanee, A Unique Community." Unpublished thesis for master of arts degree, Middle Tennessee State College, 1952.

Orkney, Virginia. "The Origin of the University of the South and Bishop Quintard's Part in Making It a Reality." Unpublished honors paper, Mary Washington College, May 1, 1952.

Petry, Helen A. "College Matriculants, 1868-1953." This chart includes enrollment figures. Registrar's Office, University of the South.

Reynolds, George L. "Sewanee and the Cumberland Plateau in the Civil War." Address delivered at the E. Q. B. Club, 1949.

Published Sewaneeana

Daniel, Robert W. "The Battle of Sewanee," *Sewanee Alumni News* (Sewanee), XII (1946), No. 2, p. 13.

DuBose, William Porcher. "The Romance and Genius of a University," *Sewanee Review*, XIII (1905), pp. 496-502.

Elliott, Sarah Barnwell. *Sewanee: Past and Present.* Sewanee, 1909.

Gailor, Thomas Frank. *Address on July 27, 1899.* Sewanee, n. d.

―――――. *The High Adventure.* Sewanee, n.d.

Guerry, Alexander. *A Compelling Necessity.* Sewanee, 1946.

Haskins, David Greene. *A Brief Account of the University of the South,* New York, 1877.

McCrady, Edward, Jr. *Founders' Day Address, 1946.* Sewanee, 1946.

Pennington, Edgar Legare. "The Battle at Sewanee," reprinted from *Tennessee Historical Quarterly* (Nashville), Vol. IX, No. 3, 217-43.

Quintard, Charles T. *An Address Delivered in St. Augustine's Chapel, Sewanee, Tennessee, at the Meeting of the Board of Trustees of the University of the South on Thursday, July 31st, 1890.* New York, 1890.

Thomas, Charles Edward. *Sewanee, The Oxford of America.* Sewanee, 1932.

Washington, Mrs. George (ed.). *The Sewanee Cook Book.* Nashville, 1926.

Weber, Mrs. Henri. *Planting the Cross at Sewanee.* N. p., n. d.

Biographies, Individual

Bazett-Jones, E. A., George B. Faxon, and Louis DeSaussure (eds.). *In Memoriam. Charles Todd Quintard, D.D., LL.D., M.D., Bishop of Tennessee, 1865-1898.* Memphis, 1898.

Benjamin, Marcus. "The Consecration of Bishop Wilmer of Alabama in 1862." Reprinted by the Church Historical Society, Publication No. 4. Philadelphia, 1927.

Bratton, Theodore DuBose. *An Apostle of Reality, The Life and Thought of the Reverend William Porcher DuBose.* New York, 1936.

Burger, Nash K. "William Mercer Green, First Bishop of Mississippi, 1850-1887," *Historical Magazine of the Protestant Episcopal Church* (New Brunswick, New Jersey), XIX (1950), pp. 340-54.

DuBose, William Porcher. "George Rainsford Fairbanks," *Sewanee Review* (Sewanee), XIV (1906), pp. 498-503.

Gorgas, Marie D., and Burton J. Hendrick. *William Crawford Gorgas, His Life and Work.* Garden City, New York, 1924. Life of a matriculant of 1869.

Guthrie, William Norman. "The Doctor [William Porcher DuBose] as I Knew Him," *Churchman* (New York), December 15, 1936, pp. 16-18.

Henneman, John Bell. "George Rainsford Fairbanks," *Sewanee Review,* XIV (1906), pp. 493-98.

Hopkins, John Henry. *The Life of the Late Right Reverend John Henry Hopkins, First Bishop of Vermont, and Seventh Presiding Bishop.* New York, 1873.

Insko, W. Robert. *Kentucky Bishop, An Introduction to the Life and Work of Benjamin Bosworth Smith.* Frankfort, 1952.

Jervey, James Postell. "Leonidas Polk, the Confederate General," *Historical Magazine of the Protestant Episcopal Church,* VII (1938), pp. 389-404.

Lefler, Hugh T. "Thomas Atkinson, Third Bishop of North Carolina," *ibid.,* VII (1938), pp. 422-34.

Mabbott, Thomas Ollive (ed.). *The Complete Poetical Works of W. W. Lord.* New York, 1938. Includes a biographical sketch of a trustee of 1857.

Manning, William T. "An Apostle of Reality" (review), *Living Church* (Milwaukee), October 24, 1936, pp. 457-59. Biographical material on William Porcher DuBose.

Manross, William W. "Early Life and Presbyterate of Leonidas Polk," *Historical Magazine of the Protestant Episcopal Church,* VII (1938), pp. 324-40.

Marshall, John S. *The Word was Made Flesh, The Theology of William Porcher DuBose.* Sewanee, 1949.

Noll, Arthur Howard (ed.). *Alexander Gregg, First Bishop of Texas.* Sewanee, 1912.

Osborn, George Coleman. *John Sharp Williams, Planter-Statesman of the Old South.* Baton Rouge, 1943. Student life in 1870.

Owens, Hubert Bond. *Georgia's Planting Prelate.* Athens, 1945. Life of Stephen Elliott.

Pennington, Edgar Legare. "John Freeman Young, Second Bishop of Florida." Publication 195, Church Missions Publishing Company *Quarterly* (May-July, 1939).

———. "Stephen Elliott, First Bishop of Georgia," *Historical Magazine of the Protestant Episcopal Church,* VII (1938), pp. 203-63.

Polk, William M. *Leonidas Polk, Bishop and General.* 2 vols. New York, 1915.

Quintard, Charles T. *Memorial Sermon on the Rt. Rev. Alexander Gregg, D.D., Bishop of Texas, August 1, 1893.* N.p., n.d. Sewanee Archives.

BIBLIOGRAPHY

Stowe, Walter H. "Polk's Missionary Episcopate," *Historical Magazine of the Protestant Episcopal Church,* VII (1938), pp. 341-59.

Vandiver, Frank E. *Ploughshares into Swords: Josiah Gorgas and Confederate Ordnance.* Austin, 1952.

Whitaker, Walter C. *Richard Hooker Wilmer, Second Bishop of Alabama.* Philadelphia, 1907.

White, Greenough. *A Saint of the Southern Church.* New York, 1897. Life of Nicholas Hamner Cobbs, first bishop of Alabama.

Biographies, Collected

Fairbanks, Lorenzo Sayles. *Genealogy of the Fairbanks Family in America.* Boston, 1897.

Fleming, Francis P. (ed.). *Memoirs of Florida.* 2 vols. Atlanta, 1902. Biographical sketches of students and trustees are included.

Garrett, William. *Reminiscences of Public Men in Alabama for Thirty Years.* Atlanta, 1872.

Guerry, Moultrie. *Men Who Made Sewanee.* Sewanee, 1932.

Knight, Lucian Lamar (ed.), *Library of Southern Literature.* 16 vols. New Orleans, 1907.

Mickle, William E. *Well Known Confederate Veterans and Their War Records.* New Orleans, 1915.

Perry, William Stevens. *The Bishops of the American Church.* New York, 1897.

Colleges

Brumbaugh, A. J. *American Universities and Colleges,* Fifth Edition. Washington, 1948.

Caswell, Henry. *The Martyr of the Pongas: being a Memoir of the Rev. Hamble James Leacock.* London, 1857. Includes an account of the Kentucky theological school.

Coulter, E. Merton. *College Life in the Old South.* New York, 1928.

Denny, George H. "Universities and Colleges of the South," Samuel C. Mitchell et al. (eds.), *The South in the Building of the Nation.* 12 vols. Richmond, 1909. X, 243.

Fisher, Sydney G. *Church Colleges, Their History, Position and Importance.* Philadelphia, 1895.

Godbold, Albea. *The Church College of the Old South.* Durham, 1944.

Smythe, George Franklin. *Kenyon College, Its First Century.* New Haven, 1924.

Thomas, Charles Edward. *European Universities.* Boston, 1936.

Nixon, H. Clarence. "Colleges and Universities," William T. Couch (ed.), *Culture in the South.* Chapel Hill, 1934.

Publications Concerning the Protestant Episcopal Church

Cheshire, Joseph B. *The Church in the Confederate States.* New York, 1912.

Davidson, Randall T. *The Lambeth Conferences of 1867, 1878, and 1888.* London, 1896.

Constitution and Canons for the Government of the Protestant Episcopal Church in the United States of America. Chicago, 1943.

McConnell, Samuel David. *History of the American Episcopal Church, 1699-1915.* 11th edition. Milwaukee, 1934.

Manross, William Wilson. *A History of the American Episcopal Church.* Milwaukee, 1935.

Murphy, DuBose. "The Spirit of a Primitive Fellowship: The Reunion of the Church," *Historical Magazine of the Protestant Episcopal Church,* VII (1938), 435-48.

Noll, Arthur Howard. *History of the Church in the Diocese of Tennessee.* New York, 1900.

Parker's Church Calendar and General Almanack, 1868. Oxford, 1868.

Pennington, Edgar Legare. "The Organization of the Protestant Episcopal Church in the Confederate States of America," *Historical Magazine of the Protestant Episcopal Church,* VII (1938), 308-38.

Perry, William Stevens. *Handbook of the General Convention of the Protestant Episcopal Church, 1785-1880.* New York, 1881.

———. *History of the American Episcopal Church, 1787-1883.* 2 vols. Boston, 1885.

Seymour, Charles M. *History of One Hundred Years of St. John's Episcopal Church, Knoxville, Tennessee, 1846-1946.* Knoxville, 1947.

Stewart, M. Bowyer. *The Work of the Church in the South during the Period of Reconstruction.* Milwaukee, 1913.

INDEX

The dates following the name of each bishop indicate the years of his episcopate. Abbreviations: *biog.*, principal biographical data; *illus.*, illustration; *n.*, note; tr., trustee.

Abernathy, Dr., 56.
Advent offering, 118, 138, 178.
Agassiz, Louis, 44.
Agriculture, Croom's professorship, 55; school of, 69, chemistry applied to, 69.
Aiken, Mary Gayle (Mrs. Hugh), 166 *n. 59*.
Air force ROTC, 179.
Alabama, diocese of, *founding diocese*, 43, 45, 50, 52, 62, 75 *n. 18*, 100, 119, 133, 134, 176; prewar expectations, 58, contributions, 71; enrollment, 175; Advent offering, 178. (See Bishops Cobbs and Wilmer.)
Alabama, University of, 42, 44, 112 *n. 87*, 119.
Alcohol, forbidden to students, 162, 167 *n. 89*.
All Saints' Chapel, 102.
Ancient languages, Harrison, instructor in classics, 130; school established, 135; Harrison, first professor, 135; enrollment, 135. (See Latin and Greek.)
Anderson, H. M., M.D., Ga. tr., 143 *n. 23*, U. treasurer, 128.
Anderson, Leroy H., M.D., Ala. tr., 77 *n. 61*.
Archaeology and history, school of, 69.
Architects, landscape, Hopkins, 61; buildings, 63.
Architecture, in school of civil engineering, 69.
Arkansas, missionary district and diocese of, *founding diocese*, 43, 45, 62, 75 *n. 18*, 80 *n. 117*, 119, 176; enrollment, 175; Advent offering, 178. (See Bishops Polk, Freeman, and Lay.)
Armfield, Col. John, Tenn. tr., 57, 60, 77 *n. 61*.
Astronomy and physical geography, school of, 69; (in department of physics), 136.
Athens, Tenn., offered site, 53.
Atkinson, Thomas, third bishop of N. C. (1853-1881); 55, 63, 80 *n. 119*, 87, 103, 110 *n. 36*, 183 *n. 27*.
Atlanta, Ga., considered as site, 53, 54.

Bachelor of arts degree, requirements, 70, 136; first awarded, 182 *n. 7*.
Bachelor of divinity degree, first awarded, 182 *n. 3*.
Bachelor of letters degree, first awarded, 182 *n. 7*.
Bachelor of science degree, requirements, 136.
Band, 51, 63; cornet, 161.
Banister, Rev. John Monro, Ala. tr., 143 *n. 4, 23*.
Banking, in school of commerce and trade, 70, 136.
Baptist colleges, 42; theological school, 58.
Barbados, Bishop of, 105.
Barbot, Pierre, tailor, 137, 152.
Barnard, Frederick A. P., 44, 64.
Barnes, D., land grant, 60.
Barney, Charles R., engineer, 52, 56, 57, 59, 60, 61, 62, 71, 72.
Barnum, Mrs., of Baltimore, 111 *n. 49*.
Baseball, 160, 161.
Bass, John, 60.
Baylor University, 43.
Beauchamp, Earl, 105.
Beckwith, John Watrus, second bishop of Ga. (1868-1890); 115, 118, 142 *n. 2*.
Beersheba Springs, Tenn., trustees' meetings, 55, 58.
Bell, Meneely, 131, 147 *n. 111*.
Bellewood, hall, 157.
Beresford-Hope, A. J. B., M. P., 104, 112 *n. 89*, 113 *n. 95*.
Bevan, Rev. W. Lloyd, faculty, 180.
Bexley Hall, 137.
Bishops, southern, Polk's letter to, 45; manifesto, 45.
Bolles, Rev. J. A., D.D., 124.
Bombay, Bishop of, 105.
Bookkeeping, in school of commerce and trade, 70, 136.
Bork, Joseph F., tinsmith, 152.
Bowers, Abraham, land grant, 60.
Bradford, John S., student, 163.

Breslin Tower, 130.
Brick-making, 153.
Brierfield, Gorgas' home, *illus.*, 33; 137.
Bright, Congressman John M., 64.
Bringhurst, Thomas, 182 *n. 7.*
Bristol, Bishop of, 105.
Brokerage, in school of commerce and trade, 70.
Buccleuch, Duke of, 105.

Calaboose, 154.
Caldwell, H. N., bookstore, pharmacy, 152.
Cambridge University, 81 *n. 139,* 103, 105, 107, 130, 170.
Canterbury, Archbishop of, 48, 103; St. Augustine's College, 112 *n. 89.*
Cap and gown, 66, 155, 167 *n. 67;* required of professors, 129, 137, of college students, 137, 159, 170.
Capetown, Bishop of, 104, 105.
Carnarvon, Earl of, 113 *n. 95.*
Carolina Life Insurance Company, 138.
Carrick Academy, Winchester, Tenn., 94.
Central building, plans, 71, 82 *n. 154.*
Centre College, 43.
Chancellor, 46, 51, 97, 101, 102, 138. (See Bishops Otey, Polk, Elliott, Green, and Gregg.)
Chapel attendance, 69, 160; services, 159, 160. (See St. Augustine's and All Saints' Chapels.)
Chaplain, Knight, acting, 121; Shoup, acting, 130; DuBose, 139.
Charter, 55.
Chattanooga, 46, entertained trustees, 50, 51; offered site, 53; St. Paul's Church, 84.
Chemistry, schools of, theoretical and experimental, 69, applied to agriculture and the arts, 69; school established, 135; Elliott, instructor, 129, first professor, 135; enrollment, 135; 136.
Chester, Bishop of, 105.
Choir, 51, 63, 64, 124, 125, 159, 169.
Church support, 177-178. (See each diocese, Advent offering.)
Civil engineering, school of, 69, established, 135; Gorgas instructor, 131, professor, 135; 136.
Civil War, 41, 49, 72, 179, military action on domain, 64, 83, 108 *n. 2;* devastation to Episcopal churches, 84, to southern colleges, 119; colleges opened following, 172, 182 *n. 15.*

Clarke, Mrs. Mary, scholarship, 126.
Classical tradition, 125, 179, 180. (See ancient languages, Latin, Greek.)
Cleveland, Tenn., considered as site, 53.
Coal, 53; on domain, 54, 153; train, 159.
Cobbs Hall (South Wing), 101.
Cobbs, Nicholas Hamner, first bishop of Ala. (1844-1861); *illus.,* 28; 51, 55, 56, 63, 80 *n. 119,* 158, 166 *n. 53.*
Coit, Rev. J. H., 116.
College of Charleston, 44.
Colleges, southern, prewar, 42-44, 45; state, 42; denominational, 43, 162, 163; Baptist, 43; Episcopal, 43; Methodist, 43; Presbyterian, 42, 182 *n. 15;* Roman Catholic, 43; American, 59; in Reconstruction, 119, 120; northern, 120, 121, 136; in former Confederate states, 182, *n. 15.* (See institutions by name.)
Columbia Female Institute, Tenn., 47.
Columbia, S. C., trustees' meeting, 72.
Columbia University, 44, 88, 120, 136.
Colyar, Arthur St. Clair, land titles, 60.
Commerce and trade, school of, 70; Sevier, acting professor, 126; 136.
Commissary, U. of S., Tremlett, 123.
Commissioner of buildings and lands, 99, 127, 129. (See domain, Fairbanks, leases.)
Community, 56; Elliott's conception, 70; Gorgas' description, 142; expansion, 151, 153; society of, 154, 164; Hayes' contributions to, 153, 157.
Composition, in schools of rhetoric, 69, metaphysics, 135.
Confederate States of America, 124; Episcopal Church in, 72, 86, 87; veterans on faculty, 115, 142, in student body, 179; widows, 142, 158; colleges in former states, 172.
Constitution, U. of S., 61, 66-70.
Constitution of United States, in school of government, 69.
Cooper, John Locke, tutor in grammar school, registrar, 131; umpire, 161.
Corinth, Miss., offered site, 53.
Cornerstone, 63, 83; laying, 61, 62-66.
Cornish, Rev. J. H., fund-raiser, 100.
Cotten, Mrs. Sarah Eliza Wright, matron, 122, 157.
Cowan, Tenn., 54, 159.
Craik, Dr. James, 101.
Cranborne, Viscount, 113 *n. 95.*
Crane, Rev. William C., Miss. tr., 98.

INDEX 199

Creary, James Edwin, student, 122.
Croom, Col. Isaac, 55; Croom's Bluff, 55.
Cross, planted in 1866, 94.
Cruger, Nicholas J., student, 122.
Curriculum, 69, 135. (See subjects.)
Curtis, Rev. Moses Ashley, N. C. tr., 77 *n. 61*, 80 *n. 119*, 98, 111 *n. 62*, 142 *n. 2*, 143 *n. 23*.

Dabney, Dr. Robert, *illus.*, 31; *biog.*, 121, 122; 142, 156, 179; metaphysics and English literature, instructor, 121, professor, 135; acting headmaster, 121.
Dalton, Ga., offered site, 53.
Dances, 140, 162; dance hall, 152.
Daniel Baker College, 76 *n. 48*.
Dartmouth, Earl of, 105.
Davidson College, 42.
Davis, Jefferson, 117, 124, 133; addressed trustees, 138; oratorical contest, 162.
Davis, Thomas Frederick, fifth bishop of S. C. (1853-1871); 76 *n. 29*, 77 *n. 61*, 80 *n. 119*, 81 *n. 128*.
Debating, student, 160.
DeBow, J. D. B., 44.
Decherd Tract, 60.
Degrees, awarded by hebdomadal board, 70; requirements for, 70, 136; awarded, 182 *n. 3, 7*; honorary, 70, 128, 129; 170.
Deportment, student, prize for, 128, 182 *n. 5*.
Depot, railroad, 122.
deRosset, Armand John, M.D., N. C. tr., 142 *n. 2*, 143 *n. 23*.
Derry, Bishop of, 105.
Diocesan treasurers, 46, 57, 99.
Diplomas, 70, 170.
Divinity, systematic, 137.
Doctor of civil law, 128.
Doctor of philosophy, 129.
Domain, 53, 54, 56, 71, 72; land grants, 60; during war, 83, 96, 108 *n. 1*; deeds, 96, 97; Fairbanks' conception of, 92, 93.
Dorr, Cicero Hawkes and Hawkes Barkley, students, 122.
Dramatics, student, 161.
Drawing, in school of civil engineering, 69.
Dry Grove, Miss., theological seminary, 111 *n. 69*.
DuBose, Mattie (Mrs. McNeely), 139, 167 *n. 67*.
DuBose, Robert, 139.
DuBose, Rev. William Porcher, *illus.*, 23; *biog.*, 139-141; 142, 142 *n. 1*, 157, 172, 173, 179; home, The Rectory, *illus.*, 35;

theology, 136; chaplain, professor of moral science, 139; publications, 140.
Dunn, Rev. J. Wood, Tex. tr., 55, 77 *n. 61*.
Dunnington, F. C., Tenn. tr., 112 *n. 85*, 143, *n. 4*.

Easton, diocese of, 80 *n. 118*.
Ecce quam bonum, 165 *n. 40*.
Economy, political, in school of political science, 69.
Education, school of philosophy of, 69.
Electives, 136.
Elliott, Charlotte (Mrs. Charles McD. Puckette), school teacher, 154.
Elliott, Charlotte Bull Barnwell (Mrs. Stephen), 51, 156.
Elliott, Habersham, 80 *n. 124*.
Elliott, John Barnwell, M.D., *illus.*, 30; *biog.*, 129; resident physician, 129; chemistry, instructor, 129, first professor, 135; 142, 179.
Elliott, Robert Woodward Barnwell, first bishop of W. Tex. (1874-1887), 129.
Elliott, Sarah Barnwell, 155.
Elliott, Stephen, first bishop of Ga. (1841-1866); *illus.*, 15; *biog.*, 49, 50; 46, 51, 63, 64. 80 *n. 119*, 180; endowment commissioner, 55, 58, 60, 72; residence at Sewanee, 62, 72; concept of community, 70, 155; for secession, 71; letter concerning church in Confederate States, 72; presiding bishop of Confederate Episcopal Church, 86; reunion of Episcopal Church, 87; third chancellor of U., 96; and Quintard, 123; Sigma Epsilon, 161; classical influence, 179.
Elliott Hall, 102.
Elmore, Mrs., matron, 157.
Elocution, in school of rhetoric, 69, 136.
Ely, Cathedral of, 104.
Emory College, 43.
Emory and Henry College, 43.
Endowment, 41, 46, 73; diocesan fund-raising, 57, 58, 70, 71; plan abandoned, 99, 134; commissioners of, Polk and Elliott, 55, 72, R. H. Wilmer, 134, Quintard, 96, 100, 101, 134, 138, 146 *n. 82*, 177; Young, Beckwith, J. P. B. Wilmer to solicit, 118; Thackera, agent, 128; $20 subscriptions, 118; $100 subscriptions, 134; $500 subscriptions, 138; insurance plan, 138; 177.
England, 48, 66, aid from, 102-108, 127, 131; traditions of, 177, 178.

English, school of language and literature, 69; combined with metaphysics, 135; Dabney instructor, 121, first professor, 135; enrollment, 135; 136.
Enrollment, southern colleges, 44, 120; northern colleges, 120; U. of S., 122, 124, 126, 131, 174, 175.
Ensign, William P., construction, 94.
E. Q. B., faculty club, 154, 155, 156.
Episcopal Church, in South, 43, 44; general conventions, 45, 86, 87, 122; division during war, 72; reunion, 86; bishops and clergy, 119; tradition at U. of S., 45, 180. (See P. E. Church in the Confederate States, dioceses by name.)
Erskine College, 43.
Estill, Dr. Wallace, land grant, 54, 60, 78 *n. 78*, 79 *n. 109*.
Ethics (in school of moral science), 136.
Ethnology and universal geography, school of, 69.
Ewell, Lt. Gen. Richard S., 133.
Exchange, in school of commerce and trade, 70.
Executive committee, 68, 93, 128, 129, 133, 137, 138, 143 *n. 4*.
Exeter, Bishop of, 105.

Faculty, 125, 131, 142, 150; not required to be Episcopalians, 69; Confederate veterans on, 115, 142; first professors, 135; salaries, 135; standards, 173. (See individual professors and subjects.)
Fairbanks, Charles Massey, first student, 122.
Fairbanks, Flora, teacher, 154.
Fairbanks, Major George Rainsford, *illus.*, 19; *biog.*, 91-93; Fla. tr., Tenn. tr., 67, 72, 73, 80 *n. 119*, 85. 93, 94, 98, 109 *n. 11*, 110 *n. 45*, 111 *n. 62*, 112 *n. 85*, 116, 133, 137, 138, 142 *n. 1*, *n. 2*, 143 *n. 4*, *n. 23*, 153, 155; residences, Rainsford Place, *illus.*, 39, 62; Rebel's Rest, *illus.*, 35, 94, 111 *n. 62*, 118, E. Q. B. founded at, 154; name of U., 55; springs and views, 80 *n. 120*; post office, 80 *n. 121*; postwar revival of U., 85, 87, 93; commissioner of buildings and lands, 99, 127, 128, 129, 134; treasurer, 124, 128; instructor in history, 144 *n. 45*; interpretation of founders' plans, 81 *n. 138*, 92, 93.
Fairmont School, Moffat (Monteagle), Tenn., 140.

Farm, University, 69.
Fees, student, 99, 124, 128, 159, 167 *n. 68*.
Fellowships, 59.
Finances, prewar, 46, 57-59, 60, 68, 70, 71, 72, 73, 102, 128, 134; postwar, 85, 89, 91, 93, 99, 100, 101, 104, 107, 108, 118, 123, 127, 128, 131, 133, 134, 138, 171, 177, 178. (See endowment, salaries, student fees, Advent offering.)
Fine arts, school of, 70.
Fischer, Herr William Frederick, cabinet worker, 152.
Flag, at Lookout Mountain, 51.
Florida, diocese of, *founding diocese*, 43, 45, 50, 52, 62, 75 *n. 18*, 119, 176; effects of war on, 85; enrollment, 175; Advent offering, 178. (See Bishops Rutledge and Young.)
Fogg, Francis Brinley, Tenn. tr., 47, 80 *n. 119*, drafted charter, 55; first registrar, 60.
Font, in chapel, 126.
Football, 161, 162.
Forbes, T. M., shoemaker, 152.
Forensic Hall, 156.
Forensics, student, 161.
Founders' plans, Fairbanks' interpretation of, 81 *n. 138*; influence of, 172, 173.
Founding, U. of S., 41, 50.
Franklin County, Tenn., 54, 56, 72.
Franklin, Tenn., offered site, 53.
Fraternities, 162.
Freedmen, colleges opened for, 182 *n. 15*.
Freeman, George W., second bishop of Ark. (1844-1858); 62, 76 *n. 29*, 80 *n. 117*, 119.
French, school of language and literature, 69; enrollment in, 135; 136. (See modern languages.)
Fulford Hall, Quintard's home, *illus.*, 34; 94.
Furman University, 43.

Garner, Henry, land grant, 60.
Garnett, Theodore S., engineer, 77 *n. 69*.
Gass, Dr. Henry M., faculty, 180.
Gass, John, student letters home, 157, 160.
General Theological Seminary, 89.
Geography, in school with astronomy, 69.
Geology, mineralogy, and paleontology, school of, 69; 136.
Geometry (in school of mathematics), 136.
Georgia, diocese of, *founding diocese*, 43, 45, 50, 52, 75 *n. 18*, 119, 176; prewar fund-

INDEX 201

raising, 58; enrollment, 175; Advent offering, 178. (See Bishops Elliott and Beckwith.)
Georgia, University of, 42, 44, 54, 59.
German, school of language and literature, 69; enrollment in, 135; 136. (See modern languages.)
Ghost, 121.
Gibralter, Bishop of, 105.
Gibson, W. A., dry goods, 152.
Gildersleeve, Basil M., 179.
Gilliam, Pleasant, store, 151.
Gipson, Allen, land grant, 60.
Gladstone, W. E., M. P., 113 *n. 95*.
Gloucester, Bishop of, 105.
Gonce, John W., 65, 66; student, Sewanee Collegiate Institute, 95.
Gordon Springs, Ga., offered site, 53.
Gorgas, Amelia Gayle (Mrs. Josiah), 117, 156.
Gorgas, Brig. Gen. Josiah, *illus.*, 22; *biog.*, 116, 117; 128, 131, 133, 137, 142, 156, 158, 171; residence at Sewanee, Brierfield, *illus.*, 33, 137; headmaster, junior department, 116, 125; engineering and physics, instructor, 131, first professor, 135; second vice-chancellor, 68, 138, 170, 171; and Quintard, 90; president U. of Ala., 117; named E. Q. B., 154.
Gorgas, William Crawford, student, *illus.*, 36; 142, 162.
Government and constitution of United States, school of, 69.
Gowns, academic. (See cap and gown.)
Gownsmen, Order of, 141.
Graduate work, 59, 120.
Graduates, first, 182 *n. 7*.
Grammar (in school of metaphysics and English literature), 136.
Grammar school, 45, 72, 122; organized as department, Sevier, master, 125; Cooper and Holmes, tutors, 131; Minor, headmaster, 141; building, 131, 151; self-supporting, 137; uniforms, 137, 159; curriculum, 148 *n. 134*; regulations, 160; 183 *n. 36*.
Gray, Rev. Charles McIlvaine, first student ordained, 169.
Gray, Joseph R., 182 *n. 7*.
Gray, Judge Peter W., Tex. tr., 151.
Greek, school of language and literature, 69; Knight, instructor, 121; Harrison, instructor, 130; enrollment, 135; 136. (See ancient languages.)

Green, G. Berkeley, instructor in mathematics, 116, 121, 123.
Green, Lily, 98, 155, 165 *n. 37*.
Green, William Mercer, first bishop of Miss. (1850-1887), *illus.*, 20; *biog.*, 97, 98; 46, 51, 63, 80 *n. 119*, 96, 99, 100, 105, 106, 112 *n. 85*, 116, 121, 123, 132, 133, 142, 143 *n. 23*, 147 *n. 124*, 174, 175, 183 *n. 26*; residence, Kendal, *illus.*, 35, 97, 157, 161, 166; proposed name of U., 51; first service at Sewanee, 57; named views and springs, 80 *n. 121*; fourth chancellor, 98; correspondence with Maury, 106.
Greeneville, Tenn., offered site, 53.
Gregg, Alexander, first bishop of Tex. (1859-1893), *illus.*, 21; *biog.*, 132; S. C. tr., 62, 77 *n. 61*, 80 *n. 119*, 143 *n. 23*, 155; library, 131; fifth chancellor, 132; support of U., 174, 176, 177.
Gregg Hall, 132.
Griffin, Daniel, Ga. tr., 109 *n. 11*, 123.
Griffin, Ga., offered site, 53.
Guerry, Alexander, ninth vice-chancellor, 175.
Guerry, Rev. Moultrie, 47.
Guilford, Rev. William H., 95.
Guion, George S., La. tr., 77 *n. 61*.
Gwynn, Col. Walter, engineer, 52.
Gymnastics, 161.

Halls, 70, 157, 158. (See individual buildings.)
Hampden-Sydney College, 42.
Hardee, Lt. Gen. William J., 117, 160.
Hardee baseball club, 160.
Harris, Rev. Samuel S., 148 *n. 148*.
Harrison, Caskie, *illus.*, 31; *biog.*, 130, 131; 142, 179; instructor in classics, 130; first prof. of ancient languages, 135, 156; directed dramatics, 161. (See ancient languages, Greek, Latin.)
Harrison, Rev. Hall, 116.
Harrowby, Earl of, 105.
Harvard University, 44, 49, 120, 135, 136.
Hawkins, J. B., land grant, 60.
Hawks, Rev. William N., Ga. tr., 89.
Hay, Dr. Henry P., 95.
Hayes, Jabez Wheeler, *illus.*, 24; *biog.*, 153; 154, 155.
Hebdomadal board, 68, 170.
Hebrew, 136, 137.
Henneman, John B., 180.
Hervey, Lord Arthur, 104.

Hervey, Rev. Lord Charles, 106, 113 *n. 95*.
Hines, Robert and Isaac, land grant, 60.
Hinton, Eugene, Miss. tr., 80 *n. 119*.
History and archaeology; American history and antiquities, schools of, 69; 136.
Holmes, Rev. Lucian, tutor, 131.
Hoge, Sam C., groceries, 152.
Honorary degrees, awarded by trustees, 70; first conferred on Tremlett, 128; Ph.D., 129.
Hoods, academic, 102, 129, 138.
Hopkins, John Henry, second bishop of Vt. (1832-1868), 50, 61, 86, 103, 129, 173; landscape sketches, 101, *illus.*, 38.
Hopkins, Rev. John Henry, Jr., 86; designed seal, 148 *n. 143*.
Hotel, 127, 134; boarding houses, 155.
Houghton land grant, 60.
Houston, Russell, 78 *n. 88*.
Hunt, Rev. G. H., Tenn. tr., 143 *n. 23*.
Huntsville, Ala., considered as site, 53, 54.

Insurance, in school of commerce and trade, 70.
Insurance plan for endowment, 70.
International law, in school of political science as "Law of Nations," 69.
Italian, school of language and literature, 69.

Jacksonville, Ala., offered site, 53.
Johnson, William Henderson, shoemaker, 152.
Johnston, Gen. Joseph E., 123, 159.
Jones, Brig. Gen. Samuel, 143 *n. 6*.
Judd, Charles S., photographer, 151.
Judd, Harvey O., 151.
Judd, Spencer, photographer, 165 *n. 17*.
Junior department, authorized, 115; opened, 121, 143 *n. 3*; became university, 135.
Juny, Rev. Francis A., *biog.*, 129, 130; modern languages, instructor in, 130, first professor of, 135. (See French, German, Spanish.)

Kendal, Bishop Green's home, *illus.*, 35; 97, 157, 161, 166.
Kentucky, diocese of, 99, 101, 119; theological school, 43; Shelby College, 43. (See Bishop Smith.)
Kenyon College, 137.
Kershaw, Maj. Gen. Joseph B., S. C. tr., 139.
King's College, London, 81 *n. 139*, *142*; 107.

Kirby-Smith, Gen. Edmund, professor of mathematics, 83; name, 109 *n. 3*; came to Sewanee, 142; 142 *n. 1*.
Knight, Rev. Franklin L., 123; rector, Sewanee Collegiate Institute, 94, 95; missionary to University Place, in charge Sewanee Training and Divinity School, 98; instructor, Greek and Latin, acting chaplain, 121; dwelling, 122.
Knight, Franklin W., student, 122.

Lambeth Conference of bishops, 102.
Landscape plan, Hopkins, 61.
Language, school of philosophy of, 69.
Latin, school of language and literature, 69; Knight, instructor, 121; Harrison, instructor, 130; Minor, professor, 141; enrollment, 135; 136. (See ancient languages.)
Law, school of, 70; commercial, 136.
Lay, Henry Champlin, third bishop of Ark. (1859-1869); first bishop of Easton (1869-1885); *illus.*, 28; Ala. tr., 80 *n. 119*, 87, 96, 98; first secretary, board of trustees, 50; LL.D. from Cambridge, 103.
Lea, Albert Miller, marshal at Lookout Mountain, 51.
Leacock, Rev. William T., La. tr., 77 *n. 61*, 80 *n. 119*, 84, 98.
Leases, 71, 100, 133, 151; not restricted to Episcopalians, 138.
LeConte, Joseph, 44.
Lee, Gen. Robert E., recommended Gorgas, 117; declined vice-chancellorship, 117; at Washington College, 118, 163; baseball team named for, 160.
Lees, Robert E., baseball team, 160.
Library, *illus.*, 33; gifts from Oxford and Cambridge, 105; 123, 131; building, 131.
Lieber, Francis, 44.
Lincoln, Bishop of, 105.
Llandaff, Bishop of, 105.
Location (See site).
Logic (in school of metaphysics), 136.
London, Bishop of, 105.
London, England, Quintard's visits to, 102-108.
London, University of, 81 *n. 139*.
Lookout Mountain, trustees' meeting, 50; site offered, 53.
Lord, Rev. William Wilberforce, Miss. tr., 77 *n. 61*.
Lothian, Marquis of, 105.

Louisiana, diocese of, *founding diocese,* 43, 45, 50, 52, 62, 75 *n. 18,* 119, 176; college, 43; prewar fund-raising, 58, 71, 101, 134; effects of war on, 84; enrollment, 175, Advent offering, 178. (See Bishops Polk and Wilmer.)
Louisiana, University of, 42; State University, 120.

Madison College, Tenn., 43, 47.
Magnolia Hall, 140.
Magruder, Thomas B., Miss. tr., 80 *n. 119.*
Manners, Lord John, 113 *n. 95.*
Maps, Barney's, 59; printed, 61; Hopkins', 61; lithographed, 165 *n. 30;* McCrady's, 78 *n. 87.*
Marlborough, Gregg's home, 132.
Marshal, 126.
Mason, Mrs. Cyrus, 126.
Master of arts, requirements, 70.
Mathematics, school of, 69, established, 135; Green, instructor, 116; Shoup, instructor, 130, first professor, 135; enrollment, 135.
Maury, Com. Matthew Fontaine, *biog.,* 105; 64, 81 *n. 132,* elected vice-chancellor, 106.
Mayhew, George A., merchant, 152.
McCrady, John, professor of biology, 142.
McIlvaine, Charles P., second bishop of Ohio (1832-1873); 48, 101.
McMinnville, Tenn., considered as site, 53.
Medicine, school of, 70.
Mercer University, 43.
Mercer Hall, Columbia, Tenn., 47.
Merrick, Rev. John Austin, pres. Sewanee Mission and Theological School, 87, 94.
Metaphysics, school of, 69, established, 135, 136; Dabney, instructor, 121, first professor, 135; enrollment, 135.
Methodist colleges, 43.
Military drill, 125, 126, 141, 159, 167 *n. 169, n. 170;* tradition, 179.
Miller, I. T., 63.
Miller, John, groceries, 152.
Mineralogy, in school with geology, 69; 136.
Mines and mining, school of, 70. (See coal.)
Minor, Charles Landon Carter, professor of Latin, headmaster of grammar school, 141.
Mississippi, diocese of, *founding diocese,* 43, 45, 50, 52, 75 *n. 18,* 119, 176; colleges in, 43; seminary, 111 *n. 69;* prewar contributions, 71; enrollment, 175; Advent offering, 178. (See Bishop Green.)
Mississippi, University of, 42, 44, 116.
Modern languages, Juny, instructor, 130, first professor, 135; school established, 135; enrollment, 135; 136. (See French, German, Italian, Spanish.)
Montgomery, Ala., trustees' meetings, 52, 98.
Montpelier Female Institute, Ga., 49.
Moral science and evidences of Christian religion, school of, 69, established, 135; DuBose first professor, 139; 137.
Moray and Ross, Bishop of, 105.
Moreland Tract, land grant, 60.
Municipal regulations, 55, 137.
Music, sacred, in school of fine arts, 70, 124.
Myles, Beverly B., 182 *n. 7.*

Name of U. of S., 51, 55; of Sewanee, 74 *n. 1.*
Nash, Joseph C., student, 122.
Nashville and Chattanooga Railroad, 54, 78 *n. 80,* 84, 109 *n. 7.*
Natural Bridge, Hopkins' sketch, *illus.,* 38.
Naval training unit, 179.
Negroes, 48, 56, 84, 163, 182 *n. 15.*
Nelson, Earl, 105, 113 *n. 95.*
New Orleans, La., trustees' meeting, 61.
New York, N. Y., trustees' meeting, 122.
New Zealand, Bishop of, 105.
North Carolina, diocese of, *founding diocese,* 43, 45, 50, 52, 75 *n. 18,* 119, 176, 183 *n. 27;* prewar contributions, 71; enrollment, 175; Advent offering, 178. (See Bishop Atkinson.)
North Carolina, University of, 42, 44, 45, 48, 54, 97, 120.
Nott, Josiah C., 44.

Observatory, 69.
Oglethorpe University, 42.
Old South, tradition of, 180.
Omega society, literary, 161.
Orders, vote by, 67.
Ordination of first student, 169.
Oriental language and literature, school of, 69. (See Hebrew.)
Otey, James Hervey, first bishop of Tenn. (1834-1863); *illus.,* 11; biog., 46-48; 63, 64, 72, 73, 80 *n. 119,* 88, 169; bishops' manifesto, 45; first chancellor, 46, 51; Tennessee colleges, 47; address at Lookout Mountain, 51; life of, 97.

Otey Hall, *illus.*, 34; diocesan training school, 94, 99, 111 *n. 49, 51,* 122.
Oxford, Bishop of, 113 *n. 95.*
Oxford Court, dormitory, 131.
Oxford University, 68, 81 *n. 139,* 105, 107, 128, 178; traditions, 178, 179.

Paleontology, in school with geology, 69.
Palmetto Hall, 139, 157.
Parew, W. H. Pool, 113 *n. 95.*
Pease, Gov. Elisha M., Tex. tr., 80 *n.119.*
Pegues, Thomas E. B., Miss. tr., 85 *n. 112,* 143 *n. 23.*
Perth, Bishop of, 105.
Phelan, Judge John D., Tenn. tr., 156, first president E. Q. B., 155.
Philosophy, 136. (See metaphysics.)
Physician, resident, Elliott, 129.
Physics, school of, 69; Gorgas, instructor, 131; enrollment, 135; 136.
Pi Lambda, literary society, 161.
Pillet. L., tailor, 152.
Pise, Rev. David, Tenn. tr., *illus.*, 29; 77 *n. 61,* 80 *n. 119,* 95; second secretary, board of trustees, 61; postwar revival, 85, 111 *n. 62.*
Political science, school of, 69; 136.
Polk, Mrs. E. M., 157.
Polk, Leonidas, first bishop of Ark. (1838-1841), first bishop of La. (1841-1864), *illus.*, 13; *biog.*, 48, 49; 41, 46, 47, 51, 52, 56, 59, 61, 63, 72, 73, 74, 76 *n. 29, 40,* 77 *n. 61,* 78 *n. 80, 82,* 80 *n. 119,* 81 *n. 142,* 83, 86, 91, 96, 154, 161, 169 172, 180, 181 *n. 1;* letter to southern bishops, 45; second chancellor, 50; financial plan, 57; endowment commissioner, 55, 57, 58, 60; laid cornerstone, 64; constitution, 66; residence at Sewanee, 62, 71, 72.
Polk Spring (now Tremlett), 62.
Pollard, Charles T., Ala. tr., 77 *n. 61,* 142 *n. 2,* deeds to domain, 96, 97; meeting at his home, 98; railroad stock, 134.
Population of Sewanee, 122, 151.
Porcher, Maria L., 158.
Powhatan, home, 121, 122, 157.
Presbyterian colleges, 42.
Preston, John S., 64.
Princeton, 120.
Protestant Episcopal Church in the Confederate States of America, 50, 72, 86, 87.
Pusey, Dr. Edward B., 65, 105.

Queen's University, Ireland, 81 *n. 139.*
Quintard, Charles Todd, second bishop of Tenn. (1865-1898); *illus.*, 17; *biog.*, 87-91; 47, 63, 132, 142, 155, 175, 176, 179; postwar revival, 85, 93, 98; reunion, 87; home at Sewanee, Fulford Hall, *illus.*, 34, 94, 121, 161; diocesan theological school, 93, 94, 98; Sewanee Collegiate Institute, 94, 95; fund-raising, 93, 96, 100, 101, 104, 105, 107, 108, 118, 123, 127, 134, 138, 177; first vice-chancellor, 99, 117, 126, 133, 138, 170, 171, 172; English trip, 101-108; and Gorgas, 117; opening of U., 121; on honorary degrees, 128; exec. committee, 128, 133, 137, 143 *n. 4.;* secured faculty, 117, 130; and Bishop Elliott, 123; community, 152; philosophy of education, 174.
Quorum, in board of trustees, 67, 115.

Rainsford Place, Fairbank's home, *illus.*, 39; 62.
Rainy Spring, 80 *n. 121.*
Reuf, Christian, butcher, 152.
Randolph, James L., engineer, 77 *n. 69.*
Randolph-Macon College, 43.
Ravenscroft College, Tenn., 43, 47.
Ravenscroft, John Stark, first bishop of N. C. (1823-1830), 97, 111 *n. 66.*
Rebel's Rest, Fairbanks' home, *illus.*, 35; 94, 96, 154.
Reconstruction, 84, 105, 115, 119, 120, 124, 142, 163, 164, 173, 181.
Rectory, DuBose's home, *illus.*, 35; 36, 139.
Redwood House, 121.
Regional nature of U. of S., 45, 59, 174.
Registrar, Francis Fogg, 60; John Locke Cooper, 131.
Rhetoric, criticism, elocution, and composition, school of, 69; included in school of metaphysics, 135; enrollment, 135; 136.
Richmond, College of, 43.
"Robert," letter from, 124.
Roberts, H. H., hacks and horses, 152, 153.
Rochester, Bishop of, 105.
Roman Catholic colleges, 43.
Rose Gates College, Miss., 43.
Rowe, Lawson, land grant, 60; 79 *n. 109;* spring, 80 *n. 121.*
Ruffin, Thomas, N. C. tr., 80 *n. 119.*
Rutledge, ·Arthur Middleton, land, 60; 63, 78 *n. 79,* 79 *n. 109,* 157.
Rutledge, Francis Huger, first bishop of

INDEX 205

Fla. (1851-1866); 63, 76 n. *29*, 80 n. *119*, 111 n. *62*.
Ryder, Rear Adm., R. N., 113 n. *95*.

St. Andrew's College, Jackson, Miss., 43.
St. Asaph, Bishop of, 105.
St. Augustine's Chapel, *illus.*, 32, 37; 125, 160, 180; cornerstone laid, 102; name, 112 n. *89*; opening of U., 121; extended, 122; font, stained glass, 126; services, 159.
St. Augustine's College, Canterbury, 112 n. *89*.
St. Augustine's College, Raleigh, 182 n. *15*.
St. Luke's Hall, 136, 140.
St. Mark's Guild, 161, 167 n. *84*.
St. Mary, Sisters of, 153.
St. Paul's College, Tex., 43; La., 43.
St. Paul's-on-the-Mountain, church, 153.
Salaries, 67, 68, 99, 116, 135, 158.
Salisbury, Bishop of, 105.
Sawmill, 153.
Schlapback, Henry, butcher, 152.
Schneider, Henry, craftsman, 152.
Scholarship, to be highest, 59; 125, 173.
Scholarships, Clarke, 126; Society for Increase of the Ministry, 128; clergy sons, 128.
School building, north of chapel, 131.
School, elementary, 154.
Science and religion, 121.
Science, natural, school of, 69.
Sciences, 69, 136. (See physics, chemistry.)
Scott, Rev. J. Jackson, Fla. tr., 80 n. *119*, 98, 122.
Seal, U. of S., 137, 148 n. *143*.
Sevier, Col. T. Frank, *illus.*, 29; *biog.*, 125, 155; master of grammar school, commandant, acting professor of commerce, 125; bursar, 128; son, Granville, 146 n. *80*.
Sewanee, origin of name, 41, 74 n. *1*; post office named, 80 n. *120*.
Sewanee College, Winchester, Tenn., 95.
Sewanee Collegiate Institute, 94, 95.
Sewanee Grammar School. (See Grammar school.)
Sewanee Military Academy, formerly Sewanee Grammar School, 183 n. *36*. (See grammar school.)
Sewanee Mining Co., land grant, 53, 60, 79 n. *109*, 83.
Sewanee, Tenn. (See site, University Place, domain.)

Shaftsbury, Earl of, 105.
Shapard, W. B., land grant, 60, 79 n. *109*.
Shaw-Stewart, J. A., honorable treasurer in England, 103.
Shelby College, Ky., 43.
Sherwood, R. W., student, 122.
Shoup, Brig. Gen. Francis A., *illus.*, 30; *biog.*, 130; 140, 142, 179; recommended Gorgas, 117; mathematics, instructor, 130, first professor. 135; acting chaplain, 130, 156; St. Paul's, 153.
Sigma Epsilon, literary society, *illus.*, 37; 161.
Simkins, Smith, Fla. tr., 112 n. *85*, 142 n. *2*.
Site, 41, 45, 54, 56, 60, 92, 93. (See domain.)
Skipwith, John Adair, student, 122.
Smedes, Susan Dabney (Mrs. Lyell), 166 n. *59*.
Smith, Benjamin Bosworth, first bishop of Kentucky (1832-1884), 63, 65, 101, 181.
Sneed, H. H., student, Sewanee College Institute, 95.
South, higher education in, 43, 44, 45, 119, 120; economic conditions, 41, 42, 84, 126.
South Carolina College, 42, 44, 49, 59, 120.
South Carolina, diocese of, *founding diocese*, 43, 45, 50, 52, 75 n. *18*, 119, 176; theological seminary, 81 n. *128*; effects of war, 85; enrollment, 140, 175; Advent offering, 178. (See Bishop Davis.)
South Wing (Cobbs Hall), 101, 122.
Spanish, school of language and literature, 69; enrollment in, 135. (See modern languages.)
Spirit of laws, in school of political science, 69.
Sports, 160, 161.
Spring Hill College, 43.
Stanhope, Earl, 105.
Statistics, in school of political science, 69.
Steele, Edwin C., 182 n. *7*.
Stephenson, Col. V. K., 78 n. *80*.
Student army training unit, 179.

Taxes, 55.
Taylor, Mrs. Frances T. D., 134.
Tennessee, diocese of, *founding diocese*, 43, 45, 50, 52, 62, 75 n.*18*, 113, 119, 176; colleges, 43, 47; prewar contributions, 71; effect of war on, 84; initiated revival of U., 85; diocesan training school, 94; Sewanee Collegiate Institute,

94; enrollment, 175; Advent offering, 178. (See Bishops Otey and Quintard.)
Tennessee, diocesan divinity school, 85, 93, 98, 99.
Texas, diocese of, *founding diocese*, 43, 45, 50, 52, 62, 75 *n. 18*, 119, 176; colleges, 43; prewar contributions, 71; support of U., 132; enrollment, 175; Advent offering, 178. (See Bishops Freeman and Gregg.)
Textbooks, 135.
Thackera, Rev. Owen P., fund-raiser, 128, 134.
Theology, school of, 45, 70, 135, 136, 137, 169.
Thompson, Jacob, 133.
Tobacco, student use of, 162.
Tomlinson, W. H., postmaster, 71, 122, 151.
Tracy, Samuel F., 53.
Tracy City, Tenn., 63.
Traditions, U. of S., 178-181.
Treasurer, U., 124, 128; diocesan treasurers, 46, 57, 99.
Tremlett, Rev. Francis W., *illus.*, 25; 102-08; 123, 128.
Tremlett Hall, *illus.*, 27; 80 *n. 121*, 115, 122, 157.
Tremlett Spring, 80 *n. 121*.
Trent, William Peterfield, 180.
Trinity College, N. C., 43.
Trustees, board of, 45, 46, 67, 68, 69, 82 *n. 146*; meetings, Lookout Mountain, 50; Montgomery, 52; Beersheba, 55, 60; New Orleans, 61; Sewanee, 62; Columbia, 72; Sewanee, 96; Montgomery, 98; Sewanee, 101; Savannah, 115; Sewanee, 118; New York, 122; Sewanee, 126; Sewanee, 133; Sewanee, 137; Sewanee, 138; summary of attendance, 61, 62, 175, 176.
Tullahoma, Tenn., offered site, 53.
Turney, Col. Peter, 72, 95.

Uniforms, grammar school, 137, 170; undergraduates, 124, 159.
University Place, 61, 63, 80 *n. 120*. (See site.)

Vassar, Miles, land tract, 60.
Vice-chancellor, powers, 68, 137; Quintard, first, 99, 171, 172; Maury declined, 105, 106; Lee declined, 117; Johnston suggested, 123; Gorgas, second, 68, 138; Elliott, acting, 129; robe, 138, 170. (See Quintard and Gorgas.)
Virginia, University of, 42, 44, 54, 59, 121, 133, 139.

Wadhams, Charles, baker, 151, 152.
Wake Forest College, 43.
Warren, Thomas D., M.D., N. C. tr., 71, 77 *n. 61*.
Washington College, 42, 120, 163.
Wells, Rev. Charles L., 180.
West Point (U. S. Military Academy), 48, 52, 107, 116, 125, 130, 179.
White, Rev. George, 95.
White's Creek Springs, Tenn., site offered, 53.
Whiteside, Col. James A., 50.
Whittle, L. N., Ga. tr., 98, 111 *n. 62*, 112 *n. 85*, 142 *n. 2*, 143 *n. 4, n. 23*.
Wilkes, John, N. C. tr., 142 *n. 2*.
William and Mary College, 43, 112 *n. 87*, 119.
Williams, Channing Moore, second missionary bishop of China and Japan, 101.
Williams, J. J., Fla. tr., 142 *n. 2*.
Williams, Rev. William C., Ga. tr., third secretary, board of trustees, 98, 111 *n. 62*, 142 *n. 2*, 143 *n. 4, n. 23*.
Wilmer, Rev. George T., 142.
Wilmer, Joseph Pere Bell, second bishop of La. (1866-1878); 98, 118, 127, 133, 137, 143 *n. 4*, 166 *n. 47*.
Wilmer, Richard Hooker, second bishop of Ala. (1862-1900); 86, 87, 98, 134, 155.
Winchester, Tenn., 54, 94, 95.
Winter vacation, 56, 145 *n. 63*, 157.
Wofford College, 43.
Worcester, Bishop of, 105.

Yale University, 120, 136.
York, Archbishop of, 113 *n. 95*.
Young, John Freeman, second bishop of Fla. (1867-1885), 63, 118, 131, 142 *n. 2*, 166 *n. 47*.

PICTORIAL AND OTHER CREDITS

The end papers at the front and back of the book reprint a map circulated about 1870. The map shows not only the houses which were standing then but also give, to the best of the unknown mapmaker's memory, the details of the lost Bishop Hopkins plan for the location of the major buildings. Notable on this map is the Corso, a scenic drive planned to skirt the edge of the escarpment and make accessible the views. The springs and views preserve the names of the first trustees and prewar benefactors.

The engraving of Bishop Otey is in the sacristy of Otey Church at Sewanee. Locations of the portraits are as follows: Bishop Polk, Bishop Gregg (by Ella Wood), Bishop Cobbs, Bishop Lay, in University Library; Bishop Elliott (by Edward McCrady) in Elliott Hall; Bishop Quintard in Fulford Hall; Bishop Green in possession of William Green deRosset; Mr. Hayes in possession of a great granddaughter. The photograph of Maj. Fairbanks and the sketch of Rainsford Place are in the possession of Mrs. Rainsford Glass Dudney.

In the University Archives are the rest of the photographs, most of them the work of the Judd family. The photographs of Dr. Pise, Dr. Tremlett, and Tremlett Hall are not by the Judds. The program of St. Mary's Church is in All Saints' Chapel. The water color of Natural Bridge by Bishop John Henry Hopkins is in the University Library.

The portraits and photographs were copied for this volume by Howard Coulson of Cowan. Layout was done by W. A. Benson, Dan Eadie, and William Baggett of Benson Printing Company, who made the work of an author producing his first book a pleasure and an education. Press work for the textual portions was by the University Press, where John Sutherland, Frances Beakley, and Carl Yates are particularly to be thanked.